Behavioral Approaches to Medical Treatment

Behavioral Approaches to Medical Treatment

Edited by
Redford B. Williams, Jr.,
W. Doyle Gentry,
Duke University Medical Center

Ballinger Publishing Company • Cambridge, Mass.
A Subsidiary of J.B. Lippincott Company

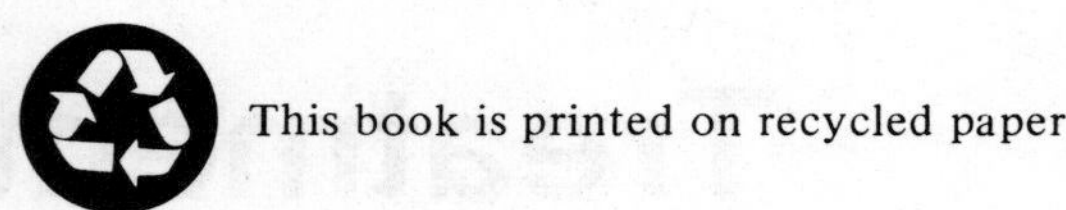

This book is printed on recycled paper.

International Standard Book Number: 0-88410-136-3

Library of Congress Catalog Card Number: 76-30327

Printed in the United States of America

Library of Congress Cataloging in Publication Data
Main entry under title:

Behavioral approaches to medical treatment.

Includes bibliographies.
1. Medicine and psychology. 2. Behavior modification.
I. Williams, Redford Brown, 1940- II. Gentry, William Doyle, 1943- [DNLM: 1. Behavior therapy—Congresses. 2. Internal medicine—Congresses. 3. Feedback—Congresses. 4. Patient compliance—Congresses. WM420 B4176].
R726.5.B42 615'.5'019 76-30327
ISBN 0-88410-136-3

Dedication

To my teachers, GEORGE B. WYNNE,
GEORGE W. GOETHALS, III,
STANLEY H. KING.

RBW

To JACK E. HOKANSON, teacher and friend.

WDG

Contents

List of Figures

List of Tables

Preface

One of the strongest trends in American medicine at the present time is that toward training more primary care physicians. The primary care physician is often defined as the "physician of first contact," and may be the product of a training program in family practice, internal medicine, obstetrics-gynecology, pediatrics or general practice. It has become increasingly evident that all too often the problems which patients bring to primary care physicians are intimately involved with the behavior of the patient.

Insomnia, alcoholism, headache, obesity and non-compliance with medical regimens—some of the most common and troublesome problems the primary care physicians (as well as their more specialized colleagues) must face each day—are essentially behavioral disorders. Certain behaviors—smoking and the Type A (coronary prone) behavior pattern—appear to be risk factors for the number one killer in America today, coronary heart disease. Still other disorders—pain, asthma, hypertension, enuresis, fecal incontinence and cardiac, arrythmias—are determined, at least in part, by the behavioral responses of the patient.

The above conditions undoubtedly account for a large proportion of patient visits to medical practitioners at all levels of specialization. In many instances, recent research has provided clear evidence that newly developed behavioral treatment approaches are capable of providing significant relief of distressing symptoms associated with these conditions. With certain of these disorders, the evidence for the efficacy of behavioral approaches, while promising, remains preliminary; much research will be required before medical practitioners can confidently prescribe behavioral treatment for these disorders.

This book was inspired by a continuing education course held at Duke University in April, 1976. It is designed specifically to provide the practitioner in both the medical and psychological specialties with a practical introduction to the new behavioral treatment approaches which have been developed over the past decade. Every attempt is made to differentiate those behavioral techniques which may be applied now as compared to those where further clinical trials are necessary. The contributers to this volume have been responsible for basic research regarding the techniques to be covered, as well as applied clinical research regarding their application in the treatment of medical problems. It is our intention that upon completion of this book the reader should not only be able to answer confidently patients' questions about these behavioral treatment techniques, but also will have taken the first step toward their clinical application in a patient care setting.

A number of individuals and groups provided support without which the final production of this book would have been impossible. These include Dr. Stephen Weiss and the Office of Prevention, Education and Control of the National Heart, Lung, and Blood Institute; Dr. George Maddox and the Duke University Center for the Study of Aging and Human Development; Dr. Hugh Angle and the Duke Medication Evaluation and Resources Program; Dr. Robert Green and the Durham Veteran's Administration Hospital Psychiatry Service; Dr. Patrick Boudewyns and the Durham Veteran's Administration Hospital Psychology Service; the Psychiatric Residency Training and the Medical Psychology Internship Training programs of the Department of Psychiatry, Duke University Medical Center; and Ms. Laura Singleton and the management and staff of The Governor's Inn, Research Triangle Park, North Carolina.

Whatever success this volume enjoys in achieving these goals for its readers will be the result of the enthusiastic and diligent participation of the contributers. The administrative and secretarial contributions of Marilyn L. Hall were invaluable in the orderly and timely assembling of the large amount of material involved in this book. We also wish to thank H. Keith H. Brodie, M.D., Chairman of the Department of Psychiatry, Duke University Medical Center, for his support at all phases in the production of this volume.

Redford B. Williams, Jr., M.D.
W. Doyle Gentry, Ph. D.

Durham, N.C.
December, 1976

Chapter 1

Behavioral Medicine: A Perspective

Edward B. Blanchard

There is a new term being discussed in the fields of psychology and primary medical care; that term is *Behavioral Medicine.* In order to put this book in perspective, I want to spend some time discussing this term and this new field of *Behavioral Medicine.*

I first saw the term behavioral medicine in the title of a book edited by Birk called, *Biofeedback: Behavioral Medicine* (Birk, 1973). This would imply that the two terms are synonymous. However, Behavioral Medicine encompasses much, much more than biofeedback, although the latter certainly is a part of the former.

Since the appearance of that book, the term has been used with accelerating frequency: (1) Neal Miller used it as part of the title of his keynote address at the National Heart and Lung Institute's Working Conference on Health Behavior about a year ago (Miller, 1975); (2) a symposium at AABT had the term in the title; (3) there is a newly established Center for Behavioral Medicine at the University of Pennsylvania under the leadership of Dr. John Paul Brady and the Department of Psychiatry and (4) a newly established Institute for Behavioral Medicine at Stanford University headed by Dr. Stewart Agras; (5) there have also been workshops on the topic in the past year.

There is a term from the philosophy of history, an explanatory construct, *Zeitgeist*, which means "the spirit of the times," or the general intellectual and moral character of a culture or era. This book seems a part of the current Zeitgeist and will probably be a milestone in the development of the field of Behavioral Medicine.

Interestingly, the National Heart and Lung Institute recognized the need for such a field in one of their large scale, multicenter programs, the Multiple Risk Factor Intervention Trial, or MRFIT. In their request for proposals, they specified that a "behaviorist" be involved in designing and implementing the intervention programs in smoking and obesity. An ad hoc "Task Force on Health Research" was recently established, by the American Psychological Association (May 1973) and completed its work in November 1975 by the establishment of a formal Section on Health Research whose focus is on identifying areas within health and health related matters that psychology can contribute to.

All of this is meant to show that Behavioral Medicine is an idea whose time has come.

Next, let me define the term Behavioral Medicine and the domain which it encompasses.

By *Behavioral Medicine* I mean the systematic application of the principles and technology of behavioral psychology to the field of medicine, health and illness. By behavioral psychology I mean primarily experimental, or at least empirical, psychology which has its roots in the psychology of learning, social psychology, and to a lesser degree physiological psychology. Behavioral psychology deals primarily with observable events, relies heavily on empirical data but does allow for nonobservables or covert events that are closely tied to data or defining operations. It is probably most closely tied to the field of the experimental analysis of behavior or operant conditioning.

Behavioral Medicine, as I view it, has several subdomains:

1. Direct psychological intervention in problems which have traditionally been considered medical. Much of the subject matter of this book fits into this subdomain. Thus obesity, insomnia, headache, and hypertension have all traditionally been considered medical problems and in most, or all of these problems, there is a definite pathophysiology. However, what behavioral medicine brings to bear on these problems is an alternative, or an adjunct, to traditional pharmocological or surgical intervention.

Almost every physician realizes that the patient's behavior plays a part in much of disease and that changes in that behavior are necessary, or at least desirable, as part of treatment. However, it has only been in the last decade and a half that an effective technology for changing behavior, as opposed to mental states, has been developed. The work in the area of behavior therapy and behavior modification in the mental health or psychiatric domain has shown that an effective technology for changing behavior can be developed. A part of behavioral medicine is the application of this knowledge and technology to the areas of health in general, rather than just mental health.

This subdomain of direct psychological intervention in "traditional" medical problems is probably the oldest part of the field and the best developed. The hallmark of this approach, as well exemplified by the topics covered in this book, is attention to overt behavior and a detailed behavioral analysis of the problem rather than reliance on hypothesized internal states or attitudes.

2. The second subdomain is the use of psychological intervention to facilitate or enhance standard medical care. The major concern of this domain is patient compliance or adherance to the prescribed medical regimen, be it diet alteration, life-style alteration, or medicine taking. You will note that other chapters in this book, such as those on smoking, obesity, and hypertension emphasize the patient's adherence to a prescribed regimen.

3. A newer area of direct psychological intervention is at the physiological level by means of biofeedback training. Thus, while I agree that biofeedback represents one aspect of *Behavioral Medicine*, it is certainly not all there is to the field. Some of the best clinical biofeedback work is very closely tied to behavioral psychology. The chapters by Engel on biofeedback treatment of cardiac arrhythmias and fecal incontinence are examples of this as is Williams' chapter on headaches.

One reason for separating biofeedback from the rest of the direct psychological intervention domain is that the behavior which is to be modified by biofeedback is not readily observable either by the patient or by the physician without electronic equipment. Otherwise the principles and psychological technology are much the same.

4. The final subdomain of behavioral medicine is that of primary prevention, or the establishment and maintenance of health behaviors. A recent paper by Pomerleau, Bass and Crown (1975) discusses some aspects of applying behavior modification to the field of preventive medicine as does Brady's chapter in this volume. This subdomain has typically belonged more to education and public health. However, there is certainly vast room for the application of behavioral psychology to the problems in this area.

You will notice that I have excluded the whole area of mental health or psychiatric problems. Psychology has long been at home in these fields and will continue to make a contribution to them. One of my own chief concerns however, is for psychology, particularly behavioral psychology, to become not just a part of the mental health team but a part of the Health Team; that psychology become, in part, a health profession with the special skills in changing health behaviors.

One might ask if behavioral medicine is just a new name for psychosomatic medicine? I do not believe this is the case. There is knowledge from behavioral medicine which is applicable to psychosomatic diseases, especially as far as it is true that psychosomatic disease is stress-induced or stress related. Behavioral psychology has some things to say about how to help patients cope with, and perhaps, overcome stress. This is well exemplified in Suinn's chapter on behavioral treatment for Type A behavior.

I believe the field of Behavioral Medicine has some important meanings and implications for practitioners of medicine and for medical educators. Considering the latter first, it is extremely difficult for medical educators to teach "so-called" behavioral science to medical students or residents. Much effort has gone into planning and trying various approaches, usually with little success. Most medical students, in my experience, are not interested in behavioral science as it is presently taught, other than the psychopathology from psychiatry. One of the main reasons, I suspect, has been the lack of applicability of the knowledge of the behavioral sciences to the practice of medicine. Now, however, with the emergence of a technology of behavior change, teaching behavioral medicine as a major component of teaching behavioral science may make life easier.

For the practitioners of medicine, the contents of this book will hopefully make a difference. You will learn some things about how to change patients' behavior when that is an indicated part of the treatment regimen and/or to whom to refer the patient for the change if you do not want to embark upon it yourself.

At one level of analysis behavioral approaches to treatment boil down to a few basic principles and a multitude of applications. In anticipation of the chapters of this book devoted to specific problems, I would like to give you a summary preview of these basic principles.

First, these approaches to treatment emphasize a detailed analysis of the problem behavior and of the Patient-Environment interaction. With this detailed analysis comes an emphasis on observables and on objective assessment. A major emphasis will be on having the patient keep records of when and under what conditions he engages in the problematic behavior. One of the most powerful tools for changing behavior is a 3 by 5 notebook in which the patient records such things as each cigarette he smokes (Boudewyns) or item he eats (Foreyt).

One needs these data for several reasons: (1) the act of self-monitoring a problematic behavior can sometimes lead to a decrease in it

(Mahoney, 1974); (2) patients' tend to generalize and try to abstract or condense much behavior into brief causal statements and thereby unwittingly can mislead you; (3) to assess the effectiveness of some particular strategy and to know when to abandon it.

Second, this detailed behavioral analysis is concerned with at least three classes of events: (1) Antecedent stimulus events, or what cues in the patient's environment are regularly associated with the problem behavior; (2) the response topography, or what the patient actually does; and (3) environmental response to the patient's behavior, or the response consequences; that is, what happens to the patient as a result of his emitting some illness or health behavior or response. Those of you familiar with behavioral psychology will recognize the above description as the basic *operant conditioning* paradigm. However, in this book its ramifications are being applied to medical problems rather than the behavior of pigeons or the behavior of hospitalized schizophrenics.

Another element present in many of the treatment strategies is *discrimination training*, that is, helping the patient to learn or recognize when he is emitting maladaptive behavior and when he is not. For example, Williams and also Suinn discuss teaching the patient to recognize when he is tense and when he is relaxed.

A topic present in many of these chapters is the value of relaxation training. It seems to be a component of most of the treatment strategies described in this book. Relaxation training, broadly conceived includes such techniques as Jacobson's (1948) progressive muscular relaxation, Schultz and Luthe's (1969) autogenic training, or Benson's (1975) meditation to elicit the "relaxation response." All of these techniques have as their goal to serve as a nonpharmocological anxiolytic agent. Certainly as a general antistress treatment it is worthwhile and it will probably be worthwhile for primary care physicians to have someone on their staff who can provide this training to patients.

A third overall feature of the treatment strategies to be described in the following chapters is the use of a multifaceted approach. It has been recognized within behavioral approaches to treatment that one-shot, single-minded interventions frequently do not work. Certainly, in dealing with behaviors that are resistant to change, only a multifaceted approach makes sense. There is also attention in many of these approaches to cognitive events—using the subject himself as the source of the stimuli which control the behavior.

Fourthly, there is widespread concern in the chapters which follow for obtaining *generalization*, or the transfer of improvement from the treatment or consulting room to the patient's natural environment.

In this area an operant analysis has been combined with some cognitive psychology to try to develop self-control and self-management techniques.

A key feature to obtaining generalization is continued follow-up of the patient as illustrated by Boudewyns' chapter. A second important aspect is providing feedback to the patient of his results. These two, continued contract and feedback, when combined with a generalized expectancy for improvement should be exploited to the fullest in seeking transfer and maintenance of improvement.

Finally, one wants to use the physician-patient relationship for all it is worth. Your contingent social approval is a powerful reinforcer, and a way of keeping patients in treatment long enough to help them help themselves.

In conclusion, I would like to repeat one of my earlier statements: Behavioral Medicine is an idea whose time has come, and I believe this book marks this new field's coming of age.

REFERENCES

Benson, H. *The relaxation response*. New York: William Morrow & Co., 1975.

Birk, L. (Ed.) *Biofeedback: behavioral medicine*. New York: Grune & Stratton, 1973.

Jacobson, E. *You must relax*. (3rd Ed.). New York: McGraw-Hill, 1948.

Mahoney, M.J. Self-reward and self-monitoring techniques for weight control. *Behavior Therapy*, 1974, *5*, 48–57.

Miller, N.E. Behavioral medicine as a new frontier: Opportunities and dangers. in S. Weiss (Ed.) *Proceedings of the National Heart and Lung Institute Working Conferences on Health Behavior*, DHEW Publication No. (NIH) 1975, 76–868.

Pomerleau, O., Bass, F., & Crown, V. Role of behavior modification in preventive medicine. *New England Journal of Medicine*, 1975, 292, 1277–1282.

Schultz, J.H., & Luthe, W. *Autogenic training*, Vol. 1, New York: Grune & Stratton, 1969.

Chapter 2

Chronic Asthma†

*A. Barney Alexander**

The focus of this chapter will be on the ways in which behavioral approaches can be of benefit in the clinical management of asthma. Both fairly well established techniques and some more recent, highly promising methods will be covered. It is the intention of this survey to provide the clinician with an elementary understanding of the rationale and implementation of these techniques as well as the ways in which their indications for use can be recognized. While it is well beyond the scope of the present chapter to discuss current notions regarding the pathophysiology of asthma or to critically review the rapidly expanding experimental literature in the area of asthma research generally, some background orientation is necessary. In particular, an attempt will be made both to present an informal model concerning the psychological aspects of asthma and to provide a brief summary of the current status of our knowledge in the latter area.

During the decades between 1920 and 1940, when psychosomatic medicine was evolving as a separate specialty, asthma began to emerge as one of the premier examples of a psychosomatic disorder. While the mainstream of medicine continued to view asthma as basically an immunological disorder, the focus within psychosomatic medicine was formed in 1941 by French and Alexander (1941). From a psychoanalytic viewpoint they promulgated the hypothesis that the *origin* of asthma was due to the suppression of intense emo-

*The National Asthma Center, Denver, Colorado.

†Preparation of this chapter was supported in part by a grant from the National Heart, Lung and Blood Institute (#HL–15620).

tion, specifically, "a suppressed cry for the mother." This influential formulation has led to a great deal of unproductive theorizing and futile investigation. Nevertheless, until very recently the dominant theme among psychosomatic researchers has been that in some manner psycho-social variables would be found to play an etiologic role in asthma.

A comparison here with peptic ulcer is instructive. It is fairly well accepted that certain forms of psychologic stress and conflict can lead more or less directly to increased gastric secretion in normal individuals. For persons who are on the high end of the gastric reactivity continuum, prolonged exposure to the appropriate forms of psychological stress may ultimately lead to ulceration of the stomach or duodenum. This analysis assigns a prominent role to psychological factors in the actual etiology of the lesion. While there surely exists a complex interaction between tissue susceptibility, "normal" gastric acid levels, secretory reactivity, and many environmental and psychological factors in the development of ulcer in any particular case, this formulation provides for the possibility that a lesion would not appear in the absence of sufficient psychological stress even if all of the other factors were favorable to ulcer development. As such, peptic ulcer would seem to be an excellent example of a truly psychosomatic disease. In contrast, for asthma there is simply no convincing evidence that the biological pathology which results in the hypersensitive airways characteristic of asthma can in any way result from psychological influence. The current view is that psychological disturbance can *result from* the continued battle with a chronic illness such as asthma and that, in at least some affected individuals, psychological influences such as emotional stress may *contribute to* the frequency and severity of specific episodes of bronchospasm. Hence, many authors are now taking the position that asthma should not be considered a psychosomatic disorder at all. There is good reason to be very sympathetic towards this view as the concept of "psychosomatic" usually includes notions regarding an etiologic role for psychological events. Sustained belief that psychological variables contribute to the *cause* of the pathophysiology in asthma will only continue to divert attention away from the more fruitful study of the ways in which psychological influences may alter airways tone in affected individuals. Equally as pertinent, the traditional psychosomatic view only furthers the destructive notion, held by most laymen and too many professionals, that asthma is "all in the head." Such a belief is monstrously unfair and often psychologically damaging to asthma sufferers and their families. It can also lead to a very dangerous clinical approach to therapy for persons who are sometimes severely ill for no fault of their own. The understanding and appreciation of the ways in which psychological events interact with the disease must become increasingly more physiologically sophisticated if continued progress is to be made in understanding this complex disorder.

Given the preceding model, a crucial question arises regarding whether or not there are possible biologic pathways and mechanisms through which psychologic events might influence lung function. The answer is a cautious "yes." While it is not possible within the scope of this chapter to discuss such mechanisms, suffice it to say that processes at the level of the hypothalamus and limbic system, at the level of the autonomic nervous system, and at the peripheral tissue level provide increasingly better understood routes for psychological influence on pulmonary reactions.

Two thorough reviews of the literature on the psychological aspects of asthma are available: Purcell and Weiss (1970) and more recently, Knapp, Mathé and Vachon (1976). Asthma is a *symptom complex* or syndrome (*not* a unitary disease) characterized by intermittent, variable and reversible airways obstruction whose etiology and pathophysiology is incompletely understood. It has long been assumed that asthma involves some sort of biological vulnerability. Certainly some of the more sophisticated notions regarding the etiologic significance of psychological variables have implicated stress factors attacking a susceptible organ. Complete and uncontradictory epidemiological and genetic evidence is not yet available—where conclusions differ so do the sampling and assessment methods and criteria employed by various investigators. Prevalence rates have varied from 2 to 20 percent. Approximately 60 percent of asthmatics are under 17 years of age and boys are affected almost twice as often as girls. This sex ratio evens out in adulthood. The best genetic data to date suggests that hereditary factors may play a less prominent role than previously assumed. Monozygotic twins produced a concordance rate of only 19 percent for asthma and 25 percent for all allergic disorders. The risk was only 1 in 3 that a child would develop an allergy if both parents were atopic and the majority of allergic children were born into families where only one or neither parent was atopic.

Psychological factors in the family constellation appear to play a role in the manifestation of the disorder in some cases though undoubtedly not in its etiology. For years clinicians have noticed that some childhood asthmatics obtained symptom reduction or remission when separated from their families for one reason or another. In the late 1950s Peshkin even spoke of "parentectomy" as a treatment for asthma in some children. Evidence for the effectiveness of separation was seen in the significant number of children whose symptoms remitted abruptly when they were sent for treatment to The National Asthma Center in Denver. However, it remained highly likely that the benefits of leaving home for a time were due to alterations of the physical rather than the emotional environment. In a landmark study, Purcell and his colleagues (1969) controlled for physical environment effects by removing the families of asthmatic children to a hotel for several weeks while the child remained home under the care of an adult child care worker. They found that this experimental separation from their families of children whose asthma displayed emotional overtones produced small but statistically significant changes in a number of asthma measures. While these results implicated general family stress, more specific attempts to verify that "rejecting" or "engulfing" mothers cause asthma have met with the expected lack of success, and attempts to dichotomise asthmatics along an emotional-organic continuum have not proved fruitful. Hence, a safe conclusion is that emotional factors account for a *modest* amount of variance in a minority subgroup of asthmatics only.

The search for a specific personality pattern associated with asthma has been carried out even more energetically and with less success. As Creer and Renne (in press) point out, asthma sufferers have been claimed at one time or another to be overdependent, hypersensitive, overly aggressive and overly passive. They have been found to be more neurotic than normals and to describe themselves in a less favorable light. In general, when comparisons have been made with those who suffer from other chronic illnesses differences disappear. It is now generally conceded that the frequently obtained personality differences between asthmatics and normals are a result of the disease itself and are probably only manifestations of the presence of chronic illness. No evidence suggests that unique personality factors contribute to the development of the disorder. All of the investigations in this area have been experimentally flawed and entail the conceptual risk for the field of deemphasizing the importance of the biologic processes which underlie asthma.

Psychophysiological studies have produced more encouraging results. It is a common clinical observation, often supported by patient report, that attacks sometimes appear during, or seem to result from, emotional stress. Certainly emotional arousal, e.g., anxiety, frequently accompanies asthma episodes. Accordingly, a number of attempts have been made to precipitate asthma employing emotional stressors such as disturbing films, recordings of the voice of a patient's mother, discussions or hypnotic suggestions of stressful life situations, etc. Generally such stimuli have proved capable at times of producing changes in respiratory patterns and/or decreases in pulmonary flow rates but do not produce frank asthma. The effects have been very modest, though usually statistically significant, and appear only in selected individuals. These results do present a paradox, however. Since the cornerstone of therapeutics in asthma has been the well established bronchodilating effects of beta adrenergic substances, the question arises as to why such episodes, accompanied as they are by sympathetic arousal, should result in bronchospasm at all. A possible answer has been proposed by Mathé and Knapp and their colleagues (1971) in a series of experiments which suggest that some sort of an adrenergic defect may be involved. They find that some asthmatics appear to produce less than normal amounts of epinephrine as indicated by decreased urinary epinephrine excretion as a result of emotional stress.

On the cholinergic side, psychophysiologic attempts to demonstrate that asthma might represent a "vagotonic" disorder, or one characterized by a relative parasympathetic dominance, have met with little success. Nevertheless, recent work by Gold and his colleagues (1972) has forced renewed interest in the vagus nerve. They have shown that significant bronchospasm can result from mechanical stimulation of vagally mediated epithelial irritant receptors. Such reflex bronchospasm is a likely cause of mechanically induced bronchospasm in humans, such as that which results from coughing, some airborne irritants, etc. It is a distinct possibility that many examples of so-called emotionally triggered asthma may be due to this mechanism. Gasping as a result of surprise, yelling during anger, crying or laughing accompanying acute emotional states may represent "emotional" asthma only very indirectly.

Undoubtedly the most compelling line of research assigning psychological variables a role in the control of airways tone is the work on suggestion, relaxation, and placebo effects. Luparello, Lyons, and their colleagues (1968) have demonstrated that inhaled aerosolized saline can result in bronchoconstriction when the subject is led to believe that the substance is one to which he or she is known to be sensitive, and that the resultant increase in airways resistance can be reversed by another inhalation of saline believed by the subject to be a standard bronchodialator. The only failures to replicate these effects have employed insensitive measurement methods, a situation confirmed by the above investigators, again underscoring that such effects are probably real but modest indeed. In our own laboratory (Alexander, 1972; Alexander, Miklich, and Hershkoff, 1972) we have shown in a series of experiments that psychologic relaxation can result in both significant decreases in airways resistance or a retarding of the natural increase in resistance which occurs when maintenance oral bronchodialators are withheld. Again, these effects, though replicated by other investigators, are modest. Finally, Godfrey and Silverman (1973) have noted that premedication with placebo can lead to a significant reduction in the degree of exercise-induced bronchospasm.

The possibility that learning or conditioning may influence bronchomotor tone has also received attention, beginning almost a century ago. In 1886 Sir James McKenzie anecdotally described a woman who was said to develop wheezing from the sight of paper rose under glass. During the ensuing nine decades there have appeared no convincing laboratory demonstrations of "conditioned asthma," but several writers have discussed the likelihood of conditioned bronchospasm. It remains only an intriguing possibility that the circumstances under which naturally occurring antigen induced bronchospasm, or sympathomimetically provided relief, represent a standard classical conditioning paradigm. For example, Pavlov's dogs were caused to have a conditioned connection between a bell and salivation by means of a bell being sounded shortly before food powder was blown into their mouths. After many such pairings of the bell and food powder, the bell alone was capable of producing the reflexive salivation. Illustratively for the asthmatic the bell might be the visual and olfactory sensations associated with grass while the pollen would be the food powder. The bronchospasm in this case would represent the "reflexive" allergic reaction to pollen just like salivation to food. After enough pairings between grass and pollen, simply seeing grass should be capable of causing some conditional bronchospasm. Similarly, the stimuli immediately preceding the inhalation of a pharmachological bronchodialator should soon come to elicit some conditioned relaxation of bronchial smoothe muscle.

While the foregoing analysis is theoretically compelling, there are some problems. These kinds of conditional connections, known as *classical conditioned responses*, have in general proved to be unstable and/or hard to develop at all. With the exception of conditional responses which are highly adaptive for the organism, e.g., some food preferences, fear reactions, etc., classically conditioned connections tend to dissipate, or extinguish, very rapidly if the conditional stimulus is not consistently paired with the stimulus producing the reflexive reaction. For our example this means that every occasion in which grass stimuli (even artificial ones) are not actually associated with sufficient real pollen, thus producing a "reflexive" bronchial reaction, will constitute an extinction, or deconditioning, trial. Further, the actual model for our example is technically called *long delay* or *trace* conditioning, an even more unfavorable set of circumstances for the development and maintenance of classically conditioned responses. While the suggestion and placebo effects can certainly be interpreted as due, at least in part, to historical conditioning trials, it is not surprising that both these effects and examples of "conditioned asthma" have been so elusive. Careful analysis suggests that conditional bronchoconstriction or dilation would tend to develop only infrequently and almost never to any great degree in any particular case. As we have seen, natural conditioning trials, which must be numerous and occur under optimal circumstances for conditional reactions to develop at all, would in most instances be continually defused by natural extinction or deconditioning trials.

More recently, the possibility of biofeedback assisted learning, or volitional control, in the lung is being investigated. This work requires the use of elaborate and very expensive instrumentation to provide almost breath by breath analysis and feedback information of airways resistance. Furthermore, the validity of the technique employed, forced pressure oscillation, has been severely criticized. Unfortunately it represents the only currently available, precise method in this sort of work. These difficulties notwithstanding, and while recognizing the problems, Vachon (1971) has shown what appears to be reliable but very small "learned" drops in respiratory resistance in a few subjects. It is becoming increasingly clear in biofeedback research generally that very elaborate experimental control procedures are required before any obtained visceral changes can be confidently ascribed to learned voluntary control. As yet, such controls have not been employed in this work.

In summary, then, it appears on the one hand that despite much belief, hope, and often inspired effort on the part of psychosomatically committed investigators, no persuasive evidence has surfaced to support the long held notion that psycho-social variables play any role in the etiology of asthma. On the other hand, psycho-social variables do appear capable of exerting at least some control over lung function and the clinical course of the disease process in some individuals. A tempting, but somewhat discouraging conclusion for those committed to finding psychological pulmonary influence, is that such influence may be modest, possibly even when it is present at full strength, and for all practical purposes unmeasurable and of no consequence for the majority of asthmatics. There is cause for some therapeutic optimism, however. It remains a distinct possibility that the lungs of *some* asthmatics might be exquisitely sensitive to psychological influence. Better understanding of, and methods for, distinguishing these individuals might yield great benefits. So, too, might refinement of our techniques when applied to this subgroup of asthmatics. Such direct effects aside, psychological intervention methods have been found to be very helpful in dealing with many aspects of the emotional and adjustment consequences of asthma. The ways in which behavioral treatment methods may be helpful to the clinician as adjunctive therapy will occupy the remainder of this chapter.

Before beginning our coverage of behavioral intervention techniques, a brief description of the asthmatic patient might be helpful. The early onset asthma patient and his or her family face some very severe hardships. These youngsters tend to grow up watching the other children play from the livingroom side of the front window. Most have poor self-concepts. Often both academic and social development suffer greatly due to the amount of time lost from school and the restricted and specialized contacts with age-mates. They face both peers and adults who are variously overindulgent or lack understanding of their difficulties. Often these children react with shame and embarrassment or demandingness to the extreme. At home their asthma may become the sole focus around which all family activities and concerns come to revolve. Their parents may feel guilty, responsible and helpless; or at other times resentful and angry. Certainly an asthma sufferer can learn to manipulate others with the disorder or use it to excuse poor performance. It is often very difficult for the patient to clearly sort out what he or she can really do from what is accomplished in the face of asthma. Many maladaptive and inappropriate behavior patterns can develop as patient and family struggle with the ravages of this disorder. Such patterns can severely cripple family life and retard the social and psychological development of the child. Often the undesirable behavior patterns substantially affect the course of the disorder. Asthma is, of course, potentially life threatening and many patients have experienced bouts of status asthmaticus which on occasion may have brought them close to death. Such experiences often generate enduring anxiety responses which can manifest themselves in fears of death, hospitals, and treatment. Some patients develop conditional fear responses which can begin at even the first signs of wheezing. The frantic, worried behavior of parents and those treating the patient can exacerbate the young patient's fear. Moods vary with the severity of symptoms and also in relation to medications taken, from the widespread adrenergic effects of the sympathominetics to the undesirable side effects of the coriosteroids.

The late onset asthma sufferer faces a somewhat different set of problems because the asthma usually disrupts a life style which has become more or less fixed. Adjusting to asthma late in life can be very difficult for the patient and his or her family, often requiring substantial changes in activities and an adjustment to taking care of a chronic disorder. Like the youthful sufferer, the late onset asthmatic may become frightened of the symptoms and often very scared by and concerned over the side effects of medications. For the families of both young and old the financial burdens encountered in continually fighting asthma are almost always oppressive.

To deal effectively with the ravages of asthma often requires the talents of both medical and behavioral specialists. The purpose of what follows is to delineate the sorts of behavioral techniques which have been found to be useful by those involved in the treatment and rehabilitation of those individuals who suffer from asthma. Behavioral intervention methods have been employed in the therapeutic management of asthma in three fairly distinct ways: (1) to alter the abnormal pulmonary functioning more or less directly; (2) to alter maladaptive emotional concommitants; and (3) to alter maladaptive asthma-related behaviors and family patterns. Examples and descriptions of the techniques that have been successfully applied in each of these categories will be discussed in turn.

The methods which are intended to alter lung function in asthma include relaxation training, biofeedback, direct operant conditioning, and to some extent the deconditioning methods. As noted previously, relaxation following appropriate training is capable of beneficially altering lung function in at least some asthmatic patients. Relaxation can be used both symptomatically to ameliorate mild to moderate attacks and/or to prolong the effectiveness of sympathomimetic medications employed as a symptomatic therapy (e.g., inhaled isoproterenol), and when practiced daily, as an adjunct to maintenance therapy itself. While it is now clear that not all patients benefit, a situation common to many chemical therapies for asthma, fortunately relaxation is easily taught to and mastered by most patients. While we do not as yet know how to reliably distinguish beforehand those patients who will benefit, or the degree of response to be expected in those patients who do respond, the low implementation cost of this therapeutic adjunct in both time and effort substantially obviates this difficulty. The clinician can relegate instruction to support personnel or even tape recordings. In any case we can be assured that relaxation training can do no harm whatsoever, and usually the patient will find it of benefit in other aspects of his life as well.

The method to be described is that which is currently used in both the clinical and research work in the psychophysiology laboratory at the National Asthma Center. It has been found to be equally appropriate to adults and children over the age of about 10 years. Below this age attention span, comprehension and motivational difficulties tend to reduce substantially its usefulness. Relaxation is taught in five 20-minute sessions.* The first 2 sessions are spent instructing the patient in deep muscle relaxation employing an abbreviated version of Jacobson's (1938) progressive relaxation training technique. The rationale is to aid the patient to become much more aware of the state of the musculature, to become sensitive to the contrast between tense and relaxed muscles, and to learn to release tension in muscles more or less at will. In terms of the physical surroundings, the illumination should be low, the environment quiet and undisturbed, and after the rationale is explained, the patient should be instructed to close the eyes and attain a comfortable position in which no part of the body must be supported by muscular effort. This can be accomplished in a reclining type chair or even a straight back chair with the arms dangling loosely to the sides and the head slumping into the shoulders. The training begins by having the patient make a tight fist with both hands, holding it tightly until the therapist says "relax," at which time the patient is instructed to simply relax the muscles all at one by just "letting go." It should be emphasized that the release of tension is not an active process but a passive one. This is repeated until both the therapist and patient are satisfied that the hands can be relaxed naturally, easily, and completely on command. Difficulties at this stage can be dealt with by focusing on just one hand or even just the fingers separately. When relaxation of the hands is accomplished the patient will have gained an appreciation of the process and be much more capable of monitoring his or her own progress. Other major muscle groups are then taken up in turn: first the forearms and then the upper arms. Next the muscles in the forehead are tensed by closing the eyes and frowning; the cheeks and jaws by clenching the teeth and pulling back the corners of the mouth; the chin and neck by pulling in the chin; and then the upper back and shoulders. Next the stomach muscles are tensed by making the stomach hard and then the leg muscles, which can be done "all at once." Finally, the feet and toes are done by curling the toes. It seems preferable to do each muscle group using varying degrees of tightness and duration of tensing: a small, medium, or maximum amount of tightness for durations varying between about two to six seconds.

Do not neglect to get feedback from the patient regarding the subjective sense of progress or to comment to the patient concerning your observations of progress. This phase is covered in two sessions about 20 minutes each in length. The next two sessions are spent instructing the patient in autogenic relaxation (Luthe, 1963). The

*Protocols for the relaxation training methods discussed are available from the author: The National Asthma Center, 1999 Julian, Denver, Colorado 80204.

rationale here is to assist the patient to become aware of two prominent subjective feeling states associated with relaxation: heaviness in the limbs and warmth in the muscles. Under the same circumstances as before, the patient is instructed to get him or herself muscularly relaxed and then to listen to the therapist in a passive, accepting manner. It is pointed out that each time the therapist says a phrase the patient is to repeat it silently to him or herself immediately afterwards, concentrating in a passive manner on the body part and feeling to which the therapist is referring. The therapist starts by saying aloud in a slow, soothing manner, "My right hand is heavy." This is repeated several times by the therapist with about 5 seconds or so between statements to provide enough time for the patient to repeat the phrase. Then the same thing is done with the right arm, followed by the left hand and arm separately. Then the therapist says, "Both of my hands and arms are heavy." Next, the same thing is done for the feet and legs separately and together. After completing the heaviness phrases, the same procedure is followed by substituting the word "warm" for "heavy." When this is accomplished the whole procedure is repeated saying the words "heavy and warm" together. The patient should be instructed not to worry about "getting the feelings" but that they will come naturally when the patient is able to "let go" and just "let them happen." The patient should be encouraged to enjoy the feelings. After each session there should be some discussion regarding progress and concerning which feelings were attained and to what extent. The final session is spent combining the two methods: once through the body with mild muscle tensing, followed by once over the limbs saying "heavy and warm" together until these feelings are present to some degree in each limb. The patient can be allowed to do this by him or herself without therapist assistance, saying the autogenic phrases enough times each to accomplish the sensations. In the last five minutes the patient should be instructed to simply "go on relaxing" by repeating the word "warm" to him or herself each time they breathe out. This latter technique is a meditative form of relaxation.

From the beginning, the patient should be requested to practice twice a day for no more than 20 minutes. Initially the patient may wish to use a timer, but this will become unnecessary very shortly. The practice should not be done during symptomatic periods until the ability to relax at will is well learned. Subsequently, the patient should continue to relax regularly twice per day and also at times when mild symptoms are present or whenever the patient desires or needs to relax for some reason: to get sleep, to "come down" after a stressful experience, or as a preparation for one.

The remaining methods which are intended to alter lung function more or less directly are much more experimental and difficult to carry out in a nonlaboratory setting. As noted previously, airway resistance biofeedback generally requires elaborate and expensive equipment which is usually unavailable to the clinician. A simple method might be to allow the patient to listen to his or her breathing sounds with a stethescope. More straightforward attempts have been made to operantly condition (teach) increased flow rates by positively reinforcing successively higher flow rates as a patient makes many forced vital capacity (FVC) "blows" into some sort of spirometric device. Such attempts have not really proved successful and it should be remembered that repeated FVC's cause reflexive bronchospasm in many asthmatics. At present, such procedures should be confined to the laboratory. Finally, it was pointed out previously that some bronchospasm may actually be classically conditioned. If so, it should be possible to employ some of the so-called deconditioning methods to reduce the conditional connection. Again, this represents a situation of much more interest to researchers than of value to clinicians. If, however, you should run across a strongly suspected case of "conditioned asthma" (like the paper rose) a method such as classical extinction, i.e., repeated presentations of the suspected stimulus, should take care of it very nicely. Just make sure that the stimulus cannot itself cause "reflexive" (nonconditioned) bronchospasm. An example would be the presentation of a real flower whose pollen dissemination was not somehow prevented. Such a presentation would result in a conditioning rather than an extinction trial.

The second category is that of the emotional concomitants of asthma episodes themselves. Such reactions can become conditioned through frightening, life-threatening episodes, the anxious reactions of parents and doctors during severe episodes, the pain associated with treatment (e.g., arterial punctures), etc. These untoward reactions often make treating the patient difficult and can apparently in some cases exacerbate and prolong the attack itself, not to speak of the increased discomfort for the patient. Such "phobic reactions" to asthma often develop at the earliest signs of tightness, or for some patients, even by thinking about the possibility of getting asthma, e.g., having to be in contact with a known precipitant or being without medications, etc. These conditioned fear reactions can be dealt with in a very efficient and effective manner by using a technique called systematic desensitization—the psychologic counterpart of hyposensitization therapy. The rationale is that conditioned fear reactions can be weakened if the stimuli which precipitate them can be made to occur in the presence of a relaxed state and without being followed by the usual aversive circumstances. This is done by presenting the eliciting stimuli in small, graded "chunks" either live or in imagination while the patient is relaxed. Each time the patient is able to endure a stimulus presentation without feeling the former anxiety, the next more powerful stimulus is presented until the patient is able to imagine or be in the presence of even the most formerly anxiety arousing situation without experiencing an anxiety response.

The treatment is accomplished in three stages. The first is to teach relaxation as outlined previously. The second is to contruct, via interview with the patient, a graded hierarchy of situations that the patient finds disturbing. Finally, the patient is assisted while relaxed to visualize or imagine the items of the hierarchy systematically from the least to the most disturbing, serially deconditioning the anxiety response at each step of the way. A typical hierarchy might go something like this: (1) just thinking about the possibility of starting to wheeze; (2) feeling tight; (3) wheezing mildly; (4) more wheezing and thinking about it getting worse; (5) failure of immediate response of a symptomatic drug; (6) having to go to the emergency room; (7) waiting for the medication to work while wheezing badly (8) requiring IV therapy. Each item is visualized for about 30 seconds while the patient is relaxed, until the patient reports feeling no anxiety to that item—usually 2 to 4 times—then the next item is visualized and so on. Relaxation is reestablished between each visualization. Sessions should not last more than about 30–40 minutes and each new session should begin with representations of the previously passed item. So that the patient does not have to routinely converse with the therapist during actual treatment, usually some sort of finger signal is employed for the patient to signal the presence of anxiety during visualization. Any time the patient signals feeling anxiety while visualizing, visualizing is stopped immediately and relaxation is reestablished before the item is presented again.

The procedure as described above is particularly useful when it would be difficult or impossible to manipulate the real anxiety arousing situations, as in the hierarchy given as an example above. There are occasions, however, when systematic desensitization can be very expeditiously carried out *in vivo*. For example, one young child at the National Asthma Center was experiencing anxiety whenever he wheezed, even mildly, but not when just talking or thinking about asthma. By withholding regular oral bronchodialators for successively longer periods preceding relaxation training sessions, this child was taught to relax while actually experiencing progressively more wheezing. The situation was enhanced by doing the training in a medical treatment atmosphere complete with all of the equipment. The therapy is simple and effective and may even lend itself to the outpatient office situation if the physician has sufficient control over the regular medication regimen to schedule office visits accordingly. This latter procedure is especially well suited to the pediatric patient who is experiencing maladaptive fear when wheezing. It should be clear that there are substantial management benefits to be gained by making use of this simple therapeutic approach either by visualization or *in vivo* for the anxious asthma patient.

The final category involves that of dealing with maladaptive or undesirable asthma-related patterns of behavior. The fact that human behavior is to a great extent controlled by its consequences forms the basis of most behavioral approaches to mental health problems. On the one hand, if a behavior is followed by a reward or desirable consequence or by the removal of an ongoing averse or undesirable circumstance, the future probability of that behavior occurring is increased. On the other hand, if a behavior is followed by an aversive consequence or the removal or enforced unavailability of a rewarding circumstance, the probability of that behavior being repeated is reduced. Techniques based upon the deliberate control of such maintenance reinforcement contingencies have been used to good effect in the rehabilitation and management of asthma patients, particularly children. Illustrative examples from work done at the National Asthma Center and elsewhere will be employed to give some indication of the variety of ways in which contingency management methods have been used.

Positive reinforcement describes the strategy of making a reward contingent upon the occurrence of a desirable behavior. Renne and Creer (1976) used this procedure to teach a young child to use properly an intermittent positive pressure breathing device. They rewarded successively more correct responses until the child had learned to use the device in its intended manner. They found also that significantly less follow-up medication was required as the child became more proficient at using this therapeutic apparatus.

Satiation occurs when a reinforcer is available in such large quantities over an extended period that it tends to lose its effect. Creer (in press) reports on a young boy who was inappropriately requesting hospitalization for very mild asthma as a way of avoiding school related stress. A dramatic drop in the number of inappropriate hospitalizations was affected by hospitalizing this boy without delay for 3 continuous days (satiation) each time he requested an *unnecessary* admission.

Extinction occurs when a previously rewarded behavior is no longer reinforced. This procedure, along with the systematic rewarding of desirable behavior, is used widely at the Center both on an informal and more formal basis. Neisworth and Moore (1972) produced a dramatic reduction in the number of coughing episodes in an asthmatic youngster by instructing the parents to withhold the attention which the coughing had been eliciting.

Time out from positive reinforcement is a procedure which involves removal of positive reinforcement for a specified period contingent upon the occurrence of a specific inappropriate behavior. Creer (1970) has reported using this procedure on another boy who was felt to be malingering. This youngster was requesting many unnecessary admissions to the hospital unit, usually to avoid social stress. Each time the boy was admitted, the usual pleasant surroundings in our hospital, comic books, games, TV, etc., were removed, and he had to spend his time simply recuperating in bed. A dramatic drop in the frequency and duration of hospitalizations resulted with no increase in symptoms.

Response cost is like time out except that it involves the contingent withdrawal of a specified amount of reinforcement rather than withdrawal of reinforcement over a specified time period. Creer and Yoches (1971) used this procedure to increase amount of time spent attending to classroom materials in two asthmatic children who had failed to develop these skills due to the amount of time lost from school because of illness. At the beginning of each classroom session the children were given 40 points, from which one point was subtracted for each 30 second period spent not attending to classroom materials. Each subtraction was signaled. The children understood well, and soon learned to retain the points, which could be exchanged for inexpensive gifts. As might be hoped, academic performance also improved.

Punishment involves contingent presentation of an aversive stimulus. In our laboratory at the Center a case of coughing elicited by several specific stimuli was treated using a procedure called response suppression shaping (Alexander et al., 1973). This boy had to refrain from coughing for longer and longer periods following presentation of a precipitating stimulus in order to avoid a brief, mild electric shock to the forearm. He was able to reduce his tendency to cough in a very orderly fashion to each of the four identified precipitants of his coughing. A prominent feature of this case was that the coughing had been maintained by contingent attention being paid to it by the boy's family. Indeed, much of the family's life had come to revolve about "the problem." For example, three of the precipitants, the odors of cooking grease, hair spray and hand soap, had required considerable accommodations in the eating and toilet habits of the family, and hence, was a source of constant stress. Behavioral intervention at the family level was required to alter reinforcement patterns such that the coughing was not reestablished once it had been eliminated by the suppression procedure.

The example cited above underscores one of the most important aspects of the total clinical management in chronic disorders such as asthma. Even the most sophisticated and potentially effective medical management program can be subverted by inappropriate patterns of reacting to and dealing with asthma at the family level. The taking of medications, the assignment of responsibilities, the ways in which the presence of symptoms are handled can have a profound effect on family life and the psychological development of the patient. Inappropriate response patterns can *cause* increased stress and can lay the foundation for psychological problems.

In almost all such cases the most effective treatment strategy is a *combination* of adequate medical management *and* behavioral intervention. But before intervention can take place a thorough behavioral analysis of response patterns and maintenance reinforcing contingencies must be carried out. Behavioral analysis is complex, and an explication of the methods involved goes well beyond the scope of this chapter. It must suffice here to firmly recommend that whenever a physician feels that reasonable medical management is being compromised by untoward reactions of the patient and/or family or that the severity of the reported symptom picture or concern of the patient and his or her family is inconsistent with the actual severity of the disorder, consultation from a psychologist familiar with behavioral methods should be sought. In this way total management can be accomplished in the most rational and effective manner.

REFERENCES

Alexander, A.B. Systematic relaxation and flow rates in asthmatic children: Relationship to emotional precipitants and anxiety. *Journal of Psychosomatic Research* 1972, *16*, 405.

Alexander, A.B., Miklich, D.R., & Herschkoff, H. The immediate effects of systematic relaxation on peak expiratory flow rates in asthmatic children. *Psychosomatic Medicine*, 1972, *34*, 388.

Alexander, A.B., Chai, H, et al. The elimination of chronic cough by response suppression shaping. *Journal of Behavior Therapy and Experimental Psychiatry* 1973, *4*, 75–80.

Creer, T.L. The use of a time-out from positive reinforcement procedure with asthmatic children. *Journal of Psychosomatic Research*, 1970, *14*, 117.

Creer, T.L., & Yoches, C. The modification of an inappropriate behavioral pattern in asthmatic children, *Journal of Chronic Disease*, 1971, *24*, 507.

Creer, T.L. Asthma: Psychological aspects and management. In Middleton, E., Reed, C. & Ellis, E., Eds., *Allergy: principles and practice*. St. Louis: C.V. Mosby (In press).

Creer, T.L., & Renne, C.M. Training social agents in the rehabilitation of chronically-ill children. In Bernal, M.E., Ed. *Training in behavior modification*. Belmont, Calif. (In press).

French, T.M. & Alexander, F. Psychogenic factors in bronchial asthma. *Psychosomatic Medicine Monographs*, 1941, *4*, 2–94.

Godfrey, S., & Silverman, M. Demonstration of placebo response in asthma by means of exercise testing. *Journal of Psychosomatic Research*, 1973, *17*, 293.

Gold, W.M., Kessler, G.R., & Yr, D.Y. C. Role of vagus nerves in experimental asthma in allergic dogs. *Journal of Applied Physiology*, 1972, *33* (6), 719–725.

Jacobson, E. *Progressive relaxation*, Chicago: University of Chicago Press, 1938.

Knapp, P.H., Mathé, A.A., & Vachon, L. Psychosomatic aspects of bronchial asthma. In Weis, E.B., & Segal, M.S., Eds., *Bronchial asthma, its nature and management*. Boston: Little, Brown & Co. (In press).

Luparello, T., Lyons, H.A., et al. Influence of suggestion on airway reactivity in asthmatic subjects. *Psychosomatic Medicine*, 1968, *30*, 819–825.

Luthe, W. Autogenic training: Method, research, and application in medicine. *American Journal of Psychotherapy* 1963, *17*, 174.

Mathé, A.A., & Knapp, P.H. Emotional and adrenal reactions to stress in bronchial asthma. *Psychosomatic Medicine*, 1971, *33*, 323.

Neisworth, J.T., & Moore, F. Operant treatment of asthmatic responding with the parent as therapist. *Behavior Therapy*, 1972, *3*, 95.

Purcell, K., Brady, D., et al. Effect on asthma in children of experimental separation from the family. *Psychosomatic Medicine*, 1969, *31*, 144–164.

Purcell, K., and Weiss, J.H. Asthma. In Costello, C.G., Ed., *Symptons of psychopathology*. New York: Wiley, 1970.

Renne, C., & Creer, T.L. The effects of training on the use of Inhalation therapy equipment by children with asthma. *Journal of the Applied Analysis of Behavior*, 1976, *9*, 1–11.

Vachon, L. Visceral learning of respiratory resistance. *Psychosomatic Medicine*, 1971, *24*, 471.

Chapter 3

Insomnia[†]

T.D. Borkovec*

The application of behavioral intervention strategies to the treatment of insomnia has a relatively recent history. Research during the past five years has demonstrated the efficacy of certain procedures for certain types of sleep disturbance problems. As you will soon see, the methods are fairly simple, even though the benefits to the patient are frequently quite substantial. Before I begin to describe these behavioral strategies, however, a few cautionary notes are necessary.

First, although insomnia typically refers to difficulty in initially falling asleep, the label is also applied to problems involving frequent awakenings during the night, difficulty in falling asleep after awakening, and early morning awakenings. Although clients reporting problems in initial sleep onset often report one or more of these additional symptoms, some clients display the latter problems without reporting initial sleep onset problems. Furthermore, behavioral research has focused on initial sleep onset and either has not measured the occurrence of the other symptoms or has usually failed to demonstrate significant changes in those problems after treatment. Thus, we will be able to talk confidently only about the treatment of sleep onset difficulties.

Second, we need to keep in mind that there is wide variation among individuals in the amount of sleep they seem to require. While

*University of Iowa.

†Some of the research studies cited were supported by Biomedical Sciences Support Grant FR–07035 from the General Research Support Branch, Division of Research Sciences, Bureau of Health Professions, and Grant MH24603–01 from the National Institute of Mental Health.

seven to eight hours is modal, some people report the need of only six hours while others report they require ten hours of sleep to feel rested and optimally alert during the subsequent day. Indeed, a pair of Australian gentlemen exist on an average of three hours of sleep without any evidence of physical or psychological dysfunction. Unfortunately, basic researchers in the sleep area have yet to determine exactly what functions sleep and its stages serve. Given such background information, it is clear that insomnia is a relative term, that the person's report of satisfaction or dissatisfaction with his/her sleep represents a prime criterion for determining the presence of a sleeping problem, and that in some cases the only sleeping problem may be an unrealistic desire to obtain more sleep than the body requires. A similar warning is applicable to latency to sleep onset. Table 3–1 summarizes the replies of 480 undergraduate students at the University of Iowa to questions regarding typical latency to sleep onset and whether or not they felt that their latency represents a problem for them. Over two-thirds of the sample reported latencies under 21 minutes; few of these students (12.7 percent) considered this latency to be a problem. With latencies beyond 21 minutes, the respondents showed a marked increase in dissatisfaction with their sleep onset. Notice, however, that substantial numbers of students with quite long latencies did not consider themselves to be sleep-disturbed.

Third, any particular case of true insomnia may be due to one or more of several causes. The use of behavioral treatment is clearly suited for only specific and limited subsets of insomnia problems and is unsuited for several other subsets. Embarking upon behavioral training programs with patients for whom such procedures are inappropriate can only increase the patient's frustration and impatience

Table 3–1. Distribution of Reports of Latency to Sleep Onset (in Minutes) and the Percent Within Each Latency Category Reporting That Latency to Represent a Sleeping Problem

Latency to Sleep Onset	*Percent Reporting This Latency*	*Percent Reporting a Latency Problem*
0–5	10.6	0.0
6–10	19.4	0.0
11–15	21.7	2.9
16–20	17.1	9.8
21–25	2.7	84.6
26–30	13.3	42.2
31–45	9.2	36.4
46–60	4.4	71.4
61–90	1.5	85.7
91+	0.2	0.0

with himself and his therapist. Consequently, determination of the suitability of behavioral approaches for a given patient is very important. Such a decision is made by identifying both characteristics that preclude their use as well as characteristics that suggest their appropriateness. I will first discuss the kinds of information that indicate causal factors not susceptible to behavior intervention and then describe factors suggesting the feasibility of such techniques.

Sleep laboratory research over the past decade has substantially increased our knowledge about sleep in general and sleep disorders in particular. The work of investigators such as William Dement and Anthony Kales has indicated very clearly the contribution of biological factors to disordered sleep. Thus far, there is no evidence that behavioral treatment has any impact on insomnia mediated by such factors.

The most important biological cause of insomnia is drug-related. Surprisingly, many insomnias are maintained by the very drugs prescribed for their treatment. Although hypnotics may offer temporary soporific effects, it has been found that most sleep-inducing agents loose their effectiveness within a week or two and influence sleep stage patterns during their administration. Tolerance to the medication develops and soon the patient has a drug dependency, a return of the original sleeping problem, and a disordered sleep pattern. The chronic use of hypnotics is such a common cause of insomnia that Dement (1972) has concluded, "Whenever an insomniac says he is taking sleeping pills, we assume that he has drug dependency insomnia" (p. 80). The initial clinical step involves gradual withdrawal of the medication; Dement (1972) reports that withdrawal has led to greatly improved sleep in every patient so treated. Of course, subsequent to such withdrawal, there may be indications for the appropriateness of further behavioral treatment to increase the improvement or to prevent future disturbance. Without such withdrawal, however, behavioral intervention is unlikely to have any effect.

Sleep apnea (the cessation of respiration) has been identified as an additional causative factor in some cases of insomnia. The patient may awaken hundreds of times at night gasping for air. In the morning, disturbed sleep or the frequent awakenings themselves are recalled but the respiration problem is not. All night recording of EEG and respiration is the only certain diagnostic procedure for this problem. As yet, there is no known simple form of treatment, but certainly the behavioral procedures to be described would be contraindicated.

There are no doubt other biologically related causes of insomnia.

Dement (1975), for example, has recently found a subset of sleep disturbed patients who display rhythmic leg twitches. Presumably such body movements whose origin is unknown are sufficient to arouse the patient and produce reports of disordered sleep. Phase shifts in circadian rhythm may also be responsible for disordered sleep, with the well-known jet lag syndrome representing the most obvious example. Further laboratory research will hopefully identify the cause and suggest the most appropriate treatment for these and other forms of insomnia.

Many cases of insomnia do not clearly involve any of the above factors, appear to be caused by psychological or environmental factors, and are quite susceptible to behavioral intervention. Similar to the biologically mediated cases, the exact nature of the psychological causes remains speculative. However, past research on sleep and studies of human behavior in general have supplied some clues to understanding the maintenance, if not the etiology, of psychological insomnia and has thus directed the development of various behavioral treatments to be described.

As might be expected, subtypes of problems exist within this class of insomnia problems as well. The most important distinction involves insomnia complaints in the absence of other symptomatology or obvious environmental stress (primary insomnia) and complaints of disturbed sleep from patients with clear psychological or environmental problems (secondary insomnia). In the former case, fairly direct application of behavioral techniques is indicated. In the case of secondary insomnia, simple behavioral intervention may be useful but caution is advised. For a patient who reports serious occupational or financial difficulties, social or marital problems, or any other psychologically stressful circumstance, it is no wonder that his/her sleep is disturbed. Counseling should, under such circumstances, focus on those adjustment difficulties. If the emotional problems are very severe, especially in the case of depression, referral to mental health professionals is highly advisable. In less severe cases, however, the presence of adjustment problems does not preclude symptomatic treatment via behavioral techniques. Disordered sleep stemming from life problems simply contributes one more form of stress to the patient and its amelioration may help the patient in his/her efforts to resolve those underlying problems.

Insomniac patients also differ in terms of whether or not they actually do show an actual sleep deficit. Again, sleep laboratory research has produced some surprising data. The EEG records of many insomniacs show no lack of objectively defined sleep, even though the patients feel they obtained very little sleep; and poor sleepers have been routinely found to grossly exaggerate how long it takes them to fall asleep (Borkovec and Weerts, in press; Rechtschaffen and Monroe chapter in Kales, 1969). Dement (1972) refers to such cases as pseudo-insomniacs, while patients who do show a sleep deficit (six hours of sleep or less and reports of daytime drowsiness) are called ideopathic insomniacs. The suffering of the pseudo-insomniac appears to be very real, however, and data from our laboratory suggest that behavioral intervention is effective in either type of case, probably for different and as yet unspecified reasons. Consequently, this distinction is generally unimportant for treatment planning, with two exceptions. First, in the case of pseudo-insomnia, sleep-inducing medication obviously should not be administered. Secondly, it may be therapeutic to inform the patient that he/she is obtaining sufficient sleep by objective standards. While one cannot assume that such information will eliminate the patient's complaint, it may serve to reduce one frequent contributing factor, i.e., the patient's concern that he/she is not obtaining enough sleep.

Finally, patients vary in terms of their reports of bedtime tension and cognitive activity. Most patients report excessive cognitive intrusions (e.g., "racing mind," worrying about past or future events) that they cannot turn off. In addition, some patients report excessive nervousness, tension, or other by-products of apparent autonomic overactivation. Again, at present there is no reason for such differences to influence treatment planning, since the behavioral techniques appear to address both potential contributors.

The two behavioral treatment procedures that I will describe in detail are progressive relaxation training and stimulus control. A growing body of research supports the efficacy of these two methods, and therefore they warrant our close attention.

PROGRESSIVE RELAXATION PROCEDURES

Progressive relaxation training was originally developed by Edmund Jacobson in the early 1900s as a method of reducing muscle tension and the autonomic arousal by-products of tension. The technique involves the learning of two specific skills through repeated practice: (1) tensing and releasing gross muscle groups throughout the body and (2) focusing of attention on the resultant feelings of tension when muscles are tensed and the feelings of relaxation that occur when muscles are released. Although the procedure has been modified by various practitioners, I will summarize the modified version that we have successfully used clinically and in research over the past seven years and that has been described in detail in Bernstein and Borkovec (1973).

The initial portion of relaxation training involves a demonstration by the therapist of the sixteen muscle groups to be employed during training with instructions of obtaining tension in each group:

1. Dominant hand and forearm—"Make a tight fist."
2. Dominant biceps—"Push your elbow down against the arm of the chair."
3. Nondominant hand and forearm.
4. Nondominant biceps.
5. Upper facial muscles—"Lift your eyebrows as high as you can."
6. Central facial muscles—"Squint your eyes tightly and wrinkle up your nose."
7. Lower facial muscles—"Bite down hard and pull the corners of your mouth back."
8. Neck muscles—"Counterpose the muscles in the front and back of your neck, e.g., pull your chin down toward your chest and at the same time prevent it from actually touching your chest."
9. Chest, upper back, and shoulders—"Pull your shoulder blades down and together."
10. Abdominal muscles—"Make your stomach hard as if you were going to hit yourself in the stomach."
11. Dominant upper leg—"Counterpose the muscles on top and underneath your upper leg."
12. Dominant calf—"Pull your toes upward toward your head."
13. Dominant foot—"Turn your foot inward while pointing your foot away from you and curling your toes."
14. Nondominant upper leg.
15. Nondominant calf.
16. Nondominant foot.

With each demonstration, the therapist insures that the patient is tensing properly and recommends alternative tensing instructions if the patient is unable to produce strong tension by the initial instructions. The therapist emphasizes that learning to relax is a skill that requires practice and that the skill involves learning both to tense and release the muscle groups as instructed and to focus on the resulting sensations. Once the patient understands the procedures and his/her task during the training session, formal relaxation training can begin. Typically, the patient sits in a recliner chair during the session, although any chair, couch, or even the floor may be suitable when combined with supporting pillows. The only important guideline is that the patient can recline in a comfortable fashion and that he/she is completely supported without the use of any muscles. Sources of possible distraction are eliminated (e.g., lights are dimmed; shoes, watches, rings are removed). With the patient comfortably reclined with eyes closed, the therapist begins training with the dominant hand and forearm and proceeds throughout the sixteen muscle groups in the order outlined above. With each muscle group, the therapist instructs the patient to tense that muscle group for five to seven seconds, to release the muscles immediately and completely, and to focus for 30 to 45 seconds on the feelings of relaxation that result. During each tension-release cycle, the therapist attempts to keep the patient's attention focused on the process and provides instructions as well as indirect suggestions of the kinds of sensations frequently reported by patients undergoing relaxation training. Thus, for example, in a quiet tone of voice, the therapist would say:

> Focus your attention on the muscles of your right hand and forearm and by making a tight fist, tense those muscles now . . . Notice what it feels like to have tension in those muscles and where that tension is located . . . Relax, letting those muscles go completely and immediately . . . concentrating only now on the pleasant feelings of relaxation as the muscles of your right hand and forearm loosen up, unwind, and become more and more relaxed . . . Just notice what it feels like as the relaxation process takes place . . .

This procedure is repeated and the therapist proceeds to the next group only if the patient reports complete relaxation (i.e., absence of tension). If tension remains after those two tension-release cycles, up to two more cycles will be administered before proceeding to the next group. After successfully completing the last muscle group (nondominant foot), the therapist asks the patient to indicate whether any muscle group is still tense. If so, two more tension-release cycles on that group are provided. Once the patient reports complete relaxation throughout his/her body, the therapist provides an additional few minutes of indirect suggestions and allows the patient to enjoy the relaxation he/she has produced.

Upon completion of the training procedure, the therapist asks a variety of questions regarding the patient's experience during the session, answers questions, and provides suggestions to overcome any problems encountered. Most importantly, the patient is instructed to practice the procedure at home twice a day between sessions, 15–20 minutes per practice session. The second practice session, of course, is to take place in bed upon retiring.

As the patient practices and acquires some skill in relaxation, muscle groups are combined during subsequent training sessions. Ordinarily, after three sessions employing sixteen muscle groups, training is conducted with seven muscle groups for two sessions, followed by two sessions with four muscle groups. The final two sessions involve the elimination of tension-release cycles altogether and a recall method is employed. With the latter procedure, the four major muscle groups are used; the patient is instructed to identify tension in each group and to relax that tension away by *recalling* how those muscles felt before when they were tensed and released. Table 3–2 describes this session progression, the muscle group combinations, and the typical training time required.

Notice that each combination results in halving the amount of time required to produce deep relaxation. Through continued use of the recall method, eventually the patient is able to eliminate unnecessary tension very rapidly and without overt muscle tension-release. If the patient encounters difficulties at any stage, the therapist simply returns to the procedures of the earlier stage.

The above description summarizes the basic training procedures for progressive relaxation. These procedures are the same, regardless of the intended use of the skill. There is nothing magical about this particular choice of muscle groups, timing parameters, number of

Table 3–2. Typical Training Sequence for Progressive Relaxation

Session Number	*Muscle Groups*	*Average Length of Session*
1, 2, 3	16 muscle groups, tension-release	45–60 min.
4, 5	7 muscle groups, tension-release: 1) dominant hand, forearm, and biceps 2) nondominant hand, forearm, and biceps 3) facial muscles 4) neck muscles 5) chest, upper back, shoulders, and abdomen 6) dominant upper leg, calf, and foot 7) nondominant upper leg, calf, and foot	20–30 min.
6, 7	4 muscle groups, tension-release: 1) hands, forearms, and biceps 2) facial and neck muscles 3) chest, upper back, shoulders, and abdomen 4) upper legs, calves, and feet	10–15 min.
8, 9	4 muscle groups, recall method	10–15 min.

cycles, progression over sessions, or particular group combinations. These initially arbitrary choices simply happen to be those we have adopted for both clinical and research use and currently represent the most frequently used procedures in the behavior therapy literature. Typically, the described progressive relaxation procedures have been employed in clinical settings for the treatment of a variety of tension related problems and as a component procedure in the systematic desensitization (Wolpe, 1958) of phobic anxiety. In applying the training to sleep disorders, a few additional comments should be made, particularly regarding the rationale for its use.

As mentioned earlier the research literature and clinical observation suggests at least three potential proximal maintaining factors of psychologically mediated sleep disturbance: heightened physiological activity, cognitive intrusion, and worry over inability to sleep. Monroe (1967), for example, found poor sleepers to be autonomically overaroused prior to and during sleep as compared to good sleepers. Our own studies indicate that patients routinely report an inability to turn off thoughts and images relating to the day's events, past and future concerns, etc. Finally, the effectiveness of placebo treatment, at least with moderate insomniacs, suggests that any form of "treatment" may be beneficial simply via its capacity to reassure the patient that he/she no longer needs to be concerned about the sleeping problem. Notice that these factors are likely to interact in most cases of insomnia.

The elements of progressive relaxation and the existing literature indicate that the training procedure may be ideally suited for each of these contributing factors. First, as originally developed by Jacobson (1938), the technique was specifically aimed at reducing physiological tension. Indeed, Paul (1969) has demonstrated that progressive relaxation is significantly superior to other forms of relaxation training (hypnotic and self-relaxation) in reducing autonomic arousal. Second, learning to focus attention on pleasant, relatively monotonous internal sensations is an integral component of learning progressive relaxation. As such, the attention-focusing training provides a skill that is incompatible with the occurrence of cognitive intrusions. In addition, tension-release cycles provide discrete, internal stimuli that can serve as clear, noticeable targets for focused attention. Swedish research (e.g., Bohlin, 1971, 1972) as well as our own studies have demonstrated that variable interval monotonous stimulation has soporific effects, very much like the folklore sleep-inducing method of counting sheep. We have also demonstrated that the tension-release cycles within the progressive relaxation procedure markedly facilitate sleep-onset improvement beyond that produced by relaxation administered without tension-release cycles (Borkovec, Kaloupek, and Slama, 1975). Finally, progressive relaxation, while demonstrated to contain an active ingredient in several studies (Steinmark and Borkovec, 1974; Borkovec et al., 1975; Borkovec and Weerts, in press), also seems to be a particularly credible and placebo-inducing procedure. Patients easily understand the procedure, can readily relate the procedure and its rationale to their own situation, and probably have less hesitancy to engage in the training than might sometimes be the case with negatively-connoted hypnotic or drug procedures.

Before initiating progressive relaxation, we will generally provide the patient with a complete description of the procedure and relate that procedure to the factors that are apparently contributing to his/her sleep problem. Thus, we don't hesitate to discuss what we know about the maintenance of sleep disturbance, in what ways we expect relaxation training to be beneficial, and what the patient might expect in terms of therapeutic benefit. Unless the patient fully understands the procedure and its rationale, faithful and conscientious practice, an absolutely essential component of the technique for a favorable outcome, is unlikely to occur.

As long as one can rule out biologically mediated disturbance or severe psychological maladjustment, prognosis for sleep onset difficulties is quite favorable. Successful clinical experience with relaxation treatment has been further supported by our laboratory investigations with moderate insomniacs. Over the past four years we have completed six outcome investigations involving over 250 sleep disturbed subjects. In relative terms, progressive relaxation has been found to be significantly superior to both no-treatment and several placebo and control conditions. In absolute terms, three to four training sessions have resulted in reductions of average sleep onset time from 41 minutes to 19 minutes at four-month and one-year follow-up, an improvement of over 50 percent. Ordinarily, improvement has been found to correlate with initial severity, so that more severe cases typically report improvements ranging from 65 to 75 percent of their initial sleep latency. Importantly, our average follow-up outcome of 19 minutes brings the treated group within the latency reports of the majority of the normal population (see Table 3–1).

STIMULUS CONTROL PROCEDURES

Stimulus control procedures have been employed for a long time in behavior modification. Once a history of learning results in an association between a stimulus and a response, presentation or removal of the stimulus can influence the current occurrence or nonoccurrence of that response. Such an association may be established either through Pavlovian conditioning procedures (e.g., sight of delicious food paired with presentation of food to the mouth leads to salivation and/or hunger response to the sight of that food) or through instrumental conditioning procedures (e.g., sight of green traffic light leads to an acceleration response, reinforced by safe passage through the intersection). Such conditioning processes are quite pervasive in human behavior, and learning theorists suggest that much if not most human behavior can be explained by, and therefore modified through, the application of these learning principles.

It is not surprising, then, that behavior therapists in the area of sleep disorders have offered stimulus control interpretations for the etiology and maintenance of the disturbances and suggest stimulus control procedures for their amelioration.

The most explicit statement of this approach along with documenting research evidence is provided by Richard Bootzin at Northwestern University. His basic assumption is that bed-related stimuli set the occasion for either sleep-compatible or sleep-incompatible responses, depending on the individual's history of associations. For most people, bed-related cues have had an extensive history of association with sleep-compatible behaviors, e.g., assuming a reclined position, turning off cognitive activity that typically occurs during the day. Upon exposure to bed-related stimuli (e.g., soft pajamas, dark room, blankets and pillow), the probability of sleep-compatible behaviors increases, thus increasing the probability of sleep. The insomniac, on the other hand, has obviously had a history in which bed-related cues have been associated with sleep-incompatible responses (e.g., worrying about problems, planning the next day's activities). Under such circumstances exposure to bed-related cues increases the probability of occurrence of sleep-incompatible behaviors, and thus decreases the probability of sleep. A variety of observations provide at least partial support for this maintenance hypothesis. Most people, for example, experience greater than usual difficulty falling asleep when exposed to novel sleeping circumstances. Monroe (1967) found that when his good sleepers stayed in his laboratory over night, they reported taking longer to fall asleep than was usually the case in their own homes. Similarly, we might expect novel sleeping cues to facilitate sleep onset among poor sleepers. Although Monroe's poor sleeper group reported significantly longer latencies to sleep onset than the good sleepers, the sleep disturbed subjects also reported that falling asleep in the laboratory was easier than at home.

Such observations suggested to Bootzin that a relatively simple treatment procedure could be implemented through the establishment of a more sleep-compatible history of association between bed cues and patient behavior. The general goal of his procedure is to insure that *rapid* sleep onset occurs in the presence of bed cues. No other behaviors which may preclude sleep are allowed to take place in the presence of those cues. Six instructions are given to the patient in order to accomplish this goal (Bootzin, 1973).

1. The patient should lie down only when he/she feels sleepy.
2. The patient should be awakened by alarm clock at the same time every morning regardless of how much sleep was obtained during the previous night.
3. Daytime naps should be avoided.
4. The bed and bedroom should be used only for sleeping. No other activities (e.g., eating, studying, reading, watching television) are allowed.
5. If the patient is unable to fall asleep within ten minutes, he/she is to leave the bedroom immediately. Returning to bed should occur only when he/she feels sleepy again.
6. The above step is repeated as often as necessary during the night until rapid sleep onset occurs.

Notice that each instruction is designed to assure a high probability of sleep upon retiring. With sufficient practice, the association between bed cues and sleep becomes stronger, while that between bed cues and sleep-incompatible behaviors weakens, and the probability of rapid sleep onset increases. Bootzin (1973) found that insomniacs requiring over 90 minutes to fall asleep reported average improvement of 74 minutes, with 61 percent of the patients averaging less than 20 minutes to sleep onset. These gains occurred after only four weeks of program implementation. Studies from our laboratory (Slama, 1975) have replicated his demonstration of the technique's effectiveness.

Stimulus control procedures possess a distinct advantage over progressive relaxation training, especially for the medical practitioner. Training the patient to follow the procedures requires only a few minutes, a typed list of the instructions can be sent home with the patient, and subsequent sessions are relatively unnecessary unless the patient confronts difficulties in following the instructions. A full course in relaxation training, on the other hand, requires nine sessions, with initial sessions lasting up to an hour. However, what is gained in therapy time may be offset by the limited usefulness of the stimulus control approach. It is designed for the specific problem of delayed sleep onset. The definite advantage of providing the patient with a relaxation skill should not be overlooked. To the extent that the insomnia is a function of overarousal and tension and to the extent that the patient successfully learns to apply the relaxation skill to stressful daily situations, progressive relaxation provides relief from both the disturbed sleep situation and the tension-producing events occurring during the day that contribute to the sleep disturbance. Thus, the additional training investment may pay off in terms of promoting a more generalizable skill useful in producing greater psychological adjustment.

Other than these considerations, there appears to be no empirical basis for electing one technique over the other. We do have some hypotheses (e.g., relaxation may be indicated for patients who report a great deal of daytime and bedtime tension; stimulus control may be more effective for patients on erratic schedules and who use their beds for purposes other than sleep), but such possibilities require future research before we can make confident recommendations. At present, the important point is that both procedures have been demonstrated under controlled conditions to produce rapid symptomatic improvement. Furthermore, with the exception of requiring the patient to leave the bed if sleep has not occurred within ten minutes, stimulus control instructions may be combined with progressive relaxation training. In our own clinical practice, we typically initiate stimulus control procedures at the beginning of assessment and begin relaxation training after the two or three sessions required for assessment.

ADDITIONAL PROCEDURES

I would like to conclude this chapter with a description of some additional procedures that we have found to be beneficial in clinical practice, although controlled research has not yet substantiated their effectiveness.

I frequently receive phone calls from individuals who frantically report that they have had little or no sleep during the last few nights and tearfully explain that something must be done, or else. The "or else" is usually a vague reference to their concern that they may be going insane either as evidenced by the sleep disturbance or because of the sleep deficit. Obviously, such people won't be satisfied with a suggestion of nine relaxation sessions or four weeks of stimulus control procedures. Consequently, as a temporary measure to deal with the acute problem, I suggest that until they begin formal therapy, they should plan to fill the nighttime hours with a variety of predetermined tasks, e.g., reading, hobbies, housework, listening to music. I stress to these patients that the only likely psychological repercussion of their lack of sleep would stem from their enormous concern with the temporary lack of sleep and that nothing serious, and certainly not insanity, will result from the sleep deficit. They might as well relax, stop worrying, and take advantage of the extra time to accomplish tasks or engage in activities for which they do not typically have time. Such a stop-gap measure is usually successful in calming the patient and aiding him/her to cope with subsequent sleepless nights. With the acute concern reduced, formal assessment and therapy, if indicated, can then proceed at the usual pace.

Boudewyns has reported the treatment of a chronic insomnia with a similar procedure known as paradoxical intention (Borkovec and Boudewyns, 1976). After suggesting that the patient was trying too hard to fall asleep, he instructed him to do the opposite, i.e., try to stay awake as long as he could. After one sleepless night, the patient fell asleep for a couple of hours the next night and obtained six and a half to eight hours of sleep over the next five days of implementing the procedure. No further treatment of the sleep disturbance was necessary.

Quite often the sleep-disturbed patient's life is so obviously filled with stress that the therapist decides to provide multiple interventions in order to both symptomatically treat the sleeping problem and to reduce the daily adjustment difficulties that are maintaining it. Secondary insomnias are common, and the therapist will apply whatever techniques are deemed appropriate for the individual case. Obviously, I cannot go into detail about general behavior therapy procedures, but I will briefly summarize a case example involving such multiple intervention. A young woman complained of long standing insomnia involving an average of two to three hours before falling asleep. Initial interviews revealed a great deal of anxiety over academic and occupational performance and a general failure to assert herself in social situations in which others commonly took advantage of her. In addition to progressive relaxation training to reduce the specific sleep problem, the patient received systematic desensitization (Wolpe, 1958) to reduce her anxiety in school and job related situations, and she was taught through role-playing how to appropriately assert herself when confronted with unreasonable social demands. Relaxation training resulted in a rapid decrease in sleep onset latency. The administration of the other intervention measures over a period of 15 sessions, however, was seen as critically important for guaranteeing the maintenance of that improvement and for providing her with adequate coping methods to deal with the adjustment problems that undoubtedly contributed to the original insomnia.

I am somewhat amazed and very encouraged by how much we have learned about sleep disturbance in general and the effectiveness of behavioral intervention in particular over a relatively brief period of time. It is obvious that we still have a long way to go before we can confidently recommend the most efficient and efficacious procedures, but the recent literature suggests that we have made a very good beginning. Future research, especially those investigations that focus on delineating specific subtypes of sleep disturbance and subtypes of patient characteristics within those disorder categories, will continue to provide more answers, better techniques, and better outcomes well beyond what we already optimistically offer to the suffering insomniac.

REFERENCES AND RECOMMENDED SUPPLEMENTAL READINGS

Technique Descriptions

Bernstein, D.A., & Borkovec, T.D. *Progressive relaxation training.* Champaign, Illinois: Research Press, 1973.

Bootzin, R. Stimulus control of insomnia. Paper presented at the meeting of the American Psychological Association, Montreal, August, 1973.

Borkovec, T.D., & Boudewyns, P.A. Treatment of insomnia by stimulus control and progressive relaxation procedures. In J. Krumboltz & C.E. Thoresen (Eds.), *Behavioral counseling methods.* New York: Holt, Rinehart, and Winston, 1976.

Jacobson, E. *Progressive relaxation.* Chicago: University of Chicago Press, 1938.

Wolpe, J. *Psychotherapy by reciprocal inhibition.* Stanford: Stanford University Press, 1958.

Sleep and Disorders of Sleep

Bohlin, G. Monotonous stimulus, sleep onset, and habituation of the orienting reaction. *Electroencephalography and Clinical Neurophysiology*, 1971, *31*, 593–601.

Bohlin, G. Susceptibility to sleep during a habituation procedure as related to individual differences. *Journal of Experimental Research in Personality*, 1972, *6*, 248–254.

Dement, W.C. *Some must watch while some must sleep.* Stanford: Stanford Alumni Association, 1972.

Dement, W.C. Introduction to sleep and sleep disorders. Symposium paper presented at the meeting of the Association for the Advancement of Behavior Therapy, San Francisco, December, 1975.

Hartmann, E.L. *The functions of sleep.* New Haven: Yale University Press, 1973.

Kales, A. (Ed.) *Sleep—physiology and pathology: A symposium.* Philadelphia: Lippincott, 1969.

Monroe, L.J. Psychological and physiological differences between good and poor sleepers. *Journal of Abnormal Psychology*, 1967, *72*, 255–264.

Usdin, G. (Ed.) *Sleep research and clinical practice.* New York: Brunner-Mazel, 1973.

Research on Relaxation and Stimulus Control Procedures

Bootzin, R. A stimulus control treatment for insomnia. *Proceedings of the American Psychological Association*, 1972, *1*, 395–396.

Borkovec, T.D., & Fowles, D.C. A controlled investigation of the effects of progressive and hypnotic relaxation on insomnia. *Journal of Abnormal Psychology*, 1973, *82*, 153–158.

Borkovec, T.D., Kaloupek, D.G., & Slama, K. The facilitative effect of muscle tension-release in the relaxation treatment of sleep disturbance. *Behavior Therapy*, 1975, *6*, 301–309.

Borkovec, T.D., Steinmark, S.W., & Nau, S.D. Relaxation training and single-item desensitization in the group treatment of insomnia. *Journal of Behavior Therapy and Experimental Psychiatry*, 1973, *4*, 401–403.

Borkovec, T.D., & Weerts, T.D. Effects of progressive relaxation on sleep disturbance: An electroencephalographic evaluation. *Psychosomatic Medicine*, in press.

Gershman, L., & Clouser, R. Treating insomnia with relaxation and desensitization in a group setting by an automated approach. *Journal of Behavior Therapy and Experimental Psychiatry*, 1974, *5*, 31–35.

Haynes, S., Woodward, S., Moran, R., & Alexander, D. Relaxation treatment of insomnia. *Behavior Therapy*, 1974, *5*, 555–558.

Hinkle, J.E., & Lutker, E.R. Insomnia: A new approach. *Psychotherapy: Theory, Research, and Practice*, 1972 *9*, 236–237.

Kahn, M., Baker, B.L., & Weiss, J.M. Treatment of insomnia by relaxation training. *Journal of Abnormal Psychology*, 1968, *73*, 556–558.

Nicassio, P., & Bootzin, R. A comparison of progressive relaxation and autogenic training as treatments for insomnia. *Journal of Abnormal Psychology*, 1974, *83*, 253–260.

Paul, G.L. Physiological effects of relaxation training and hypnotic suggestion. *Journal of Abnormal Psychology*, 1969, *74*, 425–437.

Slama, K. Studies comparing stimulus control and progressive relaxation procedures in the treatment of sleep disturbance. Unpublished Master's thesis, University of Iowa, 1975.

Steinmark, S.W., & Borkovec, T.D. Active and placebo treatment effects on moderate insomnia under counterdemand and positive demand instructions. *Journal of Abnormal Psychology*, 1974, *83*, 157–163.

Tokarz, T., & Lawrence, P.S. An analysis of temporal and stimulus factors in the treatment of insomnia. Paper presented at the meeting of the Association for the Advancement of Behavior Therapy, Chicago, November, 1974.

Weil, G., & Goldfried, M. Treatment of insomnia in an eleven-year-old child through self-relaxation. *Behavior Therapy*, 1973, *4*, 282–284.

Chapter 4

Headache†

*Redford B. Williams, Jr.**

Headache is the most common pain afflicting the human race. Ninety percent of the population is affected at one time or another in their lives. On statistical grounds alone the diagnosis of headache is deceptively simple: Ninety percent of all headaches are due to either (1) painful dilation and distention of the cranial arteries, or (2) sustained contraction of the muscles of the face, scalp, and neck. Within the ninety percent of all headaches which are either vascular or muscular in origin those secondary to increased muscle tension form the greater proportion—although the true proportion is hard to estimate, since most patients with migraine also have muscle contraction headaches at some time in conjunction with their vascular headache. Recently developed behavioral treatment approaches have made possible a significant improvement in our treatment of this common medical problem.

DIAGNOSIS

In the history, the following characteristics are helpful in differentiating among vascular, muscular, and other causes of headaches. The typical vascular headache is a throbbing, pulsatile sort of pain which is usually unilateral, at least at the outset, and often associated with other symptoms: irritability, nausea, vomiting, photophobia, and constipation or diarrhea. The pain commonly starts in one temple or

*Department of Psychiatry, Duke University Medical Center.

†Supported by a Research Scientist Development Award, Number K01–MH–70482, from the National Institute of Mental Health.

on one side of the forehead, but it can progress to become generalized, and the quality of the pain can go from throbbing to steady, probably a result of extreme distention and stiffening of the arterial walls. The pathophysiology of vascular headache appears to involve an initial phase of vasoconstriction which is followed, perhaps secondary to smooth muscle fatigue, by the vasodilatory phase, which is associated with the throbbing pain, presumably secondary to stretching of the arterial coat. The initial vasoconstrictor phase can be associated with typical prodromal symptoms, such as scotoma, visual field defect, and even hemiplegia. These occur regularly in only 10–15 percent of the cases, however, and are of no real help in diagnosis, which must depend on the presence of the typical overall clinical picture.

In contrast to the unilateral, throbbing pain of vascular headaches, muscle contraction headaches are usually symmetrical in distribution—occipital, bitemporal or "bandlike"—and are characterized by a steady, nonpulsatile ache.

Despite the low incidence of other causes of headache, these other causes are potentially of great danger, and the history and physical examination should be carried out meticulously to search for signs or symptoms which would raise the possibility of these other causes. Clearly, any focal neurological signs or symptoms would be indications to obtain skull x-rays, brain scan, EEG and neurological consultation, to evaluate the possibility of an intracranial process. Where sinus headaches are suspected there invariably will be found engorgement and inflammation of the nasal turbinates. The headache associated with high blood pressure is often indistinguishable from a typical muscle tension headache; and if the blood pressure is found to be elevated appropriate diagnostic and treatment measures should be undertaken.

The psychological characteristics of patients with frequent headaches and the life setting in which the headaches occur are important considerations in any discussion of headache. The early description by Wolff (1948) of the personality of the migraine patients applies nearly as well to many patients with muscle contraction headache. This could stem from a common role of psychophysiological factors in the etiology of both vascular and muscular headache.

Perhaps the key to understanding the personality of the patient with headache can be summed up by one word: *control*. The typical patient with headache has a great need to be in control of his or her world. At the extreme, this need is met through a behavior style which is described by the term "obsessive-compulsive." Patients with headache describe themselves as perfectionistic, neat, and liking things to be in order. In practice, if the patient has not spontaneously described himself as perfectionistic during the course of the history, it is well to ask "What kind of person are you?" If this does not elicit a description by the patient of typical perfectionistic, orderly behavior patterns, I will next ask the patient if it would be fair to describe him or her as perfectionistic. A smile and assent before I finish the last word will confirm the presence of the typical personality style. Often, it is necessary to be more specific in asking "Do you keep a neat house?" or "Do you always like to leave your desk clear at the end of the day?" The presence of the typical behavior patterns does not confirm the diagnosis of muscular or vascular headache but asking these questions can help the patient realize that these behaviors may be important in causing his headaches.

The setting in which the headaches occur is often one in which a period of high stress is followed by a period of planned relaxation during which the headaches begins, leading the patient to question that stress is the cause. This "letdown" phenomenon may result from discomfort with a setting in which inactivity is the requirement, since the patient's characteristic style is one of controlling the world through activity.

Wolff's studies suggest that the need for control and the behaviors used to achieve it among headache patients has its origin in childhood—where being neat, orderly, and obedient are behaviors adopted by the child to reduce anxiety that their parents will reject them.

It is highly likely that psychophysiological mechanisms are very important, if not central, in the etiology of both muscular and vascular headaches. The tension level in the muscles of the head and neck has been shown to increase in experimental studies in response to a wide variety of psychological as well as physical stimuli—and as little as two minutes of sustained voluntary contraction is associated with the onset of pain in the contracting muscles. Other experimental studies have shown that the arteries of the scalp constrict in response to unpleasant physical and psychological stimuli. Persons with a high need to be in control—who maintain that control by meticuously ordering their environment—are going to be subjected frequently to frustration of that need. The result of such frustration is then likely to be preparation for an emergency response—with the result that the muscles of the head and neck contract—the blood vessels of the scalp constrict, and with enough frustration, over a sufficient length of time, a headache develops. Indeed, often the headache itself becomes self-perpetuating as a means of controlling an otherwise uncontrollable situation.

To illustrate some of the points I have been making with regard to the diagnostic approach, as well as some of the pitfalls, the following case is offered.

The patient was a 42-year-old mother of three, who until recently had also been working as a bookkeeper in her husband's furniture business. She had a long history, going back over 20 years, of frontal headaches, which were described as a steady, dull ache and which occurred from one to three times per month. About two months prior to admission to Duke, the furniture store had burned down, and with inadequate insurance, her husband had had to take a job which brought in less money. The patient had not gotten another job, deciding to stay at home. Within one week after the fire, she developed a headache similar to those already described. Instead of responding to the usual aspirin, however, this headache became more intense, causing her to have to go to bed. It did not go away, but was present all the time. Her physician could provide her with relief only with narcotic doses which put her to sleep. But when she woke up the headache was still there. Because of the severity and duration of this headache she was referred for neurological evaluation, and physical examination was normal as were laboratory tests, including lumbar puncture, EEG, brain scan and skull x-rays. A consultation request was put in for biofeedback treatment for her headache, and the patient was seen after she had been in the hospital for about two weeks. She was lying very still, curled up in bed in her darkened room and spoke only in whispers. She appeared depressed. When asked if it would be fair to describe her as a perfectionist, her husband and children, who had solicitously remained in the room, could not surpress a laugh, and the patient, despite her obvious discomfort, managed a smile. Her perfectionism had been a family joke for years—in areas ranging from housework to the meticulous detail with which she kept books.

On the basis of this history, the normal physical examination and the negative laboratory tests, a diagnosis was made of muscle contraction headache, brought on in its present severe degree by the recent life events which seriously threatened her ability to control her life situation. I described our EMG feedback treatment program for tension headaches and scheduled her first session the following day, confidently predicting that we would be able to help her obtain relief.

Before her appointment the next day, I received a call from her physician saying that the patient had developed a marked ptosis of the right eye that morning and that the right pupil had become dilated relative to the left and responded only sluggishly to light. An emergency arteriogram revealed a right carotid aneurysm with leakage and she went to surgery that day. In retrospect, several observers agreed that the ptosis had been present earlier, but dismissed as related to the way she kept her eyes shut most of the time.

Comment—This case illustrates, in an extreme fashion perhaps, that even when all aspects of the clinical picture suggest one condition, in this case tension headache, it remains of crucial importance to pay close attention to all physical signs and to be prepared to perform whatever diagnostic studies are indicated. *Did* she have a tension headache? *Was* it related to the stressful life events to which she had been subjected? In both cases, I would say yes. *Was* the aneurysm the main cause of her headache? I do not know. It is clear that her psychological makeup, the long history of typical tension headaches and the recent events are quite compatible with the initial formulation. Indeed, one can even speculate that the physiological concomitants of the headache played a central role, perhaps via pressor effects, in the eventual rupture of her aneurysm. It is equally clear, however, that at the point in question, what this patient urgently required was not behavioral treatment, but the attention of the neurosurgeon.

TREATMENT

Since we are concerned here with behavioral treatment approaches, I shall have little to say regarding the pharmacologic treatment of vascular and muscle contraction headaches. However, a few points deserve comment. First of all, the only patients who will seek medical attention are those in whom the initial self-prescribed pharmacologic approaches have failed. Further analgesic medication will provide only temporary symptomatic relief, without attacking the underlying cause. Tranquilizers are often counterproductive in that they impair further the patient's ability to exert control over his life situation and are not tolerated. Where depression is present, with signs of appetite and sleep disturbance, an adequate trial of antidepressant medication is clearly indicated, and will often alleviate the headache problem. With regard to migraine, or vascular headache, the ergot preparations will often provide relief and can control symptoms over the long term, though many patients are unable to tolerate side effects of the ergots. Ergot preparations have definite dangers is used in patients with cardiovascular disease. Methylsergide preparations have serious side effects (e.g., retroperitoneal fibrosis) which prevent their long term use. Finally, the dependency upon the doctor and the medications he has prescribed often threatens the patient's need to be in control—with the result that the traditional medical management of headaches is often frustrating to both patient and physician—especially with the wish by both parties that "something" be done to relieve the suffering.

Behavioral Approaches

If properly introduced and carried out, behavioral approaches circumvent many of the problems inherent in the traditional medical management of the patient with headache.

Unlike the pharmacologic approach to headache, which is often aimed primarily at relieving the symptom, the behavioral approach proceeds from certain assumptions concerning the pathogenesis of the headache and attempts to correct the initiating pathophysiological situation itself. Basically this approach assumes that the headache results from sustained high levels of vascular or muscular response in persons whose behavioral attempts to satisfy high needs for control are not successful in their current life situation, and that this is sufficient to initiate the events in blood vessels and/or muscles which result in a headache. The initiating events can range from no more than the ordinary frustrations of daily life associated with unavoidable messes all the way to major personal catastrophies.

All the behavioral approaches might be considered as having two central goals. First, the patient must learn how to reverse the basic pathophysiological process—either to relax the tense muscles or to reduce the vasospasm which precedes the painful vasodilatation. This can be accomplished with a variety of techniques used singly, but often in combination. Second, the patient must apply his newly acquired skills on a regular basis so that when he recognizes the onset of the pathophysiologic events, as most patients do come to do, he will be able to reverse them, or prevent them from proceeding to the point of causing a headache.

The techniques used to help patients learn to modify the pathophysiologic responses fall into two general areas: psychological and psychophysiological. In practice, most centers with extensive experience in treating headaches use a combination of these techniques. I shall first consider techniques helpful to patients in learning to reduce muscle tension.

Purely *psychological* techniques patients can use to learn to relax the muscles of the head and neck include the progressive muscular relaxation technique as described many years ago by Jacobsen or the autogenic exercises described by Luthe (see Chapter 2 for references to these techniques). Basically, these involve having the patient sit or recline in a comfortable position in a quiet place while repeating to himself a series of phrases of the type, "I feel quite relaxed . . . my ankles feel very heavy, relaxed, and comfortable," and so on, right up to the head. Akin to these methods are those in which the patient is trained to induce in himself a light hypnotic trance during which he repeats the relaxation phrases to himself. A number of centers use tape recordings of the phrases as an adjunct to help the patient relax. Also useful is a meditation-type technique as described by Benson (1975). This involves having the patient first relax his body, then pay attention to his breathing and say the word, "one," to himself with each expiration.

Biofeedback is a *psychophysiological* technique which can be employed to achieve the same goal of helping patients learn how to relax the muscles whose extreme tension is responsible for their headaches. Basically, this involves having the patient again sit or recline comfortably in a quiet place, with surface electrodes attached to the relevant muscles, most often those of the forehead. Using electromyographic recording techniques, the activity in these muscles is quantitated and information concerning the level of tension is immediately "fedback" to the patient using an auditory and/or visual meter display. This information regarding second-to-second fluctuations in EMG activity provides the patient with data concerning the results of his attempt to relax the muscles in question, and, by trial and error, he learns what things he can do to relax the muscles. Furthermore, he learns to recognize the subjective feeling state associated with a reduction in EMG levels.

To understand how this works, it is useful to consider the analogy of a person trying to learn how to shoot a basketball through the basket. If he is blindfolded and just throws the ball up, he does not know whether the ball went through the basket or was to the left or right, or too short or too far. Consequently, he would have no idea of how to change his muscular behavior on the next toss to improve his performance. If the blindfold is removed, however, he can see the outcome of each attempt and will be soon able to get the ball through the basket with some regularity. Biofeedback works the same way—it provides the patient with information about the state of tension in his muscles, or blood vessels, of which he is not consciously aware and thereby enables him to bring that tension level under conscious control.

Two questions occur, "is biofeedback essential in treating tension headaches?" or "are these various relaxation exercises essential?" I have no doubt that it would be entirely possible to treat successfully some patients with biofeedback alone and some patients with relaxation exercises alone. *Clinically*, the important thing is to employ a method which will enable the patient on a regular basis to relax the involved muscles. The biofeedback technique is used mainly to speed the learning of the basic relaxation skill; the patient is instructed to practice what he has learned with the aid of biofeedback on a regular basis without biofeedback at home, and whenever he feels the tension level building up.

Whatever technique is utilized, then, the key thing is that for treatment to be successful in providing relief of headaches, the patient must be able to relax the muscles of the head and neck. Two lines of evidence support this contention. First of all, in our clinical experience at Duke, patients who are unsuccessful in reducing their EMG amplitude using biofeedback do not obtain relief of their headache. Further, it is only as they demonstrate ability to reduce EMG levels in biofeedback sessions that they report ability to relieve or prevent headaches out in the real world.

A more systematic demonstration of this principle is provided by a recent study conducted by Bernal at the Duke Clinical Biofeedback Laboratory. He studied three groups of patients with muscle contraction headaches. All three groups were instructed that their headaches were due to too much tension in their forehead muscles and that, to obtain relief, they must learn to relax those muscles. One group received EMG feedback as a learning aid. A second group were taught to place themselves in a light trance during which they repeated to themselves phrases to the effect that their muscles were becoming very relaxed. The third group was instructed to try to relax their forehead muscles by whatever means seemed to work best for them. All three groups were monitored for EMG levels during sessions, though only the first group received feedback. The group receiving feedback and the group taught in self-hypnosis both showed significant diminution in headache frequency and intensity, while the group instructed only to relax showed no change in their headaches. The EMG data indicated the likely reason. The first two groups both showed significant decreases in EMG levels during sessions, while the relax only group showed no decrease in EMG levels. I believe that this study demonstrates clearly that *any* method which will enable patients to reduce muscle tension levels can be successful in treating tension headaches.

Does this mean that biofeedback is not a specific treatment? Or that autogenic treatment is not specific? *Clinically*, these questions can be sidestepped. What does seem specific for the relief of tension headache, as might be expected from a consideration of its pathogenesis, is a reduction in muscle tension level. Biofeedback and self-hypnosis appear to be two means which can be effective in achieving this goal. Biofeedback has the added advantage of providing objective evidence of how successful the patient is in reducing muscle tension.

The efficacy of the behavioral techniques described in the treatment of muscle tension headaches is generally accepted as having been established. With regard to the use of these techniques in treating vascular headache, the evidence is clearly less solid—perhaps a result of the variable course of migraines and the intercurrent muscle tension headaches. At Duke we begin the treatment of patients with migraine by training them in muscle relaxation—using techniques I described above. If this does not prove sufficient to relieve their headaches, then biofeedback training is instituted to help the patient learn to vasodilate the skin blood vessels. This is done using a sensitive thermistor attached to the finger, with instruction to the patient to make the skin temperature increase. When effective, this technique works presumably by aborting the vasospastic phase of the migraine attack. Its efficacy cannot be regarded as established in controlled outcome studies as yet, but we have seen patients who report that for the first time in their lives they have aborted a migraine attack using the finger-warming technique.

In concluding, I would like to review in some detail how we approach a typical patient with tension headache in the Duke Clinical Biofeedback Laboratory. In so doing, I will touch briefly upon instrumentation, and, in somewhat greater detail, upon the pitfalls often encountered in using biofeedback techniques. This latter might be subtitled "When biofeedback fails: what to do until the doctor comes."

For every patient, before any treatment is administered, a complete medical history and physical examination is mandatory. This is essential to rule out any disorders which might require treatment other than behavioral to help the patient or, indeed, to save his life. Often patients are referred from physicians who have already performed a complete workup, including indicated laboratory examinations. This may indicate that a new complete workup is not necessary, but it in no way relieves those employing behavioral therapies of the obligation to take sufficient history and perform whatever examinations necessary to evaluate the patient.

Following the diagnosis of the condition as, in the case of this example, tension headache, and the gathering of data concerning the psychological makeup of the patient, and precipitating life events, we inform him of our impression that his headaches are due to too much muscle tension which is brought on by everyday stress and strain. We emphasize that this in no way means (though such may indeed be the case) that the patient is emotionally ill or "crazy," and that *we are all* subjected to such stresses—"it is unfortunate that your muscles respond in such a way that you have to suffer with these headaches." We explain that in order for him to obtain relief, two goals must be achieved. First he must learn how to relax his muscles and second, he must use that skill by practicing relaxation at home for 15–20 minutes twice a day and whenever he feels a headache coming on, or tension building up, and that only by so doing can he reverse the basic process responsible for his headaches.

The first session always proceeds according to a standard procedure. First, a five minute baseline EMG level is measured. Feedback is based on change from this baseline, and the baseline criterion can be modified depending upon the patient's performance. The first five minutes of feedback are given with no instructions other than "the meter will go up if your muscle tension is increasing and down if it is decreasing—for the next five minutes just try to relax your forehead, where the electrodes are, as best you can and make the meter go down." Some patients immediately show ability to reduce EMG levels, but most do not. Following this initial feedback period, we next instruct the patient to think about a life situation which our initial evaluation indicated would be stressful for him. Invariably, with certain important exceptions, the EMG levels increase, and it is pointed out to the patient that the same thing probably happens in real life, leading to his headaches. Thereafter the remainder of the first session is spent having the patient try a number of the relaxation techniques already described, so that he can identify which one might be best for him. The remaining sessions are spent applying those techniques which work best to obtain reliable skills in muscle relaxation, which are practiced regularly at home.

Most of our successful patients advance through several phases in their treatment, much as described by Budzinski and Stoyva (1973). First is an increased awareness of tension levels in the forehead. Next comes a phase where they are beginning to be successful in the feedback sessions in reducing EMG levels and also report that they are able to reduce or even abort incipient headaches at home. Next they report that they are able to go several days without a headache, even though, as with some patients, they had been accustomed to having a headache every day for the past several years. Finally, with continued practice, some patients report that where formerly they tensed up in a whole variety of life situations, they now find themselves "automatically" relaxing in these situations. Budzinski and Stoyva have speculated that this represents the substitution of an overlearned relaxation response for an overlearned tension response.

The above course of phases of treatment can cover a variable time interval, though we have had several patients from far away who were able to progress to just short of the last phase with only five days of daily feedback sessions and regular practice outside the feedback situation. On the average we find that about 10 sessions are required to achieve maximal benefit.

But the above descriptions refer only to those patients we are successful in treating. What about those who do not obtain relief with our approach? I believe it very important to learn as much as possible from our failures as well as our successes. Indeed, I am aware of little that has been written concerning patients who do not progress in a straightforward manner.

Often we find that patients are not learning to reduce EMG levels because all kinds of thoughts keep coming into their head. Usually it is sufficient only to work just a bit more closely with them in terms of the various relaxation exercises to help them past this block. More difficult to overcome are problems that might best be described under the heading of "transference." Often patients will develop a form of negative transferrence to the therapist, striving to prevent the biofeedback therapist from "controlling me." At times this negative transferrence can even be directed to the biofeedback apparatus itself, with the patient sitting there fuming, "No damned machine is going to get the best of me!" Often helpful in overcoming this resistance is the process of finding out what is going on and suggesting to the patient that his concern with being controlled is making his muscles even tighter, as he can see on the feedback, and stating again that this shows that we are not capable of controlling him. At other times, it is necessary to resort to more sophisticated devices to overcome this resistance. One we have found particularly effective in some cases involves the use of "paradoxical intention"—instructing the patient that instead of decreasing his muscle tension, as indicated by the meter going down, we would like him to slightly *increase* his tension, not by "scrunching" up his forehead and making the meter go all the way up, but just a little, so that the meter stays slightly above the baseline level. The patient will often respond to this instruction by promptly reducing his EMG level all the way down! The negative transferrence can then be interpreted. Clearly, then, biofeedback involves much more than simply hooking up the patient and turning on the machine.

When patients are having the degree of difficulty in reducing their EMG levels suggested by the last comments, there are almost always major underlying psychological problems which need more attention in terms of both diagnosis and treatment. Therefore whenever a patient has not made significant progress by the fifth session we will obtain an MMPI, and psychiatric evaluation will be begun. On the basis of this evaluation, appropriate psychotherapy, pharmacotherapy, or both can be prescribed.

It should be obvious from the above discussion that when the initial behavioral approaches are not working, the clinician should be alert to the existence of underlying psychological problems. Thus, these behavioral techniques should not be applied in the absence of supervision by clinicians skilled in the recognition, evaluation and treatment of such underlying psychological problems. We have even noted the emergence of potentially dangerous psychiatric complications in patients who are achieving relief of their target symptom. One such patient with a muscle spasm problem was much better with regard to the muscle spasm, but was complaining of increased anxiety despite this improvement. This patient nearly had a psychotic break, which was prevented only by hospitalization and appropriate attention to the underlying problems.

It has not been my intention in these last comments to suggest that the behavioral techniques I have been describing carry great risk. Indeed, their major advantage is the relative absence of such unwanted side effects as plague the use of other treatment modalities in patients with headache. I have only covered these aspects to make you aware that there do exist certain risks, not only in missing underlying organic pathology, but also with regard to the uncovering of underlying psychologic problems.

What, then, may the practitioner do for those patients who come to you seeking relief from their headache? First of all, I believe that he can reassure them that he understands the basis for their pain (nothing can annoy these patients so much as the message, however unconscious on your part, that "it's all in your head") that there are new treatment modalities which offer significant promise of relief, certainly for tension headache, and probably for at least some migraine sufferers. The next question is likely to be, "Well, then, when do we start?" I believe that any medical practitioner who has satisfied himself with regard to diagnosis can safely advise his patients with headache to try the relaxation exercises I have described. First, this will do no harm, and in at least some patients it will help. It would be important to emphasize to the patient the importance of daily practice and to prepare him for more intensive treatment should the relaxation alone not be of sufficient benefit.

I would advise the practitioner to obtain biofeedback equipment only if he is comfortable in dealing with the psychological problems that *will* surface in patients who are not progressing. Alternatively, there should be available a colleague to whom such patients could be referred. The March, 1975, issue of the American Psychologist is a special issue devoted to instrumentation and would be a helpful guide to those wishing to learn more of the commercially available biofeedback devices.

Finally, I would advise the practitioner interested in employing these behavioral techniques to obtain clinical training. This should involve supervision of clinical work by experts in the use of the techniques in question. One does not learn how to remove an inflamed appendix only by reading about the surgical approach. Similarly, the skilled clinical application of behavioral approaches can best be learned under skillful clinical supervision.

REFERENCES

American Psychologist. Entire issue, March, 1975 *30(3)*. This entire issue is devoted to issues of instrumentation in psychology, and contains the names and addresses of all manufacturers of biofeedback devices, from whom literature can be obtained.

Budzynski, T.H., Stoyva, J.M., Adler, C.S. and Mullaney, D.J. EMG biofeedback and tension headache: a controlled outcome study. *Psychosomatic Medicine*, 1973, *35*, 484–496. This paper is a comprehensive report of the best study to date demonstrating the efficacy of EMG biofeedback training in the treatment of tension headache.

Biofeedback and self-control. Chicago: Aldine Publishing Company, 1970–present. This volume, published annually, contains a comprehensive compilation of the important papers published in the scientific literature on the subject of biofeedback and self-control, and is highly recommended for those wishing to obtain a more indepth background regarding the basis for the behavioral techniques described in this book.

Wolff, Harold G. *Headache and other head pain.* New York: Oxford University Press, 1948. This volume remains the definitive work on the nature and etiology of headache.

Benson, H. *The Relaxation Response*, New York: William Morrow and Co., 1975.

Chapter 5

Type A Behavior Pattern

*Richard M. Suinn**

The identification of the Type A Pattern has represented an important breakthrough in the study of the role of personality and cardiovascular disease. For the first time, personality variables have been directly correlated with the incidence of heart disease through careful research. Starting in 1959, cardiologists Friedman and Rosenman began both retrospective and predictive studies of a coronary-prone behavioral pattern called Type A. In a sequence of studies involving over 3,400 persons over several years these researchers and their colleagues have demonstrated that the Type A pattern represents a cardiovascular risk factor (Friedman and Rosenman, 1959; Rosenman and Friedman, 1961; Rosenman et al., 1964). For example, they have reported that Type A men within the age group of 39–49 years show a rate of coronary disease six times higher than that of Type B men. The Type A pattern has been defined as involving: an eagerness to compete, self-imposed deadlines, desire for recognition, physical and mental alertness, quickness of mental and physical functioning, and an intense drive towards self-selected but poorly defined goals. Additionally, the following might also be included: impatience at the rate of progress of events; multiple thinking or acting; vague guilt or unease at relaxing; scheduling more things in less time; accentuating words in normal speech; hurrying the last words in speech; rapid walking, moving, eating; stressing doing as opposed to experiencing or enjoying; a dislike of repetitive duties which take away from doing; and rushing reading, or pre-

*Colorado State University.

ferring to read summaries and abstracts. Friedman and Rosenman (1974) also interpret the impatience of the Type A person to be reflective of a basic hostility (although this may be true for some cases, the behavior may be more representative of tension rather than hostility in other cases).

To date, the research on means for altering the Type A characteristics has been sparse. This is partly because many accept the view that personality as such is difficult to change. On the other hand, the Type A characteristics as described by Friedman and Rosenman lend very well to a different set of premises. It is possible to view the Type A life style as involving a series of habit patterns constantly shown over long periods of time, rather than as consisting of an unbending personality pattern resistant to change. It is from this viewpoint that the behavioral methods described in this chapter were developed.

It is my assumption that the Type A behavioral pattern is one which is learned as other habit patterns are learned. Additionally, that the increased incidence of heart disease is a function of the Type A characteristics themselves, as well as indirectly from the stress that is prompted from being a Type A person, seems clear. Type A characteristics are acquired by individuals partly since our society encourages the development of such behaviors. This is seen in our emphasis on achievement, competitiveness, productivity, aggressive drive, assertiveness, and the work ethic (the gradual increase in the number of women who are Type A individuals is also evidence of the changing patterns caused by cultural changes).

The role of stress cannot be overemphasized. If one examines the characteristics of the Type A individual, it becomes clear that this individual lives in an environment of many stresses. These stresses may derive from deadlines, or the competitiveness, or the drive towards success, or the overcommitment to work responsibilities. Stress may also develop secondarily as a result of the impatience experienced by the Type A individual when achievement is being blocked. The stress reactions themselves may have a correlated consequence on the physiology of the individual. Data have accumulated suggesting that lipid levels, such as cholesterol, increase during periods of environmental stress (Peterson, et al., 1962; Clark, et al., 1975).

Clinical attempts to alter the Type A behavioral pattern have met minimal success in the past. Although the Type A heart patient may acknowledge the necessity of changing his behavior, it is characteristic of this same individual that change is resisted. Why is it that the Type A individual does not automatically adopt new behaviors? I believe the answer is in the vicious cycles caused by stress related to Type A characteristics. As illustrated in Figure 5–1, Type A individuals respond to stress situations by displaying Type A actions, inasmuch as people under stress tend to automatically resort to those actions which are their strongest habits. Because such Type A responses tend to be valued by society, and additionally because they tend to get things done, this display of Type A behaviors is followed by two types of rewards. The actions are rewarded because they lead to achievement of a successful product. The actions are also rewarded because they help to reduce the original stress situation. However, the next stage in this vicious cycle involving stress derives from the fact that the very Type A behaviors that have just been strengthened by reinforcement are behaviors which are themselves stress producing. What I am saying is that the Type A individuals tend to put themselves in situations which involve stress, for example, because of their drive, competitiveness, achievement orientation, or self-imposition of deadlines. And how does the Type A individual react to increased stress? By displaying those very habits which have been strongly reinforced, i.e., by Type A behaviors! Thus, we say that the Type A individual is caught in a vicious cycle that prevents breaking out of Type A patterns of behavior. In order to foster change it is therefore important to deal not only with ways of promoting new behaviors, but also ways of reducing stress. A few years ago, we (Suinn, 1974) developed a method based upon behavioral modification principles. The procedure, called the Cardiac Stress Management Program, was aimed at two objectives: stress management training and behavioral change. The former was an adaptation of the Anxiety Management Training technique (Suinn and Richardson, 1971; Suinn, 1975a). Anxiety management training involves training the patient in identifying bodily cues that signal the onset of the experience of stress, such as facial muscle tension, tightening of the muscles around the neck and shoulders, or dryness of the throat; training the individual

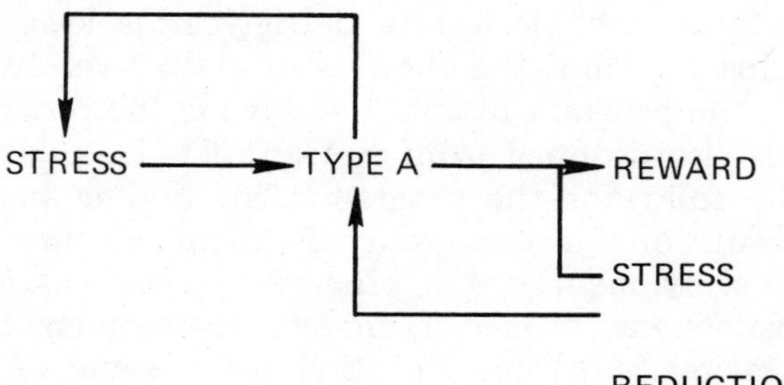

Figure 5–1. The Vicious Cycle of Stress

next in a procedure for reducing this anxiety response (we rely heavily on muscle relaxation); and training in self-control and utilizing relaxation in real life as the immediate response to the bodily cues that indicate anxiety arousal. Basically, the patient is taught to respond to bodily cues signaling the arousal of anxiety with the response that eliminates the anxiety. Anxiety management training has the person visualize circumstances which lead to anxiety arousal, permitting the anxiety reaction to increase in order to identify the bodily cues, followed by instruction to establish control through relaxation. This stress management approach is similar to the training which I provided to prepare Olympic athletes for the stresses of competition (Suinn, in press).

The second phase of the cardiac stress management program involved procedures for encouraging behavioral change. The Type A patient is encouraged to develop an alternative to typical Type A behaviors, which would still retain productivity. In order to encourage such change, a covert rehearsal (known as visuo-motor behavioral rehearsal, as I called it when used with competitive athletes) technique (Suinn, 1972) was used. This technique is based upon my premise that a new behavior is never acquired unless it is practiced behaviorally. That is, *knowing* how to act differently is not the same thing as actually *behaving* differently. The covert rehearsal involves the use of imagery to enable the patient to re-experience all aspects of a situation, while practicing new ways of responding to that situation. This imagery approach to training has the advantage of prompting behavioral change through an active rehearsal process. In other words, the patient not only develops knowledge of alternatives, but is also able to practice acting differently.

Cardiac stress management programs appear to have been successful in achieving both a reduction of stress and also an alteration of Type A characteristics. Reports from patients participating in the program support this conclusion. Additionally, lipid data showed significant reductions in cholesterol and triglyceride levels among the patient participants. Thus, the cholesterol mean level dropped from 229.1 prior to the program to 214.1 following the program; the triglyceride levels also dropped from a mean of 171.6 prior to the program to 128.8 following the program. This finding was replicated with similar results on a second group of patients (Suinn, 1975b).

The cardiac stress management program is a systematic procedure requiring a professional trained in anxiety management training and covert rehearsal methods. On the other hand, some of the general principles may be put into practice by others. The following summarizes some guidelines which may be useful in devising methods for dealing with patients to aid them in stress management and behavioral change:

RELAXATION TRAINING

A critical stage in the management of stress responses involves the acquiring of methods for relaxation. These methods may be categorized as indirect or direct approaches. An indirect approach is one in which the relaxation is an eventual consequence of some other activity; while a direct approach involves relaxing as a direct result of the activity. For example, jogging may be eventually relaxing for an individual as the person substitutes running for concerns about daily problems. In contrast, a physical massage or a sauna is directly aimed at reducing the tenseness of muscle groups. The value of this distinction relates to understanding the better methods whereby a Type A person can learn to relax. Type A individuals are characterized by an impatience at inactivity. Consequently, the indirect approaches would have less impact if these approaches stress the passive development of relaxation. A Type A individual would find it difficult to sit passively, waiting for relaxation to develop through the influence of music. In contrast, the direct approaches tend to involve active participation to achieve relaxation, and may be more suited to the Type A person's inclinations. However, it should be noted that it is possible to use indirect approaches where there is an active component involved. For example, the Type A individual could be encouraged to become actively engrossed in following the emotions being generated in a movie or television plot; or the Type A person could be helped to view that the music listening time is a scheduled part of daily activities for a specific objective. Thus, the viewpoint is shifted towards relaxation as a planned accomplishment rather than relaxation as a waste of activity time. A caution should be inserted at this point. Inasmuch as Type A individuals are easily triggered into competitiveness, this tendency should be kept in check. Thus, the engaging in occasional sports should again be viewed as aimed at the objective of a break from competition and stress, rather than another form of competition and stress.

Among the indirect approaches for achieving relaxation are: music, reading, movies or television, recreational sports, and alcohol. Among the direct approaches to training individuals in relaxation are: the Jacobsen muscle exercise, biofeedback, meditation, physical massage, saunas, yoga, and relaxation imagery. The individual patient should be encouraged to develop whichever methods provide the greatest aid to achieving relaxation that seems appropriate and works.

IDENTIFYING AND CONTROLLING SITUATIONAL STRESS STIMULI

It is also valuable for the patient to be helped in identifying those environmental situations which appear to prompt stress reactions. Many persons are unaware of the conditions which prompt stress in their lives. A useful procedure is to first help the individual to become aware of how he or she experiences stress. Is stress felt subjectively in muscle tightening, in a more pervasive feeling of "being under pressure," in sweating of the palms, or in habits such as drumming the fingers? The patient might be instructed to spend a minute every hour in looking for the presence of these signs. Thus, a patient who tends to experience stress by tension in the neck muscles might be asked to crosscheck those muscles once per hour. If this indicates that the person is currently experiencing stress, then the patient is instructed to immediately consider what may be occurring in the environment that has prompted such a reaction. Patients should be encouraged to keep a daily log of such stressors and to review the log at the end of the week to determine whether there are common circumstances that provoke stress.

Once the patient is able to identify the conditions that provoke stress, then it may be possible to engage in the means of reducing and controlling such stresses. There are at least three methods possible. First, the patient may wish to withdraw from the stress interaction and engage in one of the relaxation activities previously mentioned. This is basically a 'time out' approach permitting the individual to regain control. A second method is related to the first and involves the reduction of the amount of time spent in the stress producing situation. Stress responses increase as a direct function of the amount of time that the stress cues are present and can work on the individual. By cutting back the amount of time, it may be possible to break up the stress responses before they accumulate to the point of being destructive. Thus, a person may divide up the amount of time devoted to working on a disagreeable project into smaller units, taking frequent breaks. A third procedure might involve preventing the stressful stimuli from occurring at all. For example, if an executive discovers that a particular kind of interaction is stressful, then he or she may be able to delegate the responsibility to someone else who has lesser difficulty. Or, if a problem seems to be developing as a function of a mistaken communication, then the individual might prevent a building confrontation by clarifying the communication. In other words, this involves 'solving the problem before it becomes a problem'.

CONTROLLING INNER STRESS REACTIONS

The control of inner stress reactions can be approached from either of two directions: relief or prevention. Once an environmental stress stimulus precipitates a stress reaction, the only option left for the patient is to seek the means for relieving the accumulated stress. As indicated in the previous section, the adoptation of indirect or direct approaches for achieving a more relaxed state is essential. A typical pattern once stress responses are triggered is for those responses to build to a higher and higher level. Internal cues may be responsible for this process, for example, a person may perceive himself becoming more tense, and reacting to this increasing tension with a feeling of loss of control, which in turn may lead to a building panic. This can happen particularly if the individual is at a loss in terms of not possessing coping techniques. Another example would be the influence of negative thoughts. The Type A patient may add to the building tension by entertaining thoughts about succeeding, worries about having insufficient time, cognitions about being overcommitted, etc. These types of internal stimuli, if not controlled, can make matters worse than they might have been at the start. By introducing relaxation activities, the patient may be able to reduce the tension before it increases to a point of prompting higher levels of tension or negative thoughts. Once the disruptive cognitions occur, the patient however must be trained in the means for coping with these thoughts. One principle that is valuable is the one that asserts that competing or contradictory thoughts cannot coexist simultaneously. Therefore, a patient may be instructed to refocus his thoughts in other directions, such as on deliberately considering alternative active solutions to the issue. Another procedure would be to have the patient engage in discussing alternative solutions with another person; as long as 'solutions' are being discussed, then the patient cannot easily entertain thoughts of failure. A slightly different method for controlled thoughts involves a method often used in breaking smoking habits. By this method, the undesired activity, such as smoking, is restricted to a specific location. Thus, the smoker is told to smoke only in a specific chair in a specific room, thereby narrowing the cues that prompt smoking to a limited number. In the same way, a patient who is plagued by interfering cognitions that prompt stress can be encouraged to deliberately engage in such thoughts, but only in a specific room, while waiting in a specific chair, and during a specific time of day.

A better approach for coping with daily situations that appear to prompt stress is a reconditioning approach. By this method the objective is to recondition the person such that the stress situations lose their ability to prompt the emotional reaction to tension and anxiety. This is similar to methods used to break up the ability of certain situations to provoke fear responses in patients, and to prevent them to face the circumstances but without the emotional response. An emotional reconditioning process would have the individual first engage in a relaxing activity. After the patient is certain that he is extremely comfortable, then he briefly thinks about the stress situation. Any signs of increase in tension should be followed immediately by termination of the thoughts, as well as refocusing the attention on increasing the relaxed state. Through a number of such brief exposures under a relaxed condition, the patient will soon discover that he can face the previous stress producing situation without the same reactions.

BEHAVIORAL CHANGE FOR EMOTIONAL CHANGE

A useful concept is that certain emotions are influenced by certain actions. If a person deliberately acts angry or out of control, that person may soon discover that these actions actually prompt a *feeling* or *emotion* congruent with the actions. One favorite device of television professionals to prepare an audience prior to a live show is to engage the audience in activities on the premise that their mood will also change. Basically the premise is that behavioral change leads to emotional change. Perhaps the reason that the Type A individual experiences more pressure and feels emotionally in a rush is because the individual behaves in a "rushed" manner—movements are more rapid in the Type A individual. One method for slowing down the Type A individual emotionally would therefore be to slow down the individual behaviorally. Thus, the Type A individual may be encouraged to deliberately speak slower, use less vigorous gestures, and walk slower.

SPOUSE INVOLVEMENT

The involvement of the patient's spouse is relevant for not only the control of stress but also the alteration of Type A behaviors. With the aid of the spouse, the patient may be able to better control situations prompting stress reactions. A spouse may help the patient in identifying those conditions which are stress producing, help develop alternative means for dealing with such circumstances, or even take on certain obligations directly from the patient (this might involve reanalysis of role definitions). In another way, the spouse may be able to enhance behavioral change through acting as a social reinforcer. In other words, the approval of the spouse as he or she observes changes in the Type A behaviors of the patient can carry much weight in encouraging such change. Finally, the opposite is also true. There is nothing more damaging than the reaction of a Type A to changes being tried by the Type A patient. Consider a Type A patient who has allocated a thirty minute period to relax and not do anything other than experience the advantages of time out from activities. If the spouse, being a Type A person as well, is intolerant of this inactivity that person may interfere with progress by demanding, "Since you're not doing anything, I have something for you that needs to be done immediately!"

In summary, there are a variety of methods which could be tried to achieve stress control or even behavioral changes with a Type A patient. It is important to recognize that certain basic principles are behind these methods, and it is the principles that are important rather than routine following of a method. Some individualizing of the approach to match the characteristics of the patient in question is desirable, provided that the same principles are applied. It is also important to note that the Type A individual will be highly responsive to trying out such recommendations for change, and in some cases in a great hurry to respond! The Type A person's very characteristic is to be challenged by tasks, and to attempt to achieve success in those tasks instantly. The practitioner should take care in identifying this tendency in patients, and to caution the patient that the recommendations should be implemented more slowly and in a more patient fashion. In turn, the practitioner should also be prepared to display the same patience as is being expected of the patient.

The topic of compliance is important to consider in any treatment or training regime. Much understanding can be gained by first reconceptualizing compliance as a habit or response. Then it is possible to apply all we know about strengthening habits to strengthening compliance. For example, stimulus control may be applied. Rather than having medication prescribed 'four times a day', it might be associated with exact hours which fit the daily activity schedule of the patient. If the patient is usually up for breakfast at home by 8 A.M., then this hour would be designated, and marked on clocks and wristwatch with a colored tape or marking pen. An alarm could serve the same function of stimulus control, or a reminder note taped to the lunchbox as a noon stimulus. Requiring that the compliance response always be at a set time and associated with set stimuli also has the advantage of making it habitual. Thus, the habit of taking medication might be as strongly developed as the habit of teeth brushing on awakening. New habits are sometimes more readily reinforced where record keeping is required. Four spaces might be drawn on a home calendar on the refrigerator or an office desk calendar or even a small calendar in the car's dashboard can serve as a simple chart.

Compliance may be needed for other nonmedication activities, such as exercise. A cost-benefit analysis is useful for encouraging compliance. Exercise should be started which requires minimal initial 'cost' in getting started. Specifically, for example, a high cost would mean the amount of effort if the exercise required that the person drive home, walk to the bedroom, change clothes, walk back to the car, drive to the exercise locale, find a space, exercise, be required to shower, walk back to the car, return home, walk to the bedroom, and change. In contrast, some patients are helped to design exercise programs which easily fit into their daily routine, such as skipping every other stair in walking upstairs to one's bedroom. No change of clothes is required, no exertion to the level demanding showering, etc. For women who are housewives with children, physical exercise should not be scheduled during busy periods. For example, the cost would be extremely high if she would jog just before the dinner hour, have to return home, quickly prepare dinner, and face the harassment of a flurry of family activities. Soon, she would find jogging aversive since it would be immediately followed by negative events. The opposite can also be planned, i.e., whereby the effort of exercise can be associated with positive features, thereby enhancing the quality of exercising. For some, exercising with a spouse or friend can add a social atmosphere. For an extremely busy person, scheduling an hour and a half (including travel time) to do nothing but exercise can also have the fringe benefit of providing a peaceful respite.

Compliance for the Type A represents a difficult goal, especially if the activity required is directly opposite to the habits of the patient. As indicated earlier, being Type A is rewarding. Additionally, the Type A person wants immediate results, and is impatient to see gains. Finally, passive activities are aversive to the normally active Type A individual. The successful practitioner enlists the Type A person's characteristics to support compliance. Thus, the achievement drive is channeled into achieving in training. A mild, humorous pointing at the Type A's impatience as it is displayed can challenge the patient to aiming at succeeding in the goal of reducing these very behaviors. Type A persons also need to be reassured that adopting new behaviors will not reduce productivity, an extremely valid issue. Rather, the practitioner needs to point out the greater efficiency possible as stress reactions and fatigue are eliminated through training. The important contribution of rest periods to enhance work output may be an important context in which to examine rest and recreation. *Scheduling* relaxation as an 'activity' can help, especially if successful relaxation is viewed as a step in a planned series of steps leading to the objective of better self-control. Many Type A's respond to the analysis that they are currently being controlled by their environment, rather than being in control of themselves. The need to react to telephone calls, the inability to keep a calendar from being so jammed with appointments, the impatience at waiting, the feelings of pressure that are uncalled for, are all clear indications that the environment is controlling the patient. In this context, environmental planning, stress management, and the strengthening of adaptive alternate behaviors can all be presented in a positive context. Many Type A's respond well to a program that is viewed as systematic and planned, with concrete objectives.

REFERENCES

Clark, D.A., Arnold, E.L., Foulds, Jr., E.L., Brown, D.M., Eastmead, D.R., & Parry, E.M. Serum urate and cholesterol levels in Air Force Academy cadets. *Aviation Space and Environmental Medicine*, 1975, *46*, 1044–1048.

Friedman, M., & Rosenman, R. Association of specific overt behavior pattern with blood and cardiovascular findings. *Journal of the American Medical Association*, 1959, *169*, 1286.

Friedman, M., & Rosenman, R. *Type A behavior and your heart.* New York: Knopf, 1974.

Peterson, J.E., Keith, R.A., & Wilcox, A.A. Hourly changes in serum cholesterol concentration. Effects of the anticipation of stress. *Circulation*, 1962, *25*, 798–803.

Rosenman, R., & Friedman, M. Association of specific behavior pattern in women with blood and cardiovascular findings. *Circulation*, 1961, *24*, 1173.

Rosenman, R., Friedman, M., Straus, R., Wurm, M., Kositchek, R., Hahn, W., & Wethessin, N. A predictive study of coronary heart disease. *Journal of the American Medical Association*, 1964, *189*, 15.

Suinn, R.M. Behavior rehearsal training for ski racers. *Behavior Therapy*, 1972, *3*, 519.

Suinn, R.M. Behavior therapy for cardiac patients. *Behavior Therapy*, 1974, *5*, 569–571.

Suinn, R.M. Anxiety management training for general anxiety. In Suinn, R., and Weigel, R. (Eds.), *The innovative therapies: creative and critical contributions.* New York: Harper & Row, 1975a.

Suinn, R.M. The cardiac stress management program for Type A patients. *Cardiac Rehabilitation*, 5 (4), Winter 1975b.

Suinn, R.M. Behavioral methods at the winter olympic games. *Behavior Therapy*, In press.

Suinn, R., & Richardson, F. Anxiety management training: A non-specific behavior therapy program for anxiety control. *Behavior Therapy*, 1971, *4*, 498.

Chapter 6

Cardiac Arrhythmias

*Bernard T. Engel**

If one reviews the apochrypha of cardiology, the noncanonical, nonorthodox literature on heart disease, he will find a number of references to the important role which psychosocial or behavioral factors play in the expression of cardiovascular disorders. Even Galen was aware of these interactions. Most contemporary cardiologists are familiar with John Hunter's assessment of his own experiences with angina pectoris: "My life is in the hands of any rascal who chooses to annoy and tease me" (Palmer, 1837, p. 119). However, it is less well-known how correct Hunter's prognosis was. During a staff meeting he was angered by a remark someone made to him, stormed from the room, and dropped dead. The circumstances of Hunter's death were widely known at the time, and they apparently had a profound effect on the clinical practice of that time. In 1842, Tuke reviewed what was then known about psychosomatic links in cardiac disorders, and about the neural mechanisms which might mediate those effects. White (1951) reviewed the cyclic trends in cardiology in relation to psychosomatic processes; and he also summarized a number of relevant case studies from his practice as well as from the practice of others. Despite this venerable history, there is considerable evidence that contemporary cardiologists are indifferent to the important role which psychological factors play in heart disease. For example, three of the major American textbooks of cardiology virtually ignore psychosocial or behav-

*Gerontology Research Center (Baltimore), National Institute on Aging, National Institutes of Health, PHS, U.S. Department of Health, Education, and Welfare, Bethesda, and the Baltimore City Hospitals, Baltimore, Maryland 21224.

ioral variables: Bellett (1971) devotes 6 pages in 1300 to such variables; Scherf and Schott (1973) commit 2 pages in 1000 to them; and Hurst et al. (1974) spend about 1 page in 1800 on psychosomatic or emotional variables.

Almost everything that has been written about behavioral factors in cardiac disease is directed at the role such variables might play in triggering aberrant reactions. Very few investigators have considered the logical corollary of these morbid effects. Namely, that it might be possible to prevent or treat abnormal cardiac responses through behavioral methods—Galen was one of these few. Over the past 10 or 15 years my colleagues and I have been studying the potential application of operant conditioning techniques to the control of cardiac arrhythmias. However, because of the seriousness of many of the arrhythmias, and because of the need to understand both the physiological and the behavioral mechanisms underlying our procedures, almost all of our studies have been experimental. Thus, while we do have clinical end points in mind, we have not yet undertaken any controlled, clinical studies. We have reviewed many of our results elsewhere: In particular we have considered the results from a clinical point of view (Engel and Bleecker, 1974); from a behavioral point of view (Engel, in press), and from a psychophysiological point of view (Engel, 1972). We also have described an animal model in which one can condition cardiac rate (Engel and Gottlieb, 1970) and in which one can analyze physiological (Engel, 1974) and behavioral (Ainslie and Engel, 1974; Engel, Gottlieb, and Hayhurst, 1976) mechanisms in great detail. Rather than review all of those data again, I will describe a single case study in some detail. I have chosen this case because the results illustrate so many of our methods and principles (Bleecker and Engel, 1973).

The patient was a 29-year-old woman with a history of intermittent Wolff-Parkinson-White syndrome (WPW). WPW is characterized electrocardiographically by a short PR interval, a wide QRS complex, and the appearance of a delta wave. Physiologically, these abnormalities can be explained by the presence of an aberrant conduction pathway which conducts impulse from the atrium to the ventricle super-normally (Moore, Spear, and Boineau, 1973). In addition to these electrocardiographic abnormalities, WPW often is associated with the emergence of supraventricular tachyarrhythmias which are frequently highly resistant to therapy, and which can be life threatening.

The patient had a documented, four year history of intermittent, type-A, WPW. She complained of symptoms of dyspnea, syncope chest pain, and tachycardia. Despite treatment with combinations of various medications including propanolol, quinidine, procainamide, diphenylhydantoin, digoxin and sedatives, these symptoms persisted. At the time of admission to the hospital for study, her pulse rate was 110 beats/min and her electrocardiogram revealed a conduction pattern typical of intermittent WPW: During normal conduction the PR interval was 0.18 sec and the QRS duration was 0.07 sec; During WPW conduction the PR interval was 0.10 sec and the QRS duration was 0.12 sec.

Because the tachyarrhythmia appeared to be the more serious problem (and symptom) for this patient, we first trained her to control her ventricular rate (HR). We did this in three stages: First she was trained to slow HR, second she was trained to speed HR, and finally she was trained to speed and to slow her rate alternately. The technique we used was to provide the patient with a display of three lights; one was red, the second was green, and the third was yellow. When we wanted her to slow her rate, we would turn on the red light; when we want her to speed her rate, we turned on the green light. Whenever she performed successfully, the yellow light went on and remained on until she failed to meet our criterion. This feedback arrangement occurred on a beat-to-beat basis. Each training session was 1024 sec in duration. There were 26 sessions during which she was trained to slow HR; 15 sessions during which she was trained to speed HR; and 21 sessions during which she was required to slow for 256 sec, speed for 256 sec then slow again and then speed again. She performed successfully during 19 slowing sessions (average change 3.4 beats/min overall); during 11 speeding sessions (average change 2.5 beats/min overall); and during 20 alternate sessions (average difference between slowing and speeding 5.5 beats/min). The HR training phase of the study required about two weeks, and the results are shown in Figure 6–1.

Following completion of HR training, she was trained to control cardiac conduction. In this phase of the study we took advantage of a characteristic pattern in her electrocardiogram to feedback information about her conduction patterns. Using a right, precordial lead, the QRS deflection of WPW beats and normally conducted beats was opposite. By selectively triggering a clicker from normally conducted beats only, it was possible to provide her with beat-to-beat information on normally conducted beats (clicks) and aberrantly conducted beats (no clicks). Using such feedback she was able to increase normal conduction in four of eight training sessions, and to decrease normal conduction in two of three training sessions.

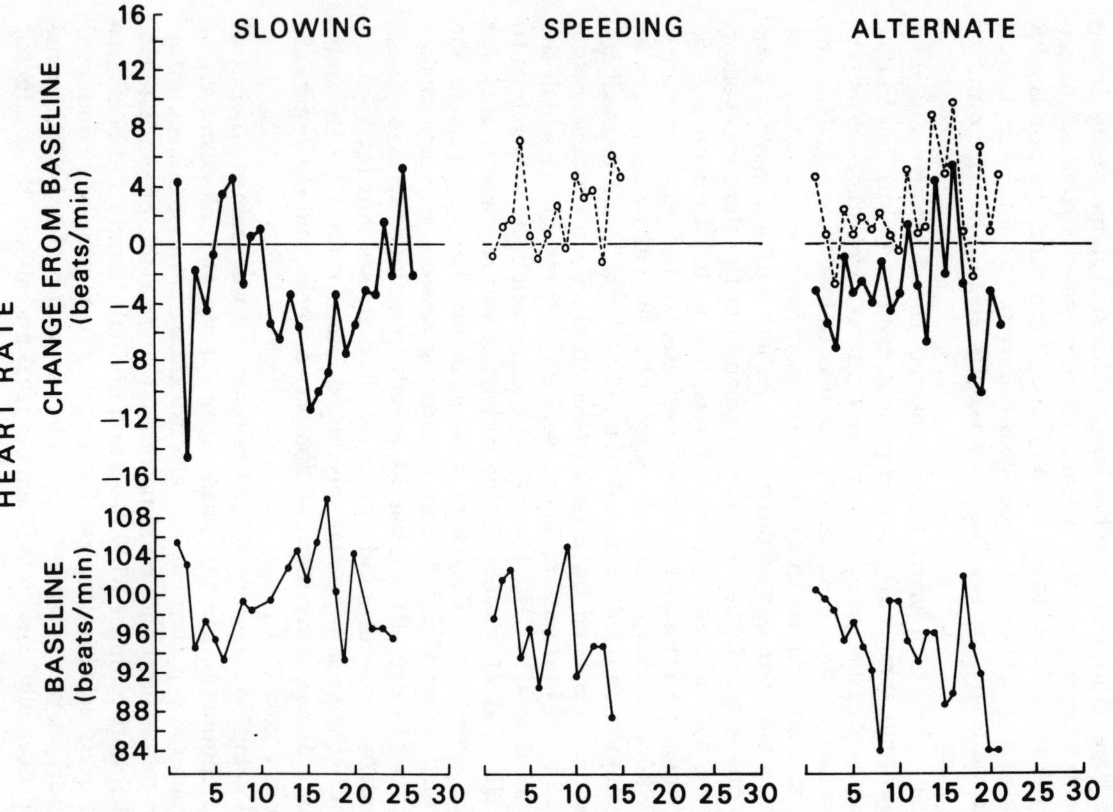

Figure 6–1. Mean baseline heart rates during training (bottom graph). Mean baseline HR (top graph) during each HR slowing (0), speeding (0) and alternate session. (Reprinted, by permission from the New England Journal of Medicine, *288*: 561, 1973.)

Her performance during alternating training sessions was divided into three categories depending on her base-line rhythm. When normal conduction was rare (base-line rhythm less than 10 percent normal conduction), she was able to increase normal conduction significantly during all five sessions from an average of 1.8 percent to an average of 18.2 percent. When normal conduction was moderate (base-line rhythm between 10 and 90 percent normal conduction), she was able to increase normal conduction significantly in five of seven sessions from an average of 38.1 percent to an average of 55.9 percent, and to decrease normal conduction significantly in four of seven sessions to an average of 31.4 percent. In six of these seven sessions she significantly differentiated between the increase and decrease of normal conduction phases. During sessions when normal conduction was predominant) base-line rhythm greater than 90 percent), she was able to decrease normal conduction significantly in five of ten sessions, from an average of 99.7 percent to an average of 90.4 percent. Figure 6–2 shows representative electrocardiographic tracings from an alternating session in which she increased and decreased normal conduction.

During the last stage of training the patient was taught to increase normal conduction without feedback. In these training sessions, 128 sec periods of feedback were alternated with 128 sec periods of no feedback, and she was instructed to increase normal conduction during the entire training session. She increased normal conduction significantly in all eight sessions during both the feedback and the no-feedback phases. The mean increase of normal conduction from baseline was 13 percent during both feedback and no-feedback phases of training.

In order to elucidate the neural mechanisms mediating her performance we carried out a series of sessions with autonomic drugs. These results are shown in Table 6–1. They indicate clearly that the inhibition of aberrantly conducted beats was associated with an inhibition of vagal tone to her heart: In two separate sessions atropine totally abolished her aberrantly conducted beats. Isoproterenol, which stimulated the beta-adrenergic receptors to her heart and raised her HR to a degree comparable to that during atropine injection, did not inhibit her aberrant conduction. Thus, the abolition of aberrant by conducted beats is not rate determined.

Follow-up testing in the clinic, ten weeks after initial training showed that she was able to modify cardiac conduction differentially (Figure 6–3). These data show clearly that she had retained the skill she had learned in the laboratory. Furthermore, she reported that over the 10 week period she had used the techniques she had learned

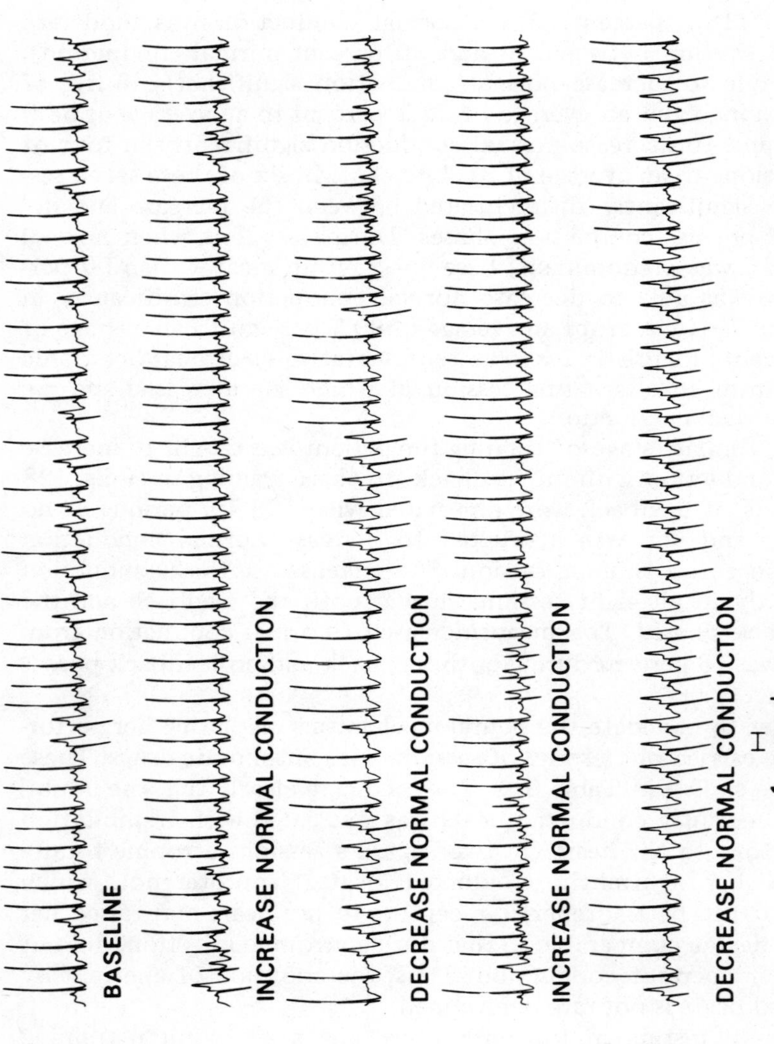

Figure 6–2. Representative rhythm strips from an alternate training session during which the patient was sequentially increasing and decreasing normal conduction. QRS complexes with upright R waves and normal PR intervals were normally conducted. (Reprinted, by permission from the New England Journal of Medicine, *288*: 561, 1973.)

Table 6–1. Ability to Increase and Decrease Normal Sinus Conduction (NSR) During Studies with Autonomic Drugs

	Percentage NSR Conduction			*Heart Rate (beats/min)*		
Drug	*Baseline*	*NSR Increase*	*NSR Decrease*	*Baseline*	*NSR Increase*	*NSR Decrease*
Pre drug test	32	63	18	95	101	91
Placebo (saline IV)	50	70	38	96	98	94
Phenylephrine HCL (0.02–0.03 mg/min IV)	5	12	3	82	91	83
Propranolol (5.0 mg IV)	4	11	0	81	83	81
Isoproterenol HCL (1–1.5 μg/min IV)	20	9	6	116	124	121
Atropine A (1.5 mg IV)	100	100	100	128	125	119
Atropine B (1.5 mg IV)	100	100	100	135	125	123

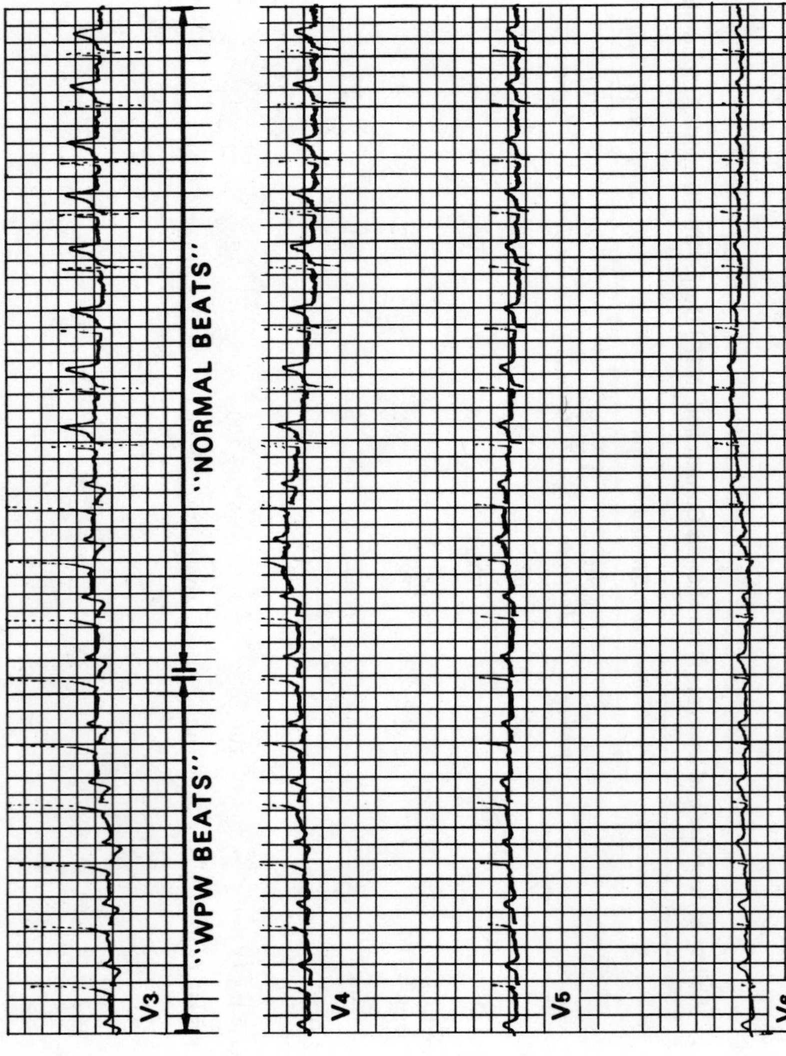

Figure 6–3. Electrocardiographic rhythm strip taken 10 weeks after completion of training (WPW denotes Wolff-Parkinson-White). The patient was able to control differentially her heart rhythm away from the laboratory and without feedback.

to control episodes of tachycardia; and she expressed a sense of confidence in her ability to control her cardiac function which, she said, encouraged her to resume a more normal life style. It seems likely that this reaction to her arrhythmia reduced her sympathetic tone. This may have helped her clinically in two ways: First, it reduced her anxiety and sense of helplessness by providing her with a rational and effective mechanism for dealing with her arrhythmia; and second, to the extent that increased sympathetic tone facilitates retrograde conduction, her learned control reduced the probability of an episode of supraventricular tachycardia.

The results of this study illustrate strikingly the interaction between physiological processes and psychological processes. The data show that neural factors operate importantly in the regulation of cardiac function, and that these factors can be utilized by some patients to affect aberrant responses irrespective of the etiology of the abnormal cardiac rhythm. Furthermore, when patients learn such control, they can implement it in naturally occurring situations.

The data suggest strongly the need for controlled clinical trials to ascertain the clinical effectiveness of biofeedback as an adjunctive therapy in the regulation of cardiac arrhythmias.

REFERENCES

Ainslie, G.W., & Engel, B.T. Alteration of classically conditioned heart rate by operant reinforcement in monkeys. *Journal of Comparative and Physiological Psychology*, 1974, *87*, 373–382.

Bellet, S. *Clinical disorders of the heart beat* (3rd ed.) Philadelphia: Lea & Febiger, 1971.

Bleecker, E.R., & Engel, B.T. Learned control of cardiac rate and cardiac conduction in the Wolff-Parkinson-White syndrome. *The New England Journal of Medicine*, 1973, *288*, 560–562.

Engel, B.T. Operant Conditioning of cardiac function: A status report. *Psychophysiology*, 1972, *9*, 161–177.

Engel, B.T. Electroencephalographic and blood pressure correlates of operantly conditioned heart rate in the restrained monkey. *Pavlovian Journal of Biological Sciences*, 1974, *9*, 222–232.

Engel, B.T. Operant conditioning of cardiovascular function: A behavioral analysis. In S. Rachman (Ed.), *Advances in medical psychology 1976*, in press.

Engel, B.T., & Bleecker, E.R. Application of operant conditioning techniques to the control of the cardiac arrhythmias. In P.A. Obrist (Ed.), *Cardiovascular psychophysiology*. Chicago: Aldine, 1974.

Engel, B.T., & Gottlieb, S.H. Differential operant conditioning of heart rate in the restrained monkey. *Journal of Comparative and Physiological Psychology*, 1970, *73*, 217–225.

Engel, B.T., Gottlieb, S.H., & Hayhurst, V.F. Tonic and phasic relationships between heart rate and somato-motor activity in monkeys. *Psychophysiology*, 1976, *13*.

Hurst, J.W., Logue, R.B., Schlant, R.C., & Wenger, N.K. *The heart*, (3rd ed.) New York: McGraw-Hill, 1974.

Moore, E.N., Spear, J.F., & Boineau, J.P. Recent electrophysiologic studies on the Wolff-Parkinson-White syndrome. *The New England Journal of Medicine*, 1973, *289*, 956–963.

Palmer, J.F. (Ed.). *The works of John Hunter, F.R.S.* Vol. 1. London: Longman, Rees, Orme, Brown, Green and Longman, 1837.

Scherf, D., & Schott, A. *Extrasystoles and allied arrhythmias*, (2nd ed.) Chicago: Year Book Medical Publishers, Inc., 1974.

Tuke, D.H. *The mind upon the body in health and disease.* London: J & A Churchill, 1872.

White, P.D. The psyche and the soma: The spiritual and physical attributes of the heart. *Annals of Internal Medicine*, 1951, *35*, 1291–1305.

❋ *Chapter 7*

Obesity

*John P. Foreyt**

Physicians have known the five magic words to achieve weight loss since the beginning of time: *Eat less and Walk More.* If all overweight patients followed that sage advice, obesity would not be the major health problem it is today. Unfortunately, most patients with weight problems do not take those words to heart (and mouth), for there are about 80 million overweight adults in the United States today. That fact wouldn't be so bad, except that obesity is such a serious health problem. It is associated with cardiovascular diseases, diabetes, cirrhosis of the liver, appendicitis, and many other conditions.

One cannot look at a rack of women's magazines without seeing some new wonder diet shouting at you on the cover. Newspapers are full of ads touting techniques to lose weight while you eat all you want, without trying, while you sleep, painlessly. Private clinics and clubs have sprung up in every large and small city in the country. Weight loss surpassed sex in 1971 as the national pastime.

In spite of all the interest in losing weight, we really do not know how to effectively teach people to eat less and walk more. Certainly prior to 1967 the success rate was practically zero. Whatever initial losses were achieved by a patient through diet, drugs, and determination, these lost pounds were usually gained back within a year. Stunkard and McLaren-Hume (1959), in their review of the obesity treatment outcome literature found that only about 25 percent of patients in obesity treatment programs lost 20 pounds and only 5 percent lost 40 pounds. They also reported that some programs had

*Baylor College of Medicine

as high as an 80 percent dropout rate, a finding many physicians know full well to be true. Chlouverakis (1975) reviewed the more recent dietary and medical treatment literature and, after pointing out that this line of research is difficult to evaluate because long-term data are not available and appropriate controls are generally lacking, concluded that none of the treatments reviewed were particularly successful. He added, "Despite the claims which are constantly made by the inventors of new methods, the treatment of obesity for the majority of patients is still difficult, tedious, and long as life" (p. 18).

BEHAVIORAL APPROACHES TO OBESITY

In 1962, Ferster, Nurnberger, and Levitt stepped into this rather discouraging area with an article in a short-lived obscure journal describing a behavioral analysis of overeating. Their analysis and treatment program involved four steps: identifying the variables that influence eating, determining how the variables can be manipulated, specifying the unwanted effects of overeating, and arranging a method for developing self-control. Although Ferster et al. did not report any data, apparently their treatment program was not particularly successful (Penick et al., 1971). No one paid much attention to the study until 1967, when Stuart reported the results of an outpatient treatment program for obesity based on Ferster et al.'s behavioral analysis. Stuart presented data on eight female patients who stayed in treatment over a one year period (two others dropped out). Their initial weights ranged from 172 to 224 pounds. After one year they had lost an average of 37 pounds, ranging from 26 to 47 pounds. Stuart's treatment consisted of 30 minute sessions, three times a week, for 12–15 sessions. After the initial treatment period, sessions were held as needed, usually every other week, for three months. Maintenance sessions were held whenever necessary, and followup classes were held monthly. The number of sessions for these eight patients ranged from 16 to 41. Stuart's results were the best ever published for outpatient programs and they generated considerable interest and enthusiasm in treating obesity with behavioral techniques.

Harris (1969), for example, reported significant weight loss data for her two behavioral treatment groups of seven college students each, compared to a no-treatment control group. Her treatment groups lost a combined average of 10.5 pounds over a six month period while her controls gained 3.6 pounds.

Wollersheim (1970) introduced the placebo control group to behavioral weight loss research with an elaborate well-designed study including four treatment conditions: behavioral treatment ("focal"), social pressure, attention placebo (nonspecific), and no-treatment control. A total of 79 female college students were assigned to one of the four conditions. Four therapists conducted the treatment groups. At the end of the twelve week program, participants in the behavioral treatment group had lost the most weight, an average of 11 pounds, compared to 5 pounds for the social pressure group, 7 pounds for the attention placebo group, and a gain of 2 pounds for the no-treatment control group. After an eight week followup, the behavioral group had still lost the most weight, an average of almost 9 pounds. Hagen (1974) used a design similar to Wollersheims to test the effectiveness of a written weight loss manual, without a therapist. His four experimental conditions included a manual-only group, behavioral treatment-only group ("Contact"), both manual and behavioral treatment ("contact") group, and no treatment control group. He found all three treatment conditions resulted in significant weight losses when compared to the no treatment controls, but three treatment groups did not differ significantly from each other, either at the end of treatment or followup, suggesting to Hagen that the need for therapists in the behavioral treatment of obesity might be minimal. Fernan (1973) replicated Hagen's study, using the same manual except that his manual-only group was stricter than Hagen's, with essentially no interpersonal contact at all, i.e., homework assignments were not returned to the participants as they had been in Hagen's study. Fernan found that the participants in this condition lost an average of 4.9 pounds, compared to 5.2 pounds in his no-treatment condition, and 11.8 pounds in his manual with contact group (which was similar to Hagen's "manual-only" group). Fernan's study clearly indicated the need for some therapist contact in a weight loss program, even though the contact might not necessarily have to be in a face to face encounter.

Levitz and Stunkard (1974) investigated the question of what kind of therapist is needed to run a successful weight loss program. They conducted a study with 16 TOPS (Take Off Pounds Sensibly) clubs in Philadelphia. Four of the clubs received a behavioral treatment package from psychiatric residents, four received the same behavioral treatment package from the club leader and co-leader who had received training in the behavioral techniques, four received nutrition-education from the club leader and co-leader, and four received the usual TOPS program. Each treatment lasted 12 weeks. The clubs who received the behavioral treatment from the psychiatric residents lost the most weight (4.2 pounds), those who received it from the clubs' leaders lost second most (1.9 pounds), the nutrition-education clubs lost 0.2 pounds, and the TOPS program only condition showed a gain of 0.7 pound. At one year followup, the professionally led clubs continued to lose, an average of 5.8 pounds, while the clubs who had received the behavioral training from the club leaders had regained the lost weight. The nutrition education and TOPS program only clubs both showed a gain at one year followup. The results suggest the importance of well trained professionals in therapeutic intervention programs.

McReynolds et al. (1976) reported the use of nutritionists as group leaders in two successful behavioral treatment programs. Nineteen patients who received behavioral treatment emphasizing stimulus control ("food management") lost an average of 18.6 pounds at the end of a 15 week program, 22 pounds at the end of a three month followup, and 20.4 pounds at the end of six months. Twenty-one patients who received a program similar to Wollersheim's (1970) ("behavior control") lost an average of 16.1 pounds at the end of treatment, 17 pounds at three months, and 14.6 pounds at six months. The three nutritionists-therapists were highly trained professionals, two had Ph.D.'s, and one a Masters degree in nutrition, but only the Masters degree nutritionist had any prior experience in behavior modification. They were trained in the techniques by manuals, readings, and several informational sessions conducted by a psychologist.

Penick et al. (1971) investigated the question of therapist bias on subsequent outcome in a particularly interesting, well-designed study. Patients were randomly assigned to either a behavioral treatment condition or a control condition. The two behavioral treatment groups were led by rather inexperienced though behaviorally biased therapists. The two control groups, which received supportive psychotherapy and nutrition information, were led by an experienced internist and a research nurse. All therapists believed strongly in their own techniques. Patients were treated in two hour weekly group meetings for three months. Results showed that the patients who received the behavioral treatment lost more weight than the traditional therapy groups. Median weight loss for the first behavior therapy group ($N = 8$) was 24 pounds, compared to 18 pounds for the first traditional group ($N = 10$). Median weight loss for the second behavior therapy group was 13 pounds compared to 11 pounds for the traditional group. Six month followup showed the continued influence of the behavior treatment. This report showed that rather inexperienced therapists using behavioral techniques were more effective than an experienced internist who had treated obesity for many years. Also of interest in this study was the great variability in weight losses among the patients in the behavioral treatment groups.

For example, the five patients who lost the most weight were all in the behavioral conditions as was the only patient who gained weight during treatment. Apparently the behavioral techniques are a useful tool for weight loss with about half of the patients. More traditional approaches generally show less variability among patients, perhaps suggesting the nonspecific effects of the therapy, such as the therapist's attention and encouragement (Stunkard, 1975).

The above studies illustrate the kind of research now going on in the obesity area. Extensive reviews of the field may be found in Stuart and Davis (1972), Abramson (1973), Stuart (1973), Hall and Hall (1974), O'Leary and Wilson (1975), Yates (1975), Foreyt (1976), Jeffrey (1976), Stunkard and Mahoney (1976), and Williams, Martin, and Foreyt (1976).

In addition to the research studies exploring the Ferster et al., (1962) and Stuart (1967, 1971) approach to treatment mentioned above (e.g., Harris and Bruner, 1971; Hall, 1972, 1973; Harris and Hallbauer, 1973; Mahoney, Moura, and Wade, 1973; Martin and Sachs, 1973; Romanczyk et al., 1973; Abrahms and Allen, 1974; Balch and Ross, 1974; Bellack, Rozensky and Schwartz, 1974; Bellack, Schwartz and Rozensky, 1974; Hall et al., 1974; Jeffrey, 1974; Mahoney, 1974; Romanczyk, 1974; Mahoney and Mahoney, 1976(b); Musante, 1976), there are numerous studies investigating other behavioral treatments as well, such as *overt aversive conditioning* (e.g., Wolpe, 1954; Meyer and Crisp, 1964; Thorpe et al., 1964; Stollak, 1967; Kennedy and Foreyt, 1968; Foreyt and Kennedy, 1971; Wijesinghe, 1973; Morganstern, 1974; Frohwirth and Foreyt, 1976), *covert sensitization* (e.g., Cautela, 1966, 1967, 1972; Ashem, Poser, and Truedell, 1972; Murray and Harrington, 1972; Janda and Rimm, 1972; Manno and Marston, 1972; Sachs and Ingram, 1972; Maletzky, 1973; Foreyt and Hagen, 1973; Diament and Wilson, 1975), *coverant conditioning* (Homme, 1965; Tyler and Straughan, 1970; Horan and Johnson, 1971; Horan et al., 1975), *induced anxiety* (e.g., Sipprelle, 1967; Bornstein and Sipprelle, 1973(a), and 1973(b), and *operant therapist reinforcement techniques* (e.g., Ayllon, 1963; Bernard, 1968; Harmatz and Lapuc, 1968; Moore and Crum, 1969; Upper and Newton, 1971; Klein et al., 1972; Foxx, 1972; Dinoff, Rickard, and Colwick, 1972; Mann, 1972; Jeffrey, Christensen, and Pappas, 1973; Aragona, Cassady, and Drabman, 1975; Foreyt and Parks, 1975).

A growing number of manuals (e.g., Hagen, Wollersheim, and Paul, 1969; Christensen, Jeffrey, and Pappas, 1973; Mahoney and Jeffrey, 1974; Paulsen et al., 1974; Ferguson, 1975) and books (Stuart and Davis, 1972; Mahoney and Mahoney, 1976(a)) are available to the physician and overweight individual.

Basic Behavioral Treatment Program

Most of the comprehensive behavioral treatment programs mentioned above consist of basically similar components. They are based on the belief that many of the behaviors associated with obesity are learned responses; therefore, they contain techniques which help the individual change his inappropriate dietary behaviors.

A behavioral treatment program may consist of a number of components including:

1. Food Record
2. Weight Record
3. Eating in One-Spot
4. Laying Down Utensils Between Bites
5. Shopping for Food
6. Storing Food
7. Meal Time Behavior
8. Number of Meals
9. Increasing Exercise
10. Contracts
11. Handling Anxiety

1. Food Record. The food record (Figure 7–1) is a critical part of all behavioral treatment programs. The patient is asked to buy a small inexpensive notebook and write in it all food and drink ingested during the entire treatment period. This includes snacks, coffee, iced tea, melba toast, everything (except plain water). She is asked to write down:

a. The time the food was eaten ("11.32 P.M.").
b. The place ("lying in bed").
c. The food, including amount and how prepared ("5 oz. hamburger fried in 1 tablespoon butter").
d. Who she was with ("husband").
e. How she felt just before eating ("bored").

The patient is asked to do her writing immediately after the food is eaten (better yet, *before* it is eaten). She then brings in the notebook to her therapist once a week. The therapist reads it over with the patient and comments favorably on good examples and makes suggestions on how to deal with various problem areas.

The food record is an important element in the program because it helps make the patient aware of how much food she is actually ingesting. It also helps the physician learn the patient's dietary habits,

FOOD RECORD

Name Pam

Date May 12, 1976

Time	Place	Food: Amount and How Prepared
7:15 am neutral	Home Kitchen table	4 oz orange juice 1 egg scrambled in 1 tsp. margarine 1 slice whole wheat toast 1 tsp. margarine 1 tsp. grape jelly 8 oz coffee, black
11:45 am anxious	Tom's Grill	3 oz grilled hamburger 1 hamburger bun 1 slice lettuce, tomato 1 tsp. mustard 15 French fries 2 Tbsp. catsup 8 oz. iced tea with lemon
3:00 pm neutral	Office desk	12 oz diet cola
7:00 pm tired	Home dining room table	4 oz baked chicken breast 1/2 cup brown rice 2 stalks broccoli 1 tsp. margarine 2 cups tossed salad 2 Tbsp. French dressing 12 oz ice tea with lemon
9:15 pm happy	Home den chair	1 cup strawberry ice cream

Figure 7–1. Food Record for Behavioral Treatment Program

many of which may have to be modified if the patient is going to successfully complete the program.

Patients oftentimes complain that having to fill out the food record is boring and monotonous. These complaints usually disappear after a month and we find that many of our patients regard it as the single most helpful technique in the program. A word of caution should be mentioned, however. The food record seems to work for us only when patients know that they must turn it in to their therapist once a week. It does not seem to work if you simply tell your patients to go home and fill out a food record for the rest of their lives or until they reach ideal weight and never turn them in to anyone. The boredom and monotony of this latter procedure become so great that the patients simply stop filling them out.

I recently spoke to a women's club in Texas and described the importance of the food record. One woman raised her hand and said that she had been filling out a food record, showing it to her husband, and had lost 90 pounds in the past year, attributing her success to the record. The patients who generally lose the most weight in our obesity classes are the ones who fill out the food record and faithfully turn it in to us.

2. Weight Record. The weight record is also an extremely helpful part of any behavioral treatment program. The patient is asked to purchase a couple sheets of graph paper and draw a weight record similar to the one illustrated in Figure 7−2. Weights are written along the left hand column, days of the month along the bottom row. The weight record is then taped to the bathroom wall above the scale. The patient is instructed to weigh herself every day at the same time, usually after rising in the morning, before breakfast. She is asked to write in an "X" on the record at the intersection of her weight and the date. She also connects the "X's" so she sees a daily continuous record of her weight (see Figure 7−2).

We stress the importance of hanging up the weight record in a prominent visible place. It should not be hidden at the bottom of the underwear drawer or taped behind the mirror facing the wall. Many patients are sensitive about family and friends knowing how much they weigh. When this is a serious problem, we permit our patients to write in along the weight line, "0, −1, −2, −3, −4," etc. By doing this, family and friends will see that the patient is losing but will not know her actual weight.

Programs vary in how often the patient is told to weigh. Some tell their patients to weigh two, even three or four times a day, others say once a week. We have found that weighing once a day seems to be the most helpful although we do explain to our patients that weight fluctuates for many reasons and they will see many ups and downs on their record. However, if they faithfully follow the program the trend will be a downward one, at the rate of 1 to 2 pounds a week.

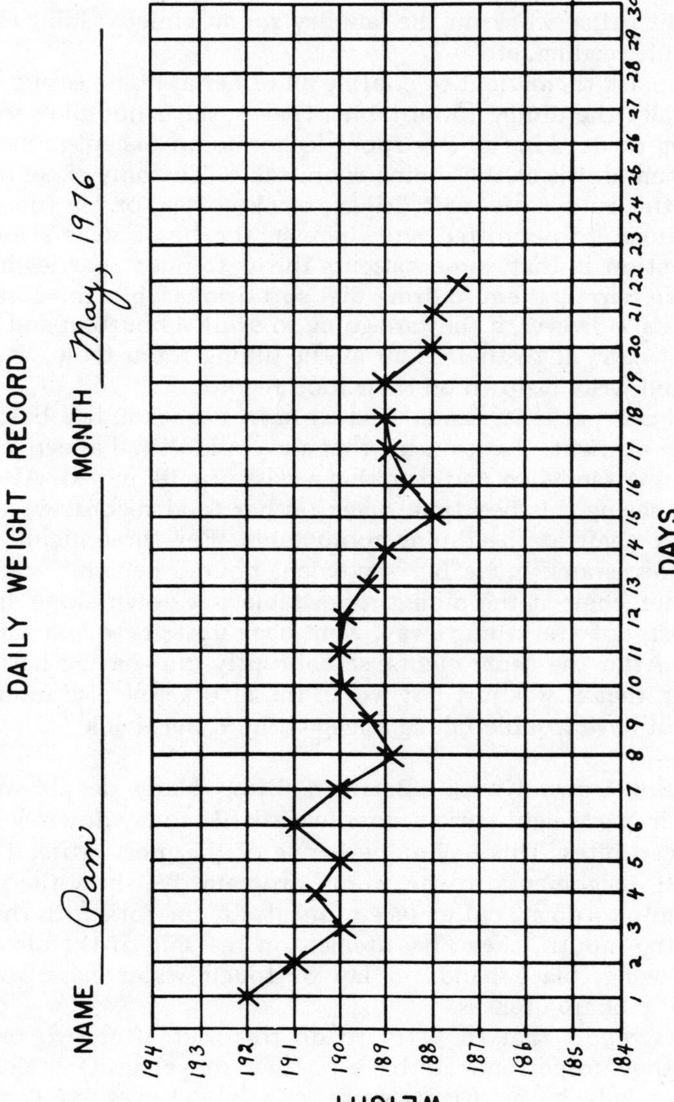

Figure 7–2. Weight Record for Behavioral Treatment Program

3. Eating in One Spot. After the patient has filled out his food record for two weeks, we then point out to her the many places in her home she eats. For example, we oftentimes see patients reporting that they eat in the living room while watching TV, in the den while doing their office work, in the laundry room while washing clothes, in bed while reading, etc.

We then ask the patient to confine all of her at-home eating to one spot, usually the dining room table. That is, she is not allowed to do any eating or drinking in any room in her home, except in her usual chair, sitting down at the dining room table. The only exception we make to this rule is *diet* soft drinks, black coffee, or tea (no sugar). These drinks are permitted anywhere in the home. One reason for this exception is that some patients throw frequent parties in their homes. We permit them to drink diet soft drinks while mingling with their guests. However, if they are going to drink a bourbon and water, they must carry it to their chair at the dining room table, sit down, drink it and write it down on their food record.

One of our patients, Linda, had to have a snack in bed before she fell asleep at night. She told me that she couldn't fall asleep without first eating a sandwich and drinking a glass of milk in bed. After two weeks of seeing this bed time snack on her food record, we limited her to her chair at the dining room table. For three nights, Linda walked downstairs, made her sandwich, poured her milk, carried it over to her chair at the dining room table, sat down alone and finished it off, put everything away, went back upstairs to bed and went to sleep. After the three nights, she abruptly quit having her snack, explaining that it was just not worth the effort. She also found that she did not have trouble falling asleep without her snack.

4. Laying Down Utensils Between Bites. Many people eat very fast. If our overweight patient does, we ask her to lay down her utensils between bites. This technique is one of the most difficult of the behavioral assignments in the whole program. We show the patient exactly how to do it: cut a piece of meat, lift the fork with the meat on it to the mouth, chew, lay utensils on the side of the plate, continue chewing, place hands in lap or touch water glass, swallow, touch and pick up utensils.

Patients report that they try to do this, but after two or three minutes they forget and are back to their shoveling. One aid to remembering is to have patients write on a folded over 3x5 card, "*lay down utensils between bites*" and have them place it next to their plate at the beginning of the meal.

Many of our patients report that this technique is extremely helpful to them. One young couple in our program came to the meeting after a week of trying to master the technique. They reported, very excitedly, that "it worked like a miracle." They did not even feel like finishing their food. They reported that they really "tasted" their food. They said they felt full before their meal ended. We explained that it takes about 20 minutes for feelings of "fullness" to occur and that the technique is a helpful one in slowing down the speed of eating. Both patients were successful in reducing their weight during and after the treatment program ended.

5. Shopping for Food. Patients are asked to do all their shopping for food *after* meals rather than on their way home from work. They are instructed to shop from a written list and to stick to their list. They are expected to write menu plans for their family.

6. Storing Food. Patients are asked to store all food out of sight and put problem foods in inaccessible places (e.g., Schachter, 1971). It is helpful to wrap refrigerated foods in tinfoil or put in opaque containers. "Free" foods, such as carrots and broccoli, should be readily accessible and easily reached when the refrigerator door is opened.

7. Meal Time Behavior. In addition to eating in one spot and laying down utensils between bites, patients are instructed to use slightly smaller plates for themselves, spread their food out on the plates, take smaller bites, and chew slowly. If they are going to sit at the table and talk after the meal, leftovers should be first removed. If there is some food still on the patient's plate, it should be covered with pepper.

8. Number of Meals. Many overweight patients do not eat breakfast. We ask all of our patients to eat at least three planned meals a day, including breakfast. More than three are permitted if they are planned and the three main meals are reduced in size.

9. Increasing Exercise. We do not ask any of our patients to go on a rigorous exercise program for several reasons, including the fact that none of them would be followed for more than a few days anyway, in spite of what we said. Instead, we ask our patients to increase their daily physical activity in small ways, such as parking at the far end of the supermarket parking lot and walking the block instead of driving around and around until a spot opens next to the door, and walking up the stairs to our office rather than taking the elevator, using the stairs rather than the escalator at the shopping mall, etc.

10. Contracts. We find contracts are a useful technique early in our weight loss program because patients generally like them and they seem to help motivate the patients to stick to the rest of the treatment assignments. One easy contract to form with a patient is to ask him to give you $20.00 in cash. The patient agrees to lose ten pounds during the next five weeks. At the end of the five weeks, he steps on the scale. At that time he receives back $2.00 for every pound he has lost. Any remaining monies should be donated to some agreed-upon organization.

The contract should be written very clearly, specifying exactly what is expected of patient and therapist, and signed by both parties. Each party keeps a copy.

In our experience, we have found that contracts should never be made for more than ten pounds at a time. After the five weeks, another contract can be negotiated if desired. The contract might also contain a bonus reward if all ten pounds are lost and all $20.00 returned. This bonus might include a new article of clothing, a new record, weekend out of town, a concert, etc. Although contracts have been criticized for rewarding weight loss rather than behavior change (they can be written to reward behavior change), we have found them helpful to use while the patient is learning and practicing the behavioral assignments because they serve as an added inducement to stay with the program.

11. Handling Anxiety. Many of our overweight patients eat when they are anxious, tense, bored, depressed, lonely, or angry. Oftentimes, this will become clear to the patient and therapist by reviewing the food records. Each patient must be handled individually in appropriate ways. Patients may be asked to keep lists of activities to perform when feeling bored, depressed, or lonely. These lists may include telephoning a friend, going to a movie, or shopping for a new outfit. For feelings of anxiety or tenseness, training in relaxation sometimes helps. For anger, the therapist may have to help counsel the patient in more appropriate ways to deal with it. If the feelings are pervasive or difficult to control, psychotherapy may be recommended.

Do the techniques really work? To answer that question, we must wait for the results of the research now in progress. There certainly is no paucity of active clinical outcome studies being conducted and we may have some answers in the near future.

The major problems in the behavioral research (Foreyt, 1976) up to now include:

1. *Inadequate followup periods.* Studies reporting one year followup data and more are needed to assess permanence of initial behavioral changes.
2. *Uncontrolled variables.* The demand characteristics of experimental programs, along with therapist and patient variables confound treatment results. Studies attempting to untangle the confounding are needed.
3. *Inability to generalize.* Research programs with patients other than college students or hospitalized psychotics are needed if we are going to make statements regarding the effectiveness of the techniques on larger populations.
4. *Attrition.* Many studies do not report data on patients who drop out of treatment. Such data are critical if we are going to talk about how many patients the techniques seem to help. Also techniques for reducing attrition are needed.
5. *Lack of Standards.* At the very least, individual weight data, including pretreatment, posttreatment and followup weights should be reported along with type of treatment used, and number and length of treatment sessions.

We have found great variability in our patients' responses to a behavioral program. Some techniques work with some patients, others do not. Overall, our best guess at this time is that behavioral techniques, when presented with a nutritionally sound, prudent eating plan, seem to be effective with about half of our patients. As the techniques continue to be refined and new ones added, perhaps the percentage will increase.

Stunkard (1976) has said it best:

> The problems of obesity are still far from solved. Even the application of our best technology leaves huge numbers of obese people unhappy and in ill health. But for the first time in many years research already underway gives promise of aid and comfort in the foreseeable future. And this is just the beginning. (p. 232).

APPENDIX 7–1

Behavioral Treatment Programs for Obesity

HELP Your Heart Eating Plan

Listed below are some organizations about which people often have strong feelings. Rate these organizations on the scales provided by placing an "X" in the space which best indicates your feelings. If you are neutral about the organization, put an "X" in the center of the scale. You will understand later the purpose of this assignment.

Democratic Party:
Strongly like : : : : : : : Strongly dislike

Republican Party:
Strongly like : : : : : : : Strongly dislike

American Independent Party (George Wallace)
Strongly like : : : : : : : Strongly dislike

John Birch Society
Strongly like : : : : : : : Strongly dislike

National Association for the Advancement of Colored People (NAACP)
Strongly like : : : : : : : Strongly dislike

American Civil Liberties Union
Strongly like : : : : : : : Strongly dislike

Mailing Addresses

Democratic National Committee
2600 Virginia Avenue N.W.
Washington, D.C. 20037

Republican National Committee
310 1st Street S.E.
Washington, D.C. 2003

American Party
P.O. Box 1976
Richmond, Virginia 23216

John Birch Society
395 Concord Avenue
Belmont, Massachusetts 02178

National Association for the Advancement of Colored People (NAACP)
1790 Broadway
New York, New York 10019

American Civil Liberties Union
22 East 40th Street
New York, New York 10016

HELP Your Heart Eating Plan
Diet Modification Clinic
Weight Reduction Contract

Note to Party of the Second Part:

This assignment may appear humorous to you, but for someone with a weight problem, it is a very serious business. If this assignment is carried out properly, the difficult business of losing weight will be made a little easier. You, as "party of the second part," might be thinking that you will probably "give the money back anyway" even if the person does not earn the sum back. If so, please realize that your integrity in keeping your part of the contract will determine to a very great degree whether or not this procedure will work *in the future* for the person trying to lose weight. If the person sees his hard earned money going to a cause with which he is unsympathetic, this lesson will not be easily forgotten. And, a similar assignment in the future will have an even greater probability of helping the person succeed in losing weight. If you do not keep your part of the contract and "give the money back anyway," the probability of this procedure working in the future is very low. By being very strict about following your part of the contract, you will be doing this person a favor by providing a viable weight reduction technique for the future, even if it does not work out completely satisfactorily this time. Please do your part and follow the contract exactly as written.

____
Dietitian

HELP Your Heart Eating Plan
Diet Modification Clinic
Weight Reduction Clinic

KNOW ALL MEN BY THESE PRESENTS:

This contract executed and entered into in duplicate this ______ day of ____________, 197___, by and between __________________ ____________________, hereinafter called party of the first part, and ______________________________, hereinafter called party of the second part, witnesseth:

For and in consideration for the mutual promises herein contained, the parties hereto agree herewith as follows:

That the party of the first part has paid to the party of the second part, the sum of $ _________, in cash, the receipt of which is hereby acknowledged, which said sum shall be held by the party of the second part until disbursed pursuant to the following terms and conditions:

1. The party of the first part agrees to work hard to lose weight by faithfully following the principles of the HELP Your Eating Plan Diet Modification Clinic and will seek to lose one to two pounds per week. For each pound of body weight that said party has lost from the date of this agreement until the ______ day of ______ , 197 ___ , said party will be paid $ _________ per pound, provided the total amount so paid hereunder shall not exceed the total amount paid to the party of the second part.
2. All sums remaining on deposit with the party of the second part on the _____ day of ___________ , 197 ___ , shall be forthwith paid to ____ ____ .
3. If the party of the first part receives the full amount of money herewith paid to the party of the second part pursuant to this agreement, then the party of the first part will also receive lavish praise from the party of second part and ______________ ____ .

In witness thereof both parties and the dietitian from the Diet Modification Clinic have hereunto set their hands and seals the day and year above written.

______________________	______________________
Party of the first part	Party of the second part
______________________	______________________
Witness	Witness

HELP Your Heart Eating Plan
Pleasure · Questionnaire

This questionnaire will help you identify various things that give you pleasure. Please check the column that best describes the amount of pleasure each item listed gives you. Omit the items that do not apply to you. At the end of the questionnaire, add any other items that give you pleasure.

	None	A Little	Much	Very Much
1. Watching Television				
2. Listening to Radio				
3. Listening to Records or Tapes				
4. Playing Cards				
5. Doing Crossword Puzzles				
6. Reading Books or Magazines				
7. Dancing				
8. Sleeping Late				
9. Shopping				
10. Buying New Clothes				
11. Buying Kitchen Appliances				
12. Buying Records				
13. Telephoning a Friend Long Distance				
14. Visiting Friends				
15. Taking a Relaxing Bath or Shower				
16. Attending Plays or Concerts				
17. Attending Movies				
18. Attending Sporting Events (football, baseball, basketball, hockey, etc.)				
19. Golfing				
20. Bowling				
21. Bicycling				
22. Playing Tennis				
23. Participating in Team Sports (football, baseball, basketball, etc.)				
24. Camping				
25. Traveling				
26. Gardening				
27. Peace and Quiet				

28. Other items that give you pleasure:

____

REFERENCES

Abrahms, J.L., and Allen, G.J. Comparative effectiveness of situational programming, financial payoffs, and group pressure in weight reduction. *Behavior Therapy*, 1974, *5*, 391–400.

Abramson, E.E. A review of behavioral approaches to weight control. *Behavior Research and Therapy*, 1973, *11*, 547–556.

Aragona, J., Cassady, J., and Drabman, R.S. Treating overweight children through parental training and contingency contracting. *Journal of Applied Behavior Analysis*, 1975, *8*, 269–278.

Ashem, B., Poser, E., and Trudell, P. The use of covert sensitization in the treatment of overeating. In R.D. Rubin, H. Fensterheim, J.D. Henderson, and L.P. Ullmann (Eds.), *Advances in behavior therapy*. New York: Academic Press, 1972, pp. 97–103.

Ayllon, T. Intensive treatment of psychotic behaviour by stimulus satiation and food reinforcement. *Behaviour Research and Therapy*, 1963, *1*, 53–61.

Balch, P., and Ross, A.W. A behaviorally oriented didactic-group treatment of obesity: An exploratory study. *Journal of Behavior Therapy and Experimental Psychiatry*, 1974, *5*, 239–243.

Bellack, A.S., Rozensky, R., and Schwartz, J. A comparison of two forms of self-monitoring in a behavioral weight reduction program. *Behavior Therapy*, 1974, *5*, 523–530.

Bellack, A.S., Schwartz, J., and Rozensky, R.H. The contribution of external control to self-control in a weight reduction program. *Journal of Behavior Therapy and Experimental Psychiatry*, 1974, *5*, 245–249.

Bernard, J.L. Rapid treatment of gross obesity by operant techniques. *Psychological Reports*, 1968, *23*, 663–666.

Bornstein, P.H., and Sipprelle, C.N. Group treatment of obesity by induced anxiety. *Behaviour Research and Therapy*, 1973a, *11*, 339–341.

Bornstein, P.H., and Sipprelle, C.N. Induced anxiety in the treatment of obesity: A preliminary case report. *Behavior Therapy*, 1973b, *4*, 141–143.

Cautela, J.R. Treatment of compulsive behavior by covert sensitization. *The Psychological Record*, 1966, *16*, 33–41.

Cautela, J.R. Covert sensitization. *Psychological Reports*, 1967, *20*, 459–468.

Cautela, J.R. The treatment of over-eating by covert conditioning. *Psychotherapy: Theory, Research and Practice*, 1972, *9*, 211–216.

Chlouverakis, C. Dietary and medical treatments of obesity: An evaluative review. *Addictive Behaviors*, 1975, *1*, 3–21.

Christensen, E.R., Jeffrey, D.B., and Pappas, J.P. *A therapist manual for a behavior modification weight reduction program.* Research and development report No. 37, Counseling and Psychological Services, University of Utah, 1973.

Diament, C., and Wilson, G.T. An experimental investigation of the effects of covert sensitization in an analogue eating situation. *Behavior Therapy*, 1975, *6*, 499–509.

Dinoff, M., Rickard, H.C., and Colwick, J. Weight reduction through successive contracts. *American Journal of Orthopsychiatry*, 1972, *42*, 110–113.

Ferguson, J.M. *Learning to eat: Student manual.* Palo Alto, California: Bull Publishing Company, 1975.

Fernan, W. The role of experimenter contact in behavioral bibliotherapy of obesity. Unpublished Master's thesis, Pennsylvania State University, 1973.

Ferster, C.B., Nurnberger, J.I., and Levitt, E.E. The control of eating. *Journal of Mathetics*, 1962, *1*, 87–109.

Foreyt, J.P. (Ed.) *Behavioral treatments of obesity*. New York: Pergamon Press, 1976 (in press).

Foreyt, J.P., and Hagen, R.L. Covert sensitization: Conditioning or suggestion? *Journal of Abnormal Psychology*, 1973, *82*, 17–23.

Foreyt, J.P., and Kennedy, W.A. Treatment of overweight by aversion therapy. *Behavior Research and Therapy*, 1971, *9*, 29–34.

Foreyt, J.P., and Parks, J.T. Behavioral controls for achieving weight loss in the severely retarded. *Journal of Behavior Therapy and Experimental Psychiatry*, 1975, *6*, 27–29.

Foxx, R.M. Social reinforcement of weight reduction: A case report on an obese retarded adolescent. *Mental Retardation*, 1972, *10*, 21–23.

Frohwirth, R.A., and Foreyt, J.P. Aversive conditioning treatment of overweight. Unpublished manuscript, Florida State University, 1976.

Hagen, R.L. Group therapy versus bibliotherapy in weight reduction. *Behavior Therapy*, 1974, *5*, 222–234.

Hagen, R.L., Wollersheim, J., and Paul, G. Weight reduction manual. Unpublished manuscript, University of Illinois, 1969.

Hall, S.M. Self-control and therapist control in the behavioral treatment of overweight women. *Behaviour Research and Therapy*, 1972, *10*, 59–68.

Hall, S.M. Behavioral treatment of obesity: A two-year follow-up. *Behaviour Research and Therapy*, 1973, *11*, 647–648.

Hall, S.M., and Hall, R.G. Outcome and methodological considerations in behavioral treatment of obesity. *Behavior Therapy*, 1974, *5*, 352–364.

Hall, S.M., Hall, R.G. Hanson, R.W., and Borden, B.L. Permanence of two self-managed treatments of overweight in university and community populations. *Journal of Consulting and Clinical Psychology*, 1974, *42*, 781–786.

Harmatz, M.G., and Lapuc, P. Behavior modification of overeating in a psychiatric population. *Journal of Consulting and Clinical Psychology*, 1968, *32*, 583–587.

Harris, M.B. Self-directed program for weight control: A pilot study. *Journal of Abnormal Psychology*, 1969, *74*, 263–270.

Harris, M.B., and Bruner, C.G. A comparison of a self-control and a contract procedure for weight control. *Behaviour Research and Therapy*, 1971, *9*, 347–354.

Harris, M.B., and Hallbauer, E.S. Self-directed weight control through eating and exercise. *Behaviour Research and Therapy*, 1973, *11*, 523–529.

Homme, L.E. Perspectives in psychology: XXIV Control of coverants, the operants of the mind. *The Psychological Record*, 1965, *15*, 501–511.

Horan, J.J., Baker, S.B., Hoffman, A.M., and Shute, R.E. Weight loss through variations of the coverant control paradigm. *Journal of Consulting and Clinical Psychology*, 1975, *43*, 68–72.

Horan, J.J., and Johnson, R.G. Coverant conditioning through a self-management application of the Premack principle: Its effect on weight reduction. *Journal of Behavior Therapy and Experimental Psychiatry*, 1971, *2*, 243–249.

Janda, L.H., and Rimm, D.C. Covert sensitization in the treatment of obesity. *Journal of Abnormal Psychology*, 1972, *80*, 37–42.

Jeffrey, D.B. A comparison of the effects of external control and self-control on the modification and maintenance of weight. *Journal of Abnormal Psychology*, 1974, *83*, 404–410.

Jeffrey, D.B. Behavioral management of obesity. In W.E. Craighead, A.E. Kazdin, and M.J. Mahoney (Eds.), *Behavior modification: Principles, issues, and applications.* Boston: Houghton Mifflin Company, 1976.

Jeffrey, D.B., Christensen, E.R., and Pappas, J.P. Developing a behavioral program and therapist manual for the treatment of obesity. *Journal of the American College Health Association*, 1973, *21*, 455–459.

Kennedy, W.A., and Foreyt, J.P. Control of eating behavior in an obese patient by avoidance conditioning. *Psychological Reports*, 1968, *22*, 571–576.

Klein, B., Steele, R.L., Simon, W.E., and Primavera, L.H. Reinforcement and weight loss in schizophrenics. *Psychological Reports*, 1972, *30*, 581–582.

Levitz, L.S., and Stunkard, A.J. A therapeutic coalition for obesity: Behavior modification and patient self-help. *American Journal of Psychiatry*, 1974, *131*, 423–427.

Mahoney, M.J. Self-reward and self-monitoring techniques for weight control. *Behavior Therapy*, 1974, *5*, 48–57.

Mahoney, M.J., and Jeffrey, D.B. A manual of self-control procedures for the overweight. Abstracted in the JSAS *Catalog of Selected Documents in Psychology*, 1974, *4*, 129.

Mahoney, M.J., and Mahoney, K. *Permanent weight control: A total solution to the dieter's dilemma.* New York: Norton, 1976a.

Mahoney, M.J., and Mahoney, K. Treatment of obesity: A clinical exploration. In B.J. Williams, S. Martin, and J.P. Foreyt (Eds.), *Obesity: Behavioral approaches to dietary management.* New York: Brunner/Mazel, 1976b.

Mahoney, M.J., Moura, N.G.M., and Wade, T.C. Relative efficacy of self-reward, self-punishment, and self-monitoring techniques for weight loss. *Journal of Consulting and Clinical Psychology*, 1973, *40*, 404–407.

Maletzky, B.M. "Assisted" covert sensitization: A preliminary report. *Behavior Therapy*, 1973, *4*, 117–119.

Mann, R.A. The behavior-therapeutic use of contingency contracting to control an adult behavior problem: Weight control. *Journal of Applied Behavior Analysis*, 1972, *5*, 99–109.

Manno, B., and Marston, A.R. Weight reduction as a function of negative covert reinforcement (sensitization) versus positive covert reinforcement. *Behaviour Research and Therapy*, 1972, *10*, 201–207.

Martin, J.E., and Sachs, D.A. The effects of a self-control weight loss program on an obese woman. *Journal of Behavior Therapy and Experimental Psychiatry*, 1973, *4*, 155–159.

McReynolds, W.T., Lutz, R.N., Paulsen, B.K., and Kohrs, M.B. Weight loss from two behavior modification procedures with nutritionists as therapists. *Behavior Therapy*, 1976, 7, in press.

Meyer, V., and Crisp, A.H. Aversion therapy in two cases of obesity. *Behaviour Research and Therapy*, 1964, *2*, 143–147.

Moore, C.H., and Crum, B.C. Weight reduction in a chronic schizophrenic by means of operant conditioning procedures: A case study. *Behaviour Research and Therapy*, 1969, *7*, 129–131.

Morganstern, K.P. Cigarette smoke as a noxious stimulus in self-managed aversion therapy for compulsive eating: Technique and case illustration. *Behavior Therapy*, 1974, *5*, 255–260.

Murray, D.C., and Harrington, L.G. Covert aversive sensitization in the treatment of obesity. *Psychological Reports*, 1972, *30*, 560.

Musante, G.J. The dietary rehabilitation clinic: Evaluative report of a behavioral and dietary treatment of obesity. *Behavior Therapy*, 1976, *7*, 198–204.

O'Leary, K.D., and Wilson, G.T. *Behavior therapy: Application and outcome.* Englewood Cliffs, N.J.: Prentice-Hall, 1975.

Paulsen, B., McReynolds, W.T., Lutz, R.N., and Kohrs, M.B. Effective weight control through behavior modification and nutrition education: A treatment manual. Unpublished paper, Lincoln University, 1974.

Penick, S.B., Filion, R., Fox, S., and Stunkard, A.J. Behavior modification in the treatment of obesity. *Psychosomatic Medicine*, 1971, *33*, 49–55.

Romanczyk, R.G. Self-monitoring in the treatment of obesity: Parameters of reactivity. *Behavior Therapy*, 1974, *5*, 531–540.

Romanczyk, R.G., Tracey, D.A., Wilson, G.T., and Thorpe, G.L. Behavioral techniques in the treatment of obesity: A comparative analysis. *Behaviour Research and Therapy*, 1973, *11*, 629–640.

Sachs, L.B., and Ingram, G.L. Covert sensitization as a treatment for weight control. *Psychological Reports*, 1972, *30*, 971–974.

Schachter, S. Some extraordinary facts about obese humans and rats. *American Psychologist*, 1971, *26*, 129–144.

Sipprelle, C.N. Induced anxiety. *Psychotherapy: Theory, Research, and Practice*, 1967, *4*, 36–40.

Stollak, G.E. Weight loss obtained under different experimental procedures. *Psychotherapy: Theory, Research and Practice*, 1967, *4*, 61–64.

Stuart, R.B. Behavioral control of overeating. *Behaviour Research and Therapy*, 1967, *5*, 357–365.

Stuart, R.B. A three-dimensional program for the treatment of obesity. *Behaviour Research and Therapy*, 1971, *9*, 177–186.

Stuart, R.B. Behavioral control of overeating: A status report. Paper presented at the Fogarty International Center Conference on Obesity, Bethesda, Maryland, 1973.

Stuart, R.B., and Davis, B. *Slim chance in a fat world: Behavioral control of obesity.* Champaign, Illinois: Research Press, Inc., 1972.

Stunkard, A.J. From explanation to action in psychosomatic medicine: The care of obesity. *Psychosomatic Medicine*, 1975, *37*, 195–236.

Stunkard, A.J. *The pain of obesity.* Palo Alto, California: Bull Publishing Co., 1976.

Stunkard, A.J., and Mahoney, M.J. Behavioral treatment of the eating disorders. In H. Leitenberg (Ed.), *Handbook of behavior modification.* Englewood Cliffs, N.J.: Prentice-Hall, 1976.

Stunkard, A.J., and McLaren-Hume, M. The results of treatment for obesity. *A.M.A. Archives of Internal Medicine*, 1959, *103*, 79–85.

Thorpe, J.G., Schmidt, E., Brown, P.T., and Castell, D. Aversion-relief therapy: A new method for general application. *Behaviour Research and Therapy*, 1964, *2*, 71–82.

Tyler, V.O., and Straughan, J.H. Coverant control and breath holding as techniques for the treatment of obesity. *The Psychological Record*, 1970, *20*, 473–478.

Upper, D., and Newton, J.G. A weight-reduction program for schizophrenic patients on a token economy unit: Two case studies. *Journal of Behavior Therapy and Experimental Psychiatry*, 1971, *2*, 113–115.

Wijesinghe, B. Massed electrical aversion treatment of compulsive eating. *Journal of Behavior Therapy and Experimental Psychiatry*, 1973, *4*, 133–135.

Williams, B.J., Martin, S., and Foreyt, J.P. (Eds.), *Obesity: Behavioral approaches to dietary management.* New York: Brunner/Mazel, 1976.

Wollersheim, J.P. Effectiveness of group therapy based upon learning principles in the treatment of overweight women. *Journal of Abnormal Psychology*, 1970, *76*, 462–474.

Wolpe, J. Reciprocal inhibition as the main basis of psychotherapeutic effects. *A.M.A. Archives of Neurology and Psychiatry*, 1954, *72*, 205–226.

Yates, A.J. *Theory and practice in behavior therapy.* New York: John Wiley, 1975.

Chapter 8

Cigarette Smoking

*Patrick A. Boudewyns**

Almost 11 times as many male cigarette smokers die of lung cancer when compared to nonsmokers of the same age group. Likewise, cigarette smokers are six times as likely to die from emphysema than are nonsmokers. Demographic studies of other killing diseases also reveal significant differences in death rates for smokers versus nonsmokers (Advisory Committee to the Surgeon General, 1964, p. 29). In addition, there is an abundance of evidence that at least some of the hydrocarbons that are present in tobacco smoke become carcinogenic in man when inhaled. Thus, to conclude that these demographic data are only correlational, and therefore not an indication of a cause-effect relationship between smoking and disease, is improbable (Advisory Committee to the Surgeon General, 1964, p. 58–60). Furthermore, thanks to a Madison Avenue campaign sponsored primarily by the National Cancer Society and the National Heart Association, the public has been informed of the dangers of smoking through every available media. Given the above situation it seems incredible that only a small minority of cigarette smokers ever attempt to quit, and of those that do, only about 20 percent succeed (Bernstein, 1969). Added to this is the alarming fact that the number of initiates to the smoking habit is increasing among teenagers and young adults in recent years.

Attempts by behaviorists and others to develop programs to help people modify smoking behavior have, until recently, also met with little success since initial reductions in smoking rates realized as a

*Duke University Medical Center and Veterans Administration Hospital Durham, N.C.

result of such programs are rarely maintained at follow-up (McFall and Hammen, 1971).

The purpose of this chapter is twofold: (1) to review some of the latest research on why people smoke, in an attempt to understand why this habit is apparently so resistant to modification and (2) to describe, in detail, those treatment programs that have had at least some success in modifying smoking behavior.

SMOKING BEHAVIOR

Why People Smoke

Mausner (1973) hypothesized that the construct of "subjective expected utility" might be useful in predicting smoking behavior. Applied to the smoking response, this construct suggests that the sum of the various consequences of smoking (physical stimulation, social approval or disapproval, biological reactions, etc.) can add up to yield an expectation, or more generally, an experience that may serve as "information" to the smoker that he should (or should not) modify his smoking behavior. Of course, this experience is subject to perceptual distortion. The significance one assigns any consequence of smoking may change within the same individual across time—i.e., the so-called "risky-shift" phenomenon. The situation may even be more complex than this. Smoking occurs in a great variety of settings throughout the daily lives of smokers, resulting in a number of different "patterns" of smoking (Mausner, p. 117–118) within the same individual. Thus, simply maximizing the negative social sanction of smoking in public, for example, may reduce public smoking, but at the same time may also serve to increase (or at least not influence) patterns of solitary smoking.[1]

Reinforcements for smoking are also numerous and varied both within and across each pattern. For example, smoking a cigarette often serves as a tension reducer in interpersonal situations. A businessman who has experienced many anxiety producing phone calls in the past, may become "conditioned" to reach for a cigarette at the sound of a ringing phone. The physical response to the smoke (the slight irritation to the throat and larynx) as well as the learned or secondarily reinforcing qualities of lighting up, inhibits, or more specifically, *reciprocally* inhibits (Wolpe, 1958) his tension. Tension (anxiety) reduction is known to be a very powerful form of negative reinforcement which will, therefore, increase the probability of any

1. There is some evidence that antismoking campaigns may have already produced this effect since both smoking prohibitions in public places and cigarette sales have increased over the past 10 years.

response that preceeds it. Further, because of the mildly addictive property of nicotine, smoking a cigarette may reduce experienced negative affect brought on simply as a function of deprivation (i.e., time since last cigarette).

If you ask smokers why they smoke you will find, among other reasons, that it's because a cigarette: "gets you going in the morning"; "makes your coffee taste better"; "increases a feeling of communication and togetherness with others who light up with you"; "tastes great" after meals; is especially "stimulating" with a drink; and is an important part of the "after glo" of sexual intercourse. Mausner hypothesized that cigarette smoking may even be an integral part of some people's style of communication, especially during adolescence. For many, smoking a cigarette is the last act before bed and the first groping response in the morning.

From a learning theory perspective then, cigarette smoking is a response that occurs often and in varying stimulus situations. Furthermore, reinforcement for smoking, both positive and negative, is both immediate (especially compared to the long delay between smoking and the "punishment" of contracting disease) and generalized (i.e., followed by a variety of reinforcers over any one time period). Thus, it would appear that the three necessary and sufficient conditions needed to build and maintain any strong and durable habit, i.e., many trials, generalized reinforcement and immediate reinforcement, are involved in cigarette smoking.

Given the above analysis, perhaps a more significant question to the learning theorist would be: why does anyone ever quit?

Why People Quit

People do quit—for good sometimes, and usually without the help of anyone or anything. Unfortunately, if you ask those who have quit why they did so, you get almost as many answers as you have respondents. What motivates one individual to quit may not influence another in the least. As one who has worked in a hospital for almost all of his professional life, I can remember men with emphysema so severe that they required emergency inhalation therapy, and yet, would complain when their physician would not allow them to smoke during their recovery phase. Contrast this with my father's response to a morning "smoker's hack" that he had developed after 25 years of smoking two packages per day. Approximately 26 years ago on one particularly bad morning, he angrily threw away what was left of a package of cigarettes and never smoked again. That was the first, last, and only time he ever quit.

A study by Mausner (1973) may provide some insight into this problem. Mausner's data support the notion that those who *do* quit make the decision to stop, not because they fear the consequences of continuing, but because they have an "increased expectation of benefits from stopping." For example, compared to those who continued smoking, subjects who quit had a greater expectation that their health would improve, or that they would enjoy food more, or would feel better in the morning. Interestingly, those subjects who made an unsuccessful attempt to quit (i.e. relapsed) also expected to have problems with tension after quitting. Perhaps these data should be considered by the Madison Avenue group whose campaigns to date have largely emphasized the negative aspects of continuing to smoke.

Given the above results, smoking modification programs might increase success rates by emphasizing the immediate benefits of quitting (rather than the possible long-term punishment for continuing) and by offering tension reduction programs such as progressive muscle relaxation or biofeedback procedures described elsewhere in this book. It is interesting to note that to date, few programs have done this.

SMOKING MODIFICATION PROGRAMS

Early Failures

Literature reports of treatment programs aimed at smoking reduction are numerous and varied in approach. To name only a few, these have included electrical aversion therapy (see below), stimulus satiation and gradual reduction with counter-conditioning (Marston and McFall, 1971), hypnotic suggestion (Von Dedenroth, 1964), covert conditioning, (having subjects associate imagined negative concepts or scenes such as a self prompt to think about the fact that smoking causes cancer each time a craving for a cigarette enters awareness) (Homme, 1965), loss of a "cash deposit" contingent upon relapse (Tighe and Elliot, 1967) and Systematic Desensitization (Koenig and Masters, 1965). In addition, Bernstein (1969) in a critical review of the area, cited a number of earlier treatment programs that included everything from performing deep breathing exercise to avoiding profane language. Unfortunately, the one thing these treatment programs had in common was that, although initial results may have been favorable, (if indeed they offered *any* data to support the treatment claims) relapse rates were so high that at follow-up, treated groups were not significantly different from controls or even from their own pretreatment baseline rates in some instances. In fact, McFall and Hammen (1971) reviewed eight well-controlled treatment outcome studies and found that at follow-up the mean number of abstainers for these studies was only 13 percent (range = 9–17 percent) of the subjects that began treatment.

Recent Successes

Recent outcome studies comparing the effectiveness of various smoking modification programs have been more encouraging. For example, Schmahl, Lichtenstein, and Harris (1972) exposed 28 habitual smokers to either warm smoky air or cool mentholated air (the air was blown into a small, nonventilated therapy room) while at the same time requiring the subject to smoke at an accelerated rate (one inhalation every six seconds). During each therapy session, subjects were required to smoke at this rapid rate until they could not tolerate another inhalation. At that point the subject was instructed to say: "I don't want to smoke anymore," and crush out his cigarette. Participants in the study were encouraged to go through this process as many times as they possibly could during each session. Treatment was considered complete upon subject's report of abstinence or after 14 sessions "without success." Also, at the third session subjects were told that they would be required to make a $5.00 deposit if they wished to continue treatment. The deposit was to be refunded if they were "responsible participants" in the study, although it was emphasized that refund was not contingent upon success.[2] Finally, verbal sanctions were used by the experimenter in that they . . . "reinforced reports of abstinence with praise, self-disclosure and encouragement and responded negatively to non-constructive behavior." After initial sessions were completed, a six month follow-up phase began. During this phase, half of the subjects in each experimental group were contacted every two weeks while the other half were contacted only every four weeks. At the end of treatment all subjects in both groups were abstinent, and at six months following treatment 64 percent were still not smoking. In direct opposition to the predictions, however, the group that was contacted every four weeks had a significantly lower follow-up smoking rate as compared to their pretreatment baseline, than the two week group. It would be interesting if this result could be replicated. Nevertheless, Schmahl et al.'s overall success rate far exceeds the mean follow-up success rate of 13 percent reported by McFall and Hammen.

These results are even more convincing in light of the fact that

2. This deposit "ploy" has been used in many behavioral programs other than smoking (e.g., overeating behavior, drinking problems, etc.) and appears to be an effective method of insuring subject cooperation. The deposit need not be excessive as witnessed by the fact that for this study no one dropped out at the third session and no deposits were forfeited although two subjects did discontinue for reasons apparently beyond their control.

they were essentially replicated in a later study. That study (Lichtenstein et al., 1973) compared three treatment procedures: warm smoky air plus rapid smoking; warm smoky air only; and rapid smoking only. The purpose of the design was to determine the relative contribution of the two aversive procedures. Additionally, a fourth "attention placebo" procedure was used as a control. The rationales and experimental procedures for the treatment groups were virtually the same as for the previous study. Subjects in the placebo group were told that the "treatment" would help them to extinguish their desire to smoke, and were encouraged not to smoke between sessions. At each session subjects in this group were required to smoke "two cigarettes for four minutes each at their normal rate" to control for the smoking rates of the subjects in the other groups. During this "normal" smoking, subjects were asked to focus on the negative aspects of smoking, and they were given the rationale that this amount of smoking would not interfere with treatment and would help them "avoid withdrawal reactions." All placebo subjects were also given Bantron pills to "help them remain abstinent between sessions."

At the end of treatment all but one subject was abstinent.[3] More importantly, however, at six months following treatment six subjects in each of the three treatment groups were still abstinent, while only three subjects in the placebo group were still not smoking at that time. Also, compared to pretreatment levels, the smoking rate (mean number of cigarettes smoked per day) for the placebo group was significantly higher than that of any of the three treatment groups. There were no significant differences between the treatment groups at either the end of treatment or at follow-up but the combined abstinence rate for these groups of 60 percent at follow-up essentially replicated the 64 percent reported in the earlier study.

Chapman, Smith, and Layden (1972) have also reported a successful treatment program. During each of five treatment sessions, all 23 subjects in this study were given painful electric shock to the forearm paired with inhaling cigarette smoke, and while observing smoking-related advertising material. Further, all subjects were required to deposit $100.00 before beginning treatment. All but $10.00 of this deposit was to be refunded if all treatment sessions were attended. Also, all subjects were given a strong expectation that the treatment program would be successful if they attended all sessions and cooperated fully. Finally, subjects were given "self management training" (Skinner, 1953, p. 235). After treatment was completed, 11 of the subjects in this study were given two weeks of posttreatment moni-

3. An "experimenter error" resulted in one subject being terminated when he was still reporting smoking one cigarette per day.

toring. Eleven others were given 11 weeks of monitoring. (One subject was not involved in all treatment manipulation and her data were not presented.) At the end of treatment, all but one subject in each follow-up group was abstinent, and a 12 month follow-up revealed that the group that was monitored longer was more successful in reducing smoking (i.e., 27 percent of the subjects in the two week group versus 55 percent in the 11 week group were abstinent at follow-up).

One other earlier study reported moderate success at follow-up. Steffy, Michenbaum, and Best (1970) used electric shock in combination with various other treatment procedures and found that at least for one group of subjects who had received shock along with "covert verbalization" there was a 55 percent abstinence rate reported at six months follow-up. However, the abstinence rate for this same group at two months follow-up was only 33 percent. Thus, it would be plausible to conclude that the abstinence of at least some subjects in this group was due to factors other than those involved in the treatment manipulation.

The fact that three of the above studies reported success rates for treated groups to be superior to previous studies regardless of the treatment process used, could lead to the conclusion that nonspecific or other specified, but uncommon procedures, account for these more encouraging results. Obviously, it does not take a design expert to realize that posttreatment monitoring and strong demands to stay with the program, elements common to both the Lichtenstein studies and the Chapman et al. study, appear to be *necessary* conditions of a successful program. Nevertheless, in the Lichtenstein, et al. study, the result that the placebo group was totally abstinent at the termination of treatment, but had a significantly higher relapse rate than the active treatment groups at follow-up, provides support for the notion that while these in-common procedures may be necessary conditions of a successful program, they are not sufficient to *maintain* gains.

TREATMENT RECOMMENDATIONS

The Rapid Smoking Technique

Although all of the procedures discussed above were successful, the rapid smoking technique is recommended here because it requires no expensive instrumentation or specially designed environment and is therefore more easily utilized by the private practitioner. Before using the rapid smoking technique, however, the reader should be aware of the effects this procedure may have on the cardiovascular system. It is reasonable to assume that rapid smoking will lead to the absorption of increased amounts of nicotine into the system which could induce cardiac arrythmias. Therefore, for individuals with known cardiac problems at least, the rapid smoking technique is contraindicated (Hauser, 1974; Lichtenstein, 1974). If it is felt that a client for medical reasons, should not be treated with the rapid smoking procedure the therapist may wish to consider using the "placebo" treatment described in Lichtenstein, et al. (1973). Recall that this procedure did meet with limited success.

Presented below is a procedural guide for those professionals who wish to use the rapid smoking technique with clients. It is *not* recommended that the procedure be self-prescribed and administered. In using this guide it should be remembered that close post-therapy monitoring and full subject cooperation are necessary conditions for a successful treatment. Further, in accordance with the data presented by Mausner (1973) (see above) I would also recommend that clients be offered some form of tension reduction training as an adjunct to the rapid smoking if they anticipate problems with tension, and also that clients should be encouraged to continually remind themselves of the benefits of stopping smoking throughout the critical three months following treatment.

RAPID SMOKING: A PROCEDURES GUIDE[4]

Apparatus

Cigarettes, ashtrays, matches, wristwatch, paper and pencil are sufficient. A stopwatch, metronome, or other timing device may be useful. A plastic mustard or ketchup bottle can be used to light cigarettes for the client but it is more convenient if they light up themselves using the candle. A basin or plastic lined wastebasket should be available in case the client becomes ill. A glass of water may be kept on hand.

Setting

Any room will do but a relatively small one with good potential ventilation is preferred. A fan is also helpful. A bathroom should be nearby and the client instructed as to its location. During the rapid smoking, per se the client should be turned toward a wall and the therapist should be out of sight so as to minimize distractions.

Instructions to the Client

The client will already know something about this from the screening and informed consent procedures. However, you should summarize the rationale and procedure for him briefly. For example:

4. This procedures guide was written by Dr. Edward Lichtenstein as a workshop handout. It is reprinted here courtesy of Dr. Lichtenstein.

We are now ready to begin the rapid smoking. This is an aversion procedure designed to change the valence of your smoking. Smoking is now enjoyable and rewarding for you. By making the act of smoking very unpleasant, cigarettes and other associated cues will no longer be perceived as enjoyable and may even become unpleasant. Therefore, it will be much easier for you to control your smoking.

We want you to smoke continually and rapidly—taking a normal drag about every six seconds—until you can't bear to continue to smoke any longer. When you finish one cigarette, leave it in the ashtray and quickly light another off the candle. While you are smoking you should concentrate just on your smoking and on the reactions of your body, that is your mouth, throat and lungs, to your smoking. This is why I will have you face the wall and will sit off to the side so you are not distracted.

This will be quite unpleasant and different people experience it in different ways. It has to be unpleasant in order to work so we do want you to push yourself. Your task in effect is to smoke until you can't bear to take another drag. However, we do not want you to get sick. At the beginning it is best to err in stopping too soon rather than too late until you learn about how your body reacts to this procedure.

When you can't bear to smoke any more say clearly, "I'm stopping" or "I can't continue" and put out your cigarette. If you have any questions, ask them now, because once the rapid smoking starts there should be no talking between us so you can concentrate on your smoking. Occasionally I will say something to remind you to concentrate on your smoking.

The Rapid Smoking Procedure

When ready to begin, let him/her light their own cigarette off the candle while you (1) start the stopwatch and (2) activate the metronome or begin pacing the subject. (The metronome should be set to tick every second.) At every six ticks or seconds, say "Smoke" in a firm voice. It is permissible to err a little on the high side but you should not have them smoke any more rapidly than six seconds. About once a trial say quietly, "concentrate on how your body is reacting to your smoking" or similar phrase, but do not repeat this too often. Use your therapy notes to keep track of how many cigarettes the subject smokes on a given trial and how long a given trial is. Also try to take notes about the subject's reactions. For example, if the subject coughs repeatedly, you should note this. If the subject should show obvious discomfort such as sweating or trembling, this should also be noted. Such manifestations of distress may also serve as signals to stop the procedure since it is not necessary and is unwise to make it excessively aversive.

When the client cannot go on any longer and signals his stopping, this constitutes the end of a trial. Make a note of the time and number of cigarettes smoked. You may wish to air out the room. During the rest period your tasks are threefold, (1) to obtain a rating of the subject's perception of unpleasantness (the particular scale or format for doing this will depend on the particular context), (2) to offer support and encouragement for the discomfort the smoker has undergone, (3) to question the smoker concerning his reactions to the experience so that he has an opportunity to cognitively rehash the unpleasant experience. This latter can be accomplished by such general questions as "How do you feel?" or "What about that was most unpleasant?" or "How did it effect you most?" One can also inquire more specifically about how the client's mouth, throat, lungs, eyes are feeling. Feelings of dizziness and nausea are fairly common.

There is no set time for the rest period, but 4–8 minutes is typical. A client may wish to have a sip of water.

You should then say to the client something like the following. "Could you now smoke another cigarette? I know you don't want one, but if you could possibly smoke one, you should have another trial."

In general, clients should be encouraged to have at least two trials unless their reaction or distress level seems clearly to indicate to the contrary. The procedures for the second trial are pretty much the same as for the previous one. After the second trial is over, the procedures again are the same (to collect unpleasant ratings, to offer support, and to query the smoker about his reactions).

Depending on the research or clinical context, two trials may be standardized and that may then constitute the end of the rapid smoking part of the session. If the number of trials is open-ended, then you would discuss again with the client whether he could stand to smoke another cigarette. However, you would not be so leading this time and should be more willing to accept the client's wish not to continue. I recommend a maximum of three trials or a total of 15 minutes of rapid smoking, whichever occurs first. In our work, clients tend to average 2.5 trials per session and trials average about three minutes each. The first trial is typically the longest and subsequent trials get shorter.

The end of the rapid smoking usually signals the end of the session as other matters should have been discussed with the client before the rapid smoking. The effects of rapid smoking in the very short run are such that you should not expect the person to be in a very chatty mood afterwards. As soon as he seems comfortable you should indicate that the session is over. Be especially sure to remind the person to not smoke between sessions.

Scheduling

When beginning treatment, therapists should schedule rapid smoking sessions on three consecutive days and then space them out. The spacing can be adjusted to the client's particular needs or may be fixed. An example might be to have rapid smoking on days 1, 2, 3, 5, 8, 11, 15. The average number of sessions per client has been six to eight.

Therapists may use this procedure with two (and three) clients at a time by arranging their chairs so they are not distracted by one another. A group of 10–12 people can be faced toward the wall if a suitable room is available. Finally, the client can be given verbal or preferably written instructions to self-administer sessions at home especially after having gone through the procedure in the clinic.

REFERENCES

Advisory Committee to the Surgeon General, The. *Smoking and Health.* (Publication No. 1103) Washington, D.C.: United States Public Health Service, 1964.

Bernstein, Douglas A. Modification of smoking behavior: an evaluative review. *Psychological Bulletin*, 1969, *71*, 418–440.

Bernstein, Douglas A. The modification of smoking behavior: a search for effective variables. *Behavior Research and Therapy*, 1970, *8*, 133–146.

Bernstein, Douglas A. & McAlister A. The modification of smoking behavior: Progress and Problems. *Addictive Behavior*, 1976, *1*, 89–102.

Chapman, R.F., Smith, J.W. & Layden, L.A. Elimination of cigarette smoking by punishment and self-management training. *Behavior Research and Therapy*, 1971, *9*, 255–264.

Hauser, R. Rapid smoking as a technique of behavior modification: caution in selection of subjects. *Journal of Consulting and Clinical Psychology*, 1974, *42*, 625.

Homme, L.E. Control of coverants, the operants of the mind. *Psychological Record*, 1965, *15*, 501–511.

Hunt, W.A. & Matarazzo, J.D. Three years later: recent developments in the experimental modification of smoking behavior. *Journal of Abnormal Psychology*, 1973, *81*, 107–114.

Hunt, W.A. & Bespalec, D.A. An evaluation of current methods of modifying smoking behavior. *Journal of Clinical Psychology*, 1974, *30*, 431–438.

Koenig, K.P. & Masters, J. Experimental treatment of habitual smoking. *Behavior Research and Therapy*, 1965, *3*, 235–243.

Lichtenstein, E. Lichtenstein replies. *Journal of Consulting and Clinical Psychology*, 1974, *42*, 625–626.

Lichtenstein, E. & Danaher, B.G. Modification of smoking behavior: a critical analysis of theory, research and practice. In M. Hersen, R.M. Eisler, & P.M. Miller (Eds.), *Progress in behavior modification* (vol. 3), New York: Academic Press, in press.

Lichtenstein, E., Harris, D.E., Birchler, G.R., Wahl, J.M. & Schmahl, D.P. Comparison of rapid smoking, warm, smoky air, and attention placebo in the modification of smoking behavior. *Journal of Consulting and Clinical Psychology*, 1973, *40*, 92–98.

Lichtenstein, E. & Keutzer, C.S. Implications of psychological research for smoking control clinics. *Health Services Reports*, June-July 1973, *88*, 535–540.

Lublin, I. & Joslyn, L. Aversive conditioning of cigarette addiction. Paper presented at the meeting of the American Psychological Association, San Francisco, September 1968.

McFall, R.M. & Hammen, C.L. Motivation, structure, and self-monitoring: role of nonspecific factors in smoking reduction. *Journal of Consulting and Clinical Psychology*, 1971, *37*, 80–86.

Marston, A.R. & McFall, R.M. A comparison of behavior modification approaches to smoking reduction. *Journal of Consulting and Clinical Psychology*, 1971, *36*, 153–162.

Mausner, Bernard. An ecological view of cigarette smoking. *Journal of Abnormal Psychology*, 1973, *81*, 115–126.

Schmahl, D.P., LIchtenstein, E. & Harris, D.E. Successful treatment of habitual smokers with warm, smoky air and rapid smoking. *Journal of Consulting and Clinical Psychology*, 1972, *38*, 105–111.

Skinner, B.F. Science and human behavior. New York: Macmillan, 1953.

Steffy, R.A., Meichenbaum, D. & Best, J.A. Aversive and cognitive factors in the modification of smoking behavior. *Behavior Research and Therapy*, 1970, *8*, 115–125.

Tighe, T.J. & Elliot, R. Breaking the cigarette habit: effects of a technique involving threatened loss of money. Paper presented at the meeting of the American Psychological Association, Washington, D.C., September 1967.

Von Dedenroth, R.E.A. The use of hypnosis with "tobaccomaniacs." *American Journal of Clinical Hypnosis*, 1964, *6*, 326–331.

Wolpe, J. *Psychotherapy by reciprocal inhibition.* Stanford, Calif: Stanford University Press, 1958.

ANNOTATED BIBLIOGRAPHY

There are many articles, reviews and critical reviews on cigarette smoking modification techniques that might be of interest to the therapist. Reading the following five articles, however, would give the practitioner a good understanding for the present state of the art.

Bernstein, Douglas A. Modification of smoking behavior: an evaluative review. *Psychological Bulletin*, 1969, *71*, 418–440.

Bernstein, Douglas A. & McAlister, A. The modification of smoking behavior: progress and problems. *Addictive Behavior*, 1976, *1*, 89–102.

Hunt, W.A. & Bespalec, D.A. An evaluation of current methods of modifying smoking behavior. *Journal of Clinical Psychology*, 1974, *30*, 431–438.

Hunt, W.A. & Matarazzo, J.D. Three years later: recent developments in the experimental modification of smoking behavior. *Journal of Abnormal Psychology*, 1973, *81*, 107–114.

Lichtenstein, E. & Danaher, B.G. Modification of smoking behavior: a critical analysis of theory, research and practice. In M. Hersen, R.M. Eisler, & P.M. Miller (Eds.), *Progress in behavior modification* (vol. 3). New York: Academic Press, in press.

Outcome studies on the effectiveness of the rapid smoking technique include:

Lichtenstein, E., Harris, D.E., Birchler, G.R., Wahl, J.M. & Schmahl, D.P. Comparison of rapid smoking, warm, smoky air, and attention placebo in the modification of smoking behavior. *Journal of Consulting and Clinical Psychology*, 1973, *40*, 92–98.

Schmahl, D.P., Lichtenstein, E. & Harris, D.E. Successful treatment of habitual smokers with warm, smoky air and rapid smoking. *Journal of Consulting and Clinical Psychology*, 1972, *38*, 105–111.

Reference to medical precautions that should be taken before using this procedure may be found in:

Hauser, R. Rapid smoking as a technique of behavior modifications: caution in selection of subjects. *Journal of Consulting and Clinical Psychology*, 1974, *42*, 625.

Lichtenstein, E. Lichtenstein replies. *Journal of Consulting and Clinical Psychology*, 1974, *42*, 625–626.

Chapter 9

Essential Hypertension

*James E. Byassee**

One of the most common diseases affecting the cardiovascular system and a major health problem is hypertension or high blood pressure, a disorder which affects more than 23 million persons in the United States (National Center for Health Statistics, 1969). Hypertension is associated with reduced life expectancy due to an increase in the frequency of heart attack, stroke, heart and kidney failure, and it is considered by some to be a major causal agent for all deaths (Galton, 1973).

Essential hypertension is usually defined by ruling out antecedent organic pathologies, and is said to account for between 90 and 95 percent of all cases (Schwartz and Shapiro, 1973). Although the criterion for a diagnosis of hypertension is somewhat arbitrary, many writers appear to accept a lower limit of approximately 140 mm. Hg systolic, and 90 mm. Hg diastolic (Geiger and Scotch, 1963; Gressel, 1949; Kalis, 1957). Race, family, weight, age, diet, salt intake, kidney problems, and hormonal factors all may influence the recorded pressure. Further, the blood pressure regulatory system is exceedingly complex and affected by many different levels of physiological interactions, separate pressure control systems, and feedback loops, which have continued to obscure the complete understanding of the etiology and pathogenesis of the disease (Guyton, Cowley, and Coleman, 1972).

Although Platt (1959, 1963, and 1964) offered the notion that essential hypertension is a recognizable entity with a pronounced hereditary influence, most physicians today agree with Pickering's

*Halifax County Mental Health Center, Roanoke Rapids, North Carolina.

(Pickering, 1968) finding of no clear distinction between normal and abnormal pressures, apart from the arbitrary statistical division of stating that a given blood pressure is markedly deviant from the population sampled (Sleight, 1971). While genetic factors appear to account for a significant portion of the variance of blood pressure readings, other factors account for the greatest proportion (Miall, 1971).

Mild essential hypertension can sometimes be adequately controlled by sedatives, tranquilizers, or a change in diet aimed at weight loss or reduction of the intake of sodium. A wide variety of effective drugs for blood pressure control also exist (Fries, 1971). Most of these drugs lower blood pressure by curbing the activity of the sympathetic nervous system, thereby reducing vasoconstriction, or by changing the patient's fluid balance in such a manner that the blood pressure returns to normal. However, these drugs are sometimes nonspecific in their action and may have undesirable side effects including headache, asthenia, dizziness, gastrointestinal disturbances, and other difficulties (Gifford, 1974). Compliance to the prescribed regimen has also been a problem with cardiovascular patients (Gulledge, 1975).

Although research has been directed to organic etiologies (Ledingham, 1971), most investigators would agree that the disease is significantly exacerbated by stress. Therefore, it may be that a key causal factor is environmental stress or perhaps a genetic tendency to overreact to stress events. The cardiovascular response to stress is characterized by an increase in heart rate and vascular output, a widespread constriction of arterial vessels, and a subsequent increase in blood pressure. Prolonged experience of stress events may eventually lead to an "upward resetting" of the pressure regulatory mechanisms, and the pressure remains permanently elevated (Wallace and Benson, 1972). Such theorizing suggests that manipulation of environmental factors or changes in the behavioral response to stress might be potential treatment possibilities.

In recent years research has indicated that it may be possible for human subjects to be trained to alter the level of their own arterial blood pressure without the use of antihypertensive drugs. Such training might prove to have considerable therapeutic benefit either apart from or as an adjunct to current drug regimens. Further, in that medications sometimes have undesirable side effects, such training might be the treatment of choice in some cases. Finally, to the extent that stress factors are etiological, teaching the person an "antistress" response might prove to have considerable therapeutic potential. This chapter is concerned with this preliminary research regarding self-control strategies for the treatment of essential hypertension. These cardiovascular self-control techniques have evolved along two paths. The first of these has to do with self-administered relaxation training, and the second is concerned with biofeedback and instrumental conditioning strategies derived from the psychological principles of learning theory.

RELAXATION TECHNIQUES

Nonpharmacologic interventions aimed at teaching relaxation or lowered states of arousal are far from new. A multitude of religious practices have used a variety of relaxation and meditative techniques (Benson, Beary, and Carol, 1974a). In the Eastern practices of Yoga and Zen, various exercises have been used for thousands of years which allow individuals to develop remarkable control of their physiological systems (Raskin, Johnson, and Roudestvedt, 1973; Wenger, Bagchi, and Anand, 1961). Frederic and Barber (1972) have discussed some of the studies of yogis' abilities for cardiovascular control, and point out that similar phenomena have been demonstrated with hypnosis, most notably the ability to alter heart rate and skin temperature. Hypnosis, of course, also has a long history as a relaxation technique, and is still frequently employed in various psychotherapy techniques where states of low arousal or suggestibility are desired by the therapist (Lazarus, 1971; Meyer and Tilker, 1969; Wolpe, 1969). Finally, a number of relaxation training methods have evolved from medicine, psychiatry, and psychology.

Benson (1974a, 1975) points out how the many relaxation methods, both secular and religious, appear to involve similar key mechanisms: (1) a mental device upon which to focus and shift away from externally-oriented thought; (2) a passive or indifferent attitude as to success in achieving the response; (3) decreased muscle tonus—trainees should be in a comfortable position so as to reduce gross motor activity; (4) a quiet environment with minimal external distraction (e.g., a place of worship).

Riddick (1971) has offered this definition of relaxation (p. 7):

> Relaxation may best be thought of as a descriptive term for a complex pattern of responses characterized by subjective feelings of calmness and peacefulness associated with lowered physiological arousal especially in the sympathetic branch of the autonomic nervous system and a diminution of gross motor movements.

A number of research reports have appeared in the literature using relaxation methods to treat hypertension. Some studies have used a collection of relaxation methods, while others have focused upon a particular approach.

Progressive Relaxation

Edmund Jacobson published the culmination of his studies on muscular relaxation entitled *Progressive Relaxation*, which was a technical description of his theory and procedures, in 1938 (Jacobson, 1938). Relaxation of muscle fibers, i.e., complete absence of muscle contractions, was seen as the direct physiological opposite of tension and therefore an appropriate treatment for the overly tense or anxious person. Jacobson discovered that by systematically tensing and relaxing various muscle groups, and by learning to attend to and discriminate the resulting sensations of tension and relaxation, a person may dramatically reduce muscle contractions and experience a feeling of deep relaxation.

Jacobson gave his patients very prolonged training, often lasting 50 to 200 sessions, in the treatment of various stress related disorders (Wolpe, 1966). Wolpe (Wolpe, 1958) modified this set of exercises in his development of a technique called reciprocal inhibition or systematic desensitization, which was designed as a treatment for anxiety. Wolpe's modification resulted in a relaxation training program that could be completed in approximately six 20-minute sessions with two 15-minute daily home practice sessions. Patients are taught to relax their muscles and, while relaxing, they are encouraged to confront their anxieties in small graded steps in their visual imagination. As a result of this procedure the individual gradually learns to control fear and avoidance responses in real life. This technique has been evaluated experimentally by many researchers and has been proven to be a very successful treatment for a variety of fear and anxiety reactions (Paul, 1969a; Paul, 1969b).

Research on relaxation has been encouraged by the upsurge in the use of desensitization, and the shortened amount of training to provide a good relaxation or antistress response was one of Wolpe's major contributions (Bernstein and Borkovec, 1973).

Most of the relaxation approaches currently in use are derivatives of either Wolpe's (1958) or Lazarus', (1971) technique, although these are similar. One manual for therapists (Bernstein and Borkovec, 1973) has outlined the procedure in some detail. This approach involves the alternate tensing and relaxing of the hands, forearms, biceps, forehead, facial muscles, chest, shoulders, upper back, abdominal region, thighs, calves, feet and so on with a focus on the pleasurable feelings that accompany relaxation. As the sessions proceed, an attempt is made to achieve the same levels of deep muscle relaxation without focusing upon all 16 muscle groups; this is achieved by using tensing-relaxing contrasts for seven muscle groups. Focus is then placed upon four muscle groups, and in the final sessions, the patient is taught to elicit the relaxation response by recalling the sensations of relaxation without tensing any particular muscle groups. The entire training is to take approximately 10 sessions, and the pace of therapy is set by the patients' gradual mastery of each step of the program. Other clinicians also recommend using relaxing images (e.g., sunbathing on the beach), or hypnotic suggestions of warmth and heaviness to deepen the individual's relaxation response (e.g., Lazarus 1971).

Jacobson (1938, 1939a, 1964, 1939b), has long maintained that progressive relaxation is useful in the treatment of hypertension. He has argued that his clinical findings support the view that high blood pressure can result in part from habitual tensions in the skeletal musculature, which can be progressively relaxed with a resultant hypotensive effect.

Some experimental evidence was offered by Jacobson (1939a) on the effects of his training method on blood pressure. He reported that there is a general relationship between decreases in blood pressure and decreases in muscle activity as shown by electromyograms, and stated also that training in progressive relaxation resulted in greater decreases in electromyogram activity than relaxation without training. He presented blood pressure data on 14 normotensive subjects, 9 of whom had been trained in progressive relaxation. Both systolic and diastolic blood pressure were collected after a 15-minute adaptation period during which the subjects rested in a supine position, and again after 45 minutes of relaxation. Although further analysis of Jacobson's data by Blanchard and Young (1973) did reveal statistically significant decreases in both systolic blood pressure (Mean = 8.0 mm. Hg), and diastolic blood pressure (Mean = 7.8 mm. Hg), no significant differences existed between the trained and untrained subjects in the degree of reduction achieved.

Steinhaus and Norris (1964) found a significant reduction in systolic blood pressure (8 mm.) for their subjects with initial readings above 130 mm. Hg systolic who were trained in progressive relaxation. Similar findings for diastolic pressure were found (8.5 mm.). These authors also reported no significant decreases in either mode of blood pressure for those subjects with blood pressure readings within the normal range. Several other studies using combined or comparative relaxation procedures have used progressive relaxation, and these are reviewed in a later section.

Autogenic Training

Autogenic training is a method of autosuggestion by which the individual is given practice in attending to both his physiological sensations and his immediate state of consciousness. The procedure involves daily practice of certain exercises, including muscular relaxation, and concentration on subjective sensations of warmth and heaviness. It has been suggested as an effective method for training individuals to gain control over various aspects of physiological reactivity, and has been tentatively reported to be of therapeutic benefit for difficulties such as asthma, ulcers, skin disorders, various cardiovascular problems, anxiety neurosis, and sleep disturbances (Schultz and Luthe, 1959).

The system involves a number of verbal formulas which make up the "standard exercises" and the "meditative exercises." The verbal content of the standard formulas is focused upon the neuromuscular system (heaviness) and the vasomotor system (warmth), on the heart, the respiratory mechanism, warmth in the abdominal area, and cooling of the forehead. The meditative exercises are composed of a series of seven exercises which are designed primarily for psychotherapy and personal growth and are reserved for trainees who have mastered the standard exercises. Later, as more research and clinical experience accumulated, the special exercises emerged. These were a number of complementary exercises specifically designed to produce normalization of specific pathofunctional deviations such as vasomotor, endocrine, and metabolic disorders (Schultz and Luthe, 1969).

Autogenic training is said to be based on the reduction of exteroceptive and proprioceptive afferent stimulation, continuous mental repetition of psychophysiologically adapted verbal formulas, and mental activity conceived as "passive concentration" (Schultz and Luthe, 1959). Note that these are the same basic elements crucial to the relaxation response outlined previously by Benson (1974a and 1975).

Numerous studies are reported which suggest the efficacy of autogenic training in the increase in peripheral circulation, decrease of muscle potentials, changes in EEG patterns and respiratory and cardiac activity, and other autonomic and visceral changes. Interested readers are referred to Luthe and Schultz (1969), and Luthe (1970), although some of this research is disappointing due to the absence of appropriate control, comparison, or placebo subject groups.

From a clinical case perspective, Luthe and Schultz (1969), argue that autogenic training appears to be a helpful therapeutic adjunct to hypertensive conditions which are a function of organic disturbance as well as for the treatment of essential hypertension. The vasodilatory and circulatory effects associated with passive concentration on the different standard formulae include a number of desirable variables which participate in lowering elevated blood pressure readings. Generally autogenic training represents a shift towards a pattern of reactivity and change away from the pattern of changes elicited by stress.

Luthe and Schultz (1969) point out that the clinical results in the treatment of hypertension vary between excellent and an apparently complete failure of response, but that it is generally agreed that the effectiveness of the autogenic standard exercises increases as the hypertensive condition is due to functional factors. In many cases, they report marked improvement for essential hypertension after four to eight weeks of standard training. Readings taken before and after one set of standard exercises usually show a 5–25 percent reduction of systolic values, and a 5–12 percent decrease in diastolic blood pressure.

Klumbies and Eberhardt (1966) applied autogenic training to a group of 83 male hypertensives, although a large number dropped out of training (57). This motivational problem has been reported elsewhere (Schwartz, 1973) and may relate to the fact that many hypertensives suffer no discernible symptoms that they feel need treatment. However, impressive results were obtained by these researchers with the remaining 26. Blood pressure readings were taken repeatedly before starting autogenic training and during subsequent periods, for 5 to 15 months. The most significant decrease of systolic and diastolic readings occurred during the first month of autogenic training. Further decreases continued during the second, third, and fourth months, with little or no change occurring during subsequent periods. The authors noted considerable individual variation in response to treatment, particularly with some individuals showing dramatic improvement. Normalization of blood pressure deviations were noted in 22 out of the 26 patients. The authors also suggest that group training (up to ten persons) is helpful, and state that in view of the unfavorable side effects experienced by some individuals on antihypertensive medication, autogenic training may be the treatment of choice for many individuals.

Luthe and Schultz (1970), however, found no significant differences in blood pressure readings of *normotensives* before and after four weeks of heaviness training. A number of subjects, in fact, reported that they experienced distinct heaviness in the extremities in spite of the fact that their blood pressure and sometimes heart rate went up slightly (5–15 percent) during training. This phenomenon occurred when subjects fell asleep, began snoring, executed minor movements, or were disturbed by unpleasant intruding thoughts during the exercises. In three subjects whose blood pressures were repeatedly determined during passive concentration on heaviness, inconsistent responses were observed (up on some days, down on others, some days no change). Luthe offered no explanation to account for these results, but as noted previously, similar findings for normotensives were reported by Steinhaus and Norris (1964) using progressive relaxation.

Modifications of the autogenic training approach have also been offered. Some clinicians have combined some of the autogenic phraseology with progressive relaxation (Love, 1972). Others have combined autogenic training with biofeedback techniques, and labeled the approach "autogenic feedback training" (Green, Green, and Walters, 1970). This method involves training the individual to practice autogenic training at home, while also receiving biofeedback treatment in the laboratory for some particular bodily process. Biofeedback involves the use of instruments to provide moment-to-moment information to an individual about a specific physiologic process, such as electromyogram potentials (EMG feedback). This autogenic feedback approach has been used by some researchers in the treatment of hypertension. Moeller and Love (1973) and their associates at Nova University provided nine hypertensive subjects with training in autogenic exercises according to a slightly modified standard approach, and gave them feedback electromyography using forearm and frontalis muscles during 17 weekly half-hour sessions. The mean blood pressures for the last eight weeks of training were analyzed, and were found to be significantly lower than pretreatment readings. However, this study is limited by the absence of control groups to determine the possible effects of placebo phenomena, or habituation to the setting. Also, it is not possible to determine the relative influence of the EMG training and the autogenic exercises as therapeutic factors.

In a second study, Love, Montgomery, and Moeller (1973) treated one group of 20 subjects with two laboratory EMG biofeedback training sessions a week, coupled with tape-recorded relaxation exercises that they were to practice at home twice per day. Blood pressure was recorded at the beginning and end of the training sessions. Another group received one laboratory biofeedback session per week with the same relaxation procedure to be followed at home. The next group received two biofeedback sessions per week, but did not receive the relaxation tapes and "thus did not practice the exercises." The final group simply had their EMG readings monitored for four weeks and served as a control comparison group. After four weeks of training, there were no significant differences among the three treatment groups, and only minor changes existed in the systolic and diastolic pressures of the control group (mean reduction of 2.2 mm. Hg systolic and 0.67 mm. Hg diastolic). The three treatment groups pooled together showed a mean reduction of 12.67 mm. Hg in systolic pressure and a 9.78 mm. Hg drop in diastolic pressure. Statistical analysis indicated a significant difference between the pooled treatment groups and control group. In a subsequent paper the authors reported a one-year follow-up of 23 of the original 32 subjects who were treated. The blood pressure readings of this group indicated a total mean decrease of 27.52 mm. Hg systolic and a 17.70 mm. Hg diastolic, representing continued gains (Montgomery, Love, and Moeller, 1974).

Generally, the above series of reports on the Nova University sample indicate the apparent effectiveness of relaxation training using autogenic relaxation instructions administered by a tape recorder and EMG biofeedback in treating hypertension. It is suggested further that with several months of training, the effects might be persistent and continually therapeutic, at least as long as one year. The use of a group to assess the effects of training in relaxation *without* biofeedback would have been a helpful addition to this study, as well as the use of an attention-placebo manipulation. Shapiro et al. (1954) showed that simply the inclusion of a subject in a special study had a hypotensive effect, and data should be gathered on the magnitude of this effect, which might likely vary depending upon the particular characteristics of the laboratory or setting and the subjects.

Yogic and Meditative Techniques

Datey et al. (1969) combined muscle relaxation with breathing exercises for treating hypertensive subjects. This management approach involved a yogic exercise known as "Shavasan," which the hypertensives practiced for 30 minutes each day. The technique consisted of lying prone on the floor and engaging in slow rhythmic diaphragmatic breathing. After establishing the rhythm, the subject is asked to attend to the sensation at the nostrils, the coolness of the inspired air, and the warmth of the expired air. This procedure is intended to keep the patient inwardly alert and to forget his usual thoughts, thus becoming less conscious of the external environment and attaining relaxation. The patient is also asked to relax the muscles so that he is able to feel the heaviness of different parts of the body. Favorable results were reported, not only with patients having essential hypertension, but also with several hypertensives having renal hypertension. However, none of the arteriosclerotic patients experienced a significant reduction in blood pressure. A statistically significant decrease of 27 mm. Hg in average mean blood pressure was reported after training of an unspecified length. The typical training course was described as requiring three weeks of 30-minute daily sessions.

Benson has reported a series of studies using transcendental meditation (TM) to treat hypertension (1974a, 1973, 1974b, 1974c, 1972). This method is a form of Yoga coming from the Vedic tradition of India (Benson, 1975) and has achieved widespread popularity in the United States. TM involves systematic but passive concentration upon a word or sound, known as the *mantra*. The trainee is to practice twice a day for a period of 15 to 20 minutes, in comfortable and quiet position. These preliminary studies showed that statistically significant reductions of both systolic and diastolic pressures of hypertensives occurred after they had begun the practice of TM. Generally, blood pressure reductions in these studies are small both for subjects taking no antihypertensive medication (6.98 mm. Hg mean systolic reduction; and 3.86 mm. Hg mean diastolic reduction), and for hypertensives who were medicated throughout the training and follow-up (10.6 mm. Hg systolic; 4.85 diastolic) (Benson, 1974b; Benson, 1974c). The hypotensive effect of TM is apparently a definitive one, even if relatively small. However, the relative effect of TM versus other relaxation techniques or placebo manipulations has yet to be assessed experimentally.

Multimethod and Comparative Studies

Although the research studies reviewed rather clearly appear to demonstrate the efficacy of several types of relaxation treatments for hypertension, particularly essential hypertension, comparative effects of the various relaxation or antistress methods have not yet been thoroughly evaluated, although several preliminary studies have been reported in the literature.

Deabler et al. (1973), for example, treated six hypertensives who were receiving no medication, using both muscular relaxation (Wolpe and Lazarus, 1966) and a hypnotic procedure, and compared this group to a group of six hypertensives who simply had their blood pressures recorded in the same way, with no instructions to relax. An additional group of nine patients, stabilized on individualized antihypertensive medication, also received the muscular relaxation and hypnosis procedures. Significant lowering of both systolic and diastolic pressures were obtained in both the no drug (systolic 17 percent, diastolic 19.5 percent reductions) and drug (systolic 16 percent, diastolic 14 percent) groups receiving treatment, but there was not significant reduction in the no treatment control group. This study suggests that relaxation or self-control methods can have a positive effect on patients who are on medication as well as those who are not, a result also found for the practice of transcendental meditation. However, since all treated patients received both the muscular relaxation as well as the hypnotic procedure, it is not possible to assess the relative effectiveness of these two treatment techniques. Further, the control group was not told that the procedure would be a treatment for blood pressure, hence expectancy factors were not operative. However, this did allow habituation to the research setting to be ruled out as an operating hypotensive factor.

Elder et al. (1973) reported on an experiment designed to compare two instrumental conditioning strategies for controlling high blood pressure. All patients were hospitalized essential hypertensives and were not medicated. One group of six subjects received an external signal contingent upon each self-generated reduction in pressure that met a preset criterion. Another group of the same size received both the signal as well as verbal praise. These results were compared to a control group that received instructions to relax and avoid thinking about personal problems and to try to lower their blood pressure. The treatment group with both the external signal and verbal praise appeared to do better but only for the diastolic readings. The data also suggested that diastolic pressure might be a more suitable dependent variable than systolic blood pressure for this type of instrumental conditioning. Some individual patients were conditioned to lower diastolic pressure by 20 to 30 percent over a period of four days, although definitive follow-up data was not provided.

In a subsequent study, Elder and Eustis (1975) used a similar procedure in the treatment of 22 primarily medicated outpatients who volunteered themselves as essential hypertensives. Although both systolic and diastolic data were collected, positive stimulus feedback and verbal praise only for diastolic reductions were provided to the subjects. Massed training (daily) for 10 sessions (20 trial sessions) was provided for 4 patients with the balance receiving spaced training. Within the latter group, female patients performed slightly better than did males. Overall results, however, were less impressive than in the hospitalized, definitely diagnosed group of patients in the previous study, a result the authors primarily attributed to the stronger motivation for the hospitalized sample. No follow-up data were provided for this sample.

Shoemaker and Tasto (1975) compared a taped muscle relaxation program, modified from Jacobson's (1938) approach, to a group receiving noncontinuous biofeedback of systolic and diastolic blood pressure. Data from these treatments were compared to a waiting list control group, which apparently received no instructions to relax or to lower their blood pressure, but had their pressure monitored. The authors found that muscle relaxation brought about a reduction of both systolic and diastolic blood pressure, while the biofeedback approach brought about a lesser reduction, but only in diastolic readings. A possible reason for this difference, offered by Shoemaker and Tasto, was that the subjects in the biofeedback group attended to biofeedback signals for both the systolic and diastolic pressures and they seemed to be able to concentrate more effectively on the diastolic signal. Elder, Uptwich, and Wilkerson (1974) also have offered some data suggesting such diastolic contingencies to be more effective.

Patel (1973) used a collection of relaxation procedures, including autogenic training suggestions, deep breathing exercises, and ongoing galvanic skin response feedback (GSR), in the treatment of 20 patients with hypertension. Five patients stopped their antihypertensive medication altogether following the 3 month, three times weekly training sessions. Seven other patients were able to reduce their drug requirement by 33–60 percent. Although overall blood pressure reductions were not analyzed, Patel did report that 16 patients' average systolic blood pressure fell from 160 to 134 mm. Hg and average diastolic fell from 102 to 86 mm. Hg. Again, since this was a clinical study and no control groups were used, it is not possible to determine whether the GSR feedback, the relaxation training, or some combination was the key factor. Another disappointing feature of this report was that the heterogeneous sample included patients with renal hypertension, essential hypertension, and intracranial hypertension, as well as essential hypertension following pregnancy toxemia. Hence, generalization of the results is limited.

Byassee, Farr, and Meyer (1976) compared autogenic training and progressive relaxation in the treatment of essential hypertension. The control group (unstructured self-relaxation) was instructed to practice relaxation at home for equivalent periods as the two treatment groups. A collection of expectancy procedures were used, including a placebo capsule designed to produce a highly credible control comparison group. All three groups showed reductions in systolic pressure (autogenic 6.1 percent, progressive 12.2 percent, self 9.5 percent), although there were no significant between-group differences. This study was specifically designed to be readily applicable to applied settings. Relaxation training was provided for groups of several subjects at once, and acceptable reliability data using routine clinical sphygmomanoters indicated that the sophisticated and complex measurement methods typically used in such research may not be necessary for an acceptable degree of research precision. Treatment gains failed to persist at a four month follow-up.

Brady, Luborsky, and Kron (1974) reported on the use of "metronome-conditioned" relaxation (MCR) in the treatment of four male patients with essential hypertension. This technique involves the use of an abbreviated progressive relaxation procedure coupled with more general suggestions of physical and psychological relaxation given while an auditory metronome is beating at 60 beats a minute. The instructions to "let-go" and "re-lax" the muscles of the body are paced with the metronome's beats. The basic notion is that in time, the metronome's beats will function as stimuli conditional to elicit the relaxation response (Brady, 1973).

Three of the four patients in this study showed statistically significant mean reduction changes in blood pressure. Further, two subjects showed a statistically significant further decrease when the MCR procedure was reinstated over an extended period of time. The possibility of expectation, suggestive factors, or placebo influences, of course, cannot be ruled out in this study.

Psychotherapy

Although there is no firm experimental evidence to support the contention that psychotherapy by itself reduces hypertension, it appears to be a common psychiatric and psychological impression that such therapy is often useful as an adjunct to medication. Further, there are some case reports describing hypotensive results from psychotherapy alone (Lachman, 1972). Schwartz and Shapiro (1973) suggest as future avenues for research, not only teaching patients an antistress response, but also teaching them how to recognize anger-fear situations, express their feelings in an adaptive manner, and to engage in behaviors so as to minimize the number or impact of stress situations. This approach has yet to be evaluated experimentally.

BLOOD PRESSURE BIOFEEDBACK TRAINING

Theoretical and applied literature in the area of biofeedback has literally mushroomed in recent years, as apparent from the extant volumes of major work in the field (Barber, 1971b; Barber, 1971a; DiCara et al., 1975; Shapiro et al., 1973; Stoyva et al.,1972; Miller et al., 1974). Current biofeedback techniques offer more refined approaches for providing an individual with feedback or moment-to-moment information about specific physiological processes which can enable him to then modify and perhaps control many functions which were once regarded as "autonomic, involuntary, or reflexive" (e.g., heart rate, blood pressure, and brain waves). The list of variables that have thus far been demonstrated to be under the self-control by human subjects is indeed impressive, although considerable research is yet to be done. With respect to clinical applications, promising preliminary results in the treatment of essential hypertension, cardiac arrhythmias, migraine and tension headaches, Raynaud's disease, and abnormal EEG phenomenon, have been reported in either research reports or clinical case studies (Schwartz, 1973). Budzynski and Stoyva (1973) have outlined a series of therapeutic biofeedback techniques that can be used in conjunction with other psychotherapy approaches already discussed, such as systematic desensitization or autogenic training.

Shapiro and his colleagues at Harvard have shown that healthy college students could learn to raise or lower their systolic blood pressure in a single session (1969 and 1970a). In a later study, subjects were trained to raise and lower their heart rate without similarly affecting their systolic blood pressure (Shapiro et al., 1970b). Schwartz (1973) has suggested that this research opens the way for the development of teaching patients *patterns* of responses:

> For example, the desired goal for those hypertensive patients having normal heart rates may be to lower stroke volume and/or peripheral resistance rather than to change heart rate *per se.* However, in reducing pain from angina pectoris, the desired goal may not be to lower just blood pressure, or heart rate, but rather to lower both functions simultaneously, since by decreasing rate and pressure, the heart requires less oxygen, which in turn leads to reduced pain (p. 668).

Recently, this same group of researchers has focused upon self-control of diastolic blood pressure (Shapiro et al., 1972), the degree of integration and differentiation of the cardiovascular system (Schwartz, 1972), as well as a general theory of voluntary control of such response patterns (Schwartz, 1974). Much work remains to be done in this area, however, particularly in the application of appropriate control groups, and the exploration of the issues relating to mediation and follow-up data (Blanchard and Young, 1973; Schwartz, 1973).

Other research reports have been concerned with the use of the operant feedback technique developed by the Harvard group in the treatment of hypertensives. Benson et al., (1971) treated a group of seven hypertensive patients for an average of 21 sessions and produced significant decreases in systolic pressures (Mean = 22.6 mm. Hg). Brener and Kleinman (1970) used a form of proportional visual feedback and took pressure recordings from the left index finger of two groups of five normotensives for two sessions. Results were consistently higher than those recorded by the more conventional arm cuff technique, e.g., used by the Harvard group.

Although definitive results from research investigations in this area have not yet been forthcoming (Blanchard and Young, 1973), some case reports and preliminary clinical findings have shown additional promise. Miller (1972), for example, has described in detail a case study of a 33-year-old hypertensive female who was given several months of training in voluntary control of blood pressure. An impressive reduction in her diastolic pressure developed, which was maintained for 30 days without drugs in her own natural environment; training resulted in a reduction from a pretraining diastolic baseline of 97 mm. Hg to a level of 76 mm. Hg. However, it is possible that other factors (client–therapist relationship, etc.) could account for the improved readings.

An additional impressive element of this case was the attempt to control for some of the demand characteristics of the setting by rewarding the patient first for producing small diastolic decreases and then, as soon as she appeared to be reaching an asymptote for that session, rewarding her for producing diastolic pressure increases, but never above the original baseline. Miller pointed out that this had the added benefit of continued reward for the patient, so as to prevent frustration from failed learning trials.

In a subsequent publication, Miller (1972) reports that when the above patient was apparently "overwhelmed" by a series of difficult experiences, she lost her ability for voluntary control and her hypertension returned. Despite this relapse, this case study does indicate that it is possible to train voluntary control of hypertension. Greater generalization and lasting changes might have been obtained by also using therapeutic approaches which teach the better handling of tension-provoking situations or arrangement of environmental factors so as to minimize stress (Schwartz and Shapiro, 1973).

Another implication of this case report is that for severely hypertensive patients, even if voluntary control is achieved, it might be better for the individual to remain on maintenance medication in the event that he might face an overwhelming emotional or physical experience that could produce a cardiovascular accident, in lieu of the use of medication. However, for less severe cases, relaxation training and biofeedback alone might prove to be a method of controlling essential hypertension without both the undesirable side affects of some chemotherapy approaches and the need for costly and sometimes complicated biofeedback machinery.

CONCLUSION

Instrumental conditioning strategies, biofeedback training, and relaxation training have achieved success in the treatment of hypertension. Yet the successes lie primarily in the electronic sophistication involved and in the information provided about the psychological relationships between cognitive, somatic, autonomic variables, and learning principles, and in the *statistical* significance of the studies. The *clinical* impact or applicability of self-control treatments of hypertension has yet to be demonstrated to be uniformly or persistently effective (Blanchard and Young, 1973; Byassee, Farr, and Meyer, 1976).

Equally important is the problem that for several reasons it is very difficult to compare one study with another. Studies vary in application of treatment modalities, length of training, use of follow-up data, and in method of data presentation offered. Some researchers focus upon the reduction of necessary antihypertensive medication as the key dependent variable (Patel, 1973). Others may present their data in terms of percentage of blood pressure reduction above the commonly accepted but somewhat arbitrary cutoff of 140/90 mm. Hg, (Deabler et al., 1973) or in terms of absolute blood pressure readings (Byassee, Farr, and Meyer, 1976). Further, the absence of standard subject selection makes comparisons across studies dubious. Brady *et al.*, (1974) for example, used a group that he labeled "labile hypertensives"; Patel (1973) used several different diagnostic categories of which hypertension was a feature; Shoemaker and Tasto (1975) used subjects who volunteered themselves as suffering from essential hypertension, although no medical corroboration was obtained (a similar selection procedure was followed by Elder and Eustis (1975)); Benson *et al.* (1973 and 1974b) used samples of "borderline" hypertensives. Further, although Byassee, Farr, and Meyer (1976) screened out what were judged to be "controlled" hypertensives and some "borderline cases," other researchers included individuals whose initial pressures were somewhat near "normal," and who might be expected for this reason to be less responsive to treatment (i.e., more dramatic reductions would seem to be more likely for individuals whose pressures were considerably above normal). Most of these confounding factors are likely due to difficulties in subject recruitment, but they continue to make meaningful conclusions difficult.

If self-control strategies are to be found as effective, the problem still remains of the most efficient method of delivery. Group training appears to have great promise, in that relaxation instructions can be easily administered and can be delivered by trained paraprofessionals.

Nursing publications have emphasized how paramedical and nursing professionals can provide ancillary care and treatment to cardiovascular patients (Batterman, Stegman, and Fitz, 1975), and group relaxation training may be an approach to further their care-delivering potential. However, only two studies have used group-administered techniques. Klumbies and Eberhart (1966) used group techniques, but failed to provide information as to how or when blood pressures were recorded or use control groups. In the more optional design of the Byassee, Farr, and Meyer (1976) study, group techniques were used, but treatment gains were equivocal at follow-up and the self-relaxation group achieved success equivalent to that of the progressive relaxation training and autogenic training groups. In the only other study to use progressive relaxation by itself in a treatment group (Brady, 1973) taped presentations were used, which have been shown to be inferior to personally administered relaxation instructions for normal subjects in learning the "relaxation response" (Paul and Trimble, 1970). Continued efforts to assess delivery mode variables are needed.

Follow-up Results

Typically, follow-up data have not been collected in self-control of hypertension studies, and in instances where they have, results have been contradictory.

In the Byassee, Farr, and Meyer (1976) study, the reduced pressures generally failed to persist over the four month follow-up period. This was the case despite the existence of data showing that some subjects continued to practice their exercises, if irregularly. Similar results were reported by Benson and Wallace (1972). While comparisons with other studies are limited by the conditions noted above, the absence of persistence over the four month period is inconsistent with the findings of Montgomery *et al.* (1974) who reported on follow-up data for 72 percent of those originally treated and reported upon by Love *et al.* (1973). This follow-up was one year later. In this study subjects received 16 weeks of both autogenic training (to be practiced at home and administered by tape) and EMG feedback training during 16 weekly treatment sessions at the clinic. Although control group data were not collected beyond four weeks initially, these subjects did show mean reductions of 14.74 mm. Hg systolic and 12.70 mm. Hg diastolic pressure during training and *continued* gains from the end of treatment to the one year follow-up (a total drop of 27.52 systolic and 17.70 diastolic). Despite the fact that information on possible medication changes or home practice was not available, these results are impressive. At present this is the only study available with long term follow-up results in the treatment of essential hypertension by self-control methods. Finally, as noted, the results contrast considerably with the data reported in other studies where the achieved reductions failed to persist (Byassee, Farr, and Meyer (1976); Wallace and Benson (1972).

It may be that individually administered biofeedback relaxation training is important in terms of long term results. However, perhaps even more significant is that longer training may increase the probability that clients will make needed lifestyle or environmental changes to support their learned lower level of arousal more effectively (changing jobs, work schedules, home routines, driving habits, etc.). Clearly several researchers have indicated that such changes are desirable for hypertensives (Schwartz and Shapiro, 1973; Schwartz, 1973), and preliminary data on the therapeutic applications of such change techniques have been published with cardiac patients (Suinn, 1974).

As noted previously, Miller (1972a, 1972b) discussed how one subject in his laboratory, trained in self-control by blood pressure feedback, lost her cardiovascular control when events in her life "seemed to overwhelm her"; it is known that stress events, even boredom (London, Schubert, and Washburn, 1972), can exacerbate arousal. Indeed an attempt to teach patients to relax without also instructing them in the application of such techniques to combat stress events (Goldfried and Trier, 1974) may be quite incomplete. In most of the research reported here, patients were told that they could use the relaxation response to combat stress, but typically no specific instructions were offered as to the methods or best techniques for doing so. It is not clear how much of such instruction might have been offered to the patients in Love's study where treatment gains were maintained at follow-up.

Control Groups and Self-Control of Hypertension

Effective control group procedures are essential in the study of such disorders as hypertension for several important reasons. Two in particular are the regression to the mean problem and the placebo effect. Miller (1974) argues that subjects are much more likely to seek out treatment when they are feeling worse. Although hypertensives often experience no discernible physical symptomatology (Schwartz, 1973), it would logically follow that they would be more likely to seek out treatment when they are most concerned or worried about their condition. Since physiological systems tend to fluctuate between periods of exacerbation and those of amelioration, it is possible to obtain a sample of volunteers whose blood pressures will show reduction simply due to spontaneous fluctuations regressing toward their mean pressure levels. It may also be that more motivated patients in this regard tend to remain in training once it has begun, accelerating this occurrence even further.

Miller also points out that the placebo effect is a potent factor in the treatment of hypertension. Expectancy of therapeutic gain (Wilkins, 1973), demand characteristics of the setting (Baker and Kahn, 1972), and a variety of other factors often have a hypotensive effect. Several reasonable hypotheses are available. For one, patients may be able to reduce their blood pressures in response to the demand characteristics of the setting, i.e., they are told that they are participating in effective treatments and experience reassurance and anxiety reduction. Secondly, blood pressures may be reduced as a consequence of nonspecific factors that all therapies have in common, e.g., suggestion, contact with experienced professionals, group process, expectancy for improvement and other factors. Third, blood pressures are reduced as a result of active components of therapy.

Ideally, it would be desirable to incorporate both a simple "no treatment" baseline group which would have no expectation for improvement and a placebo group. However, sample size limitations sometimes do not permit the use of both types of controls. Future research should consider both types of comparison groups.

It is possible to argue that the results are sometimes a consequence of nonspecific factors, in that groups improve and also contain credible and potent placebo components. The fact that the gains failed to persist would also seem to support this idea, since placebo effects are sometimes known to be transient (Shapiro, 1974). However, studies have attested to the power of progressive relaxation and autogenic training, although no comparisons with placebo groups in the treatment of essential hypertension could be located except for the Byassee, Farr, and Meyer (1976) study. These nonspecific factors are also sometimes confounded with specific procedures, i.e., instructions to relax at home and record home practice impressions, or with an emphasis on passive concentration. Kanfer (1973) has discussed how learning to monitor one's own behavior is an essential prerequisite for the acquisition of self-regulation and self-control; the requirement that patients practice at home and provide verification and data regarding their home practice sessions may have been a very important factor in terms of encouraging them to monitor their own behavior.

Considerations for Future Research

In that both Byassee, Farr, and Meyer (1976) and Elder and Eustis (1975) reported sex differences, and that other subject variables appear to play a role in the disorder of hypertension (Miall, 1971), the interaction between these variables and response to self-control treatment needs to be investigated. Further, despite a number of studies in this area, the relative effects of placebo variables, practice at home effects, and the type of treatment that best "fits" a type of individual is in need of further investigation. Additionally, the extension of learned cardiovascular control to more generally improved coping skills, such as through psychotherapy, needs to be evaluated (Schwartz and Shapiro, 1973).

Two conclusions seem clear: (1) The crucial operations for reducing hypertension using self-control methods are not yet known; (2) various forms of relaxation training, instrumental conditioning, and biofeedback, can reduce blood pressure for periods of several months, although follow-up data may not continue to reflect the reductions attained.

Finally, it is clear that the disorder of essential hypertension cannot be seen as an independent phenomenon represented simply by blood pressure readings. The particular reading gathered on any given day is a response determined by situational and diurnal variations and the complex physiology and characteristics of the person, as well as his particular environmental context. All of these factors need careful research consideration. Particularly in view of the varying nature of environments in their stress-producing potential (Insel and Moos, 1974), research is needed to evaluate the interaction between these effects and the person variables mentioned.

REFERENCES

Barber, T., DiCara, L., Kamiya, J., Miller, N., Shapiro, D., & Stoyva, J. (Eds.) *Biofeedback and self-control 1970*. Chicago: Aldine, 1971a.

——. *Biofeedback and self-control reader*. Chicago: Aldine, 1971b.

Baker, B.L., & Kahn, M. A reply to "Critique of 'Treatment of insomnia by relaxation training': Relaxation training, Rogerian therapy, or demand characteristics." *Journal of Abnormal Psychology*, 1972, *79*, 94–96.

Batterman, B., Stegman, M.R., & Fitz, A. Hypertension Part 1: Detection and evaluation. *Cardiovascular Nursing*, 1975, *11*, 35–40.

Benson, H., Shapiro, D., Tursky, B., & Schwartz, G.E. Decreased systolic blood pressure through operant conditioning techniques in patients with essential hypertension. *Science*, 1971, *173*, 740–742.

Benson, H., & Wallace, R.K. Decreased blood pressure in hypertensive subjects who practiced meditation. *Circulation*, 1972, *XLV & XLVI*, Supplement II.

Benson, H., Rosner, B.A., & Maryetta, B.R. Decreased systolic blood pressure in hypertensive subjects who practiced meditation. *Journal of Clinical Investigation*, 1973, 52: 8a.

Benson, H., Beary, J.F., & Carol, M.P. The relaxation response. *Psychiatry*, 1974a, *37*, 37–46.

Benson, H., Rosner, B.A., Maryetta, B.R., & Klemchuk, H.P. Decreased blood pressure in borderline hypertensive subjects who practiced meditation. *Journal of Chronic Disease*, 1974b, *27*, 163–169.

——. Decreased blood pressure in pharmacologically treated hypertensive patients who regularly elicited the relaxation response. *The Lancet*, 1974c, 289–291.

Benson, H. *The relaxation response*. New York: Morrow, 1975.

Bernstein, D.A., & Borkovec, T.D. *Progressive relaxation training: A manual for the helping professions*. Champaign: Research Press, 1973.

Blanchard, E.B., & Young, L.D. Self-control of cardiac functioning: A promise as yet unfulfilled. *Psychological Bulletin*, 1973, *79*, 145–163.

Brady, J.P. Metronome-conditioned relaxation: A new behavioral procedure. *British Journal of Psychiatry*, 1973, *122*, 729–730.

Brady, J.P., Luborsky, L., & Kron, R.E. Blood pressure reduction in patients with essential hypertension through metronome-conditioned relaxation: A preliminary report. *Behavior Therapy*, 1974, *5*, 203–209.

Brener, J., & Kleinman, R.A. Learned control of decreases in systolic blood pressure. *Nature*, 1970, *226*, 1063–1064.

Budzynski, T.H., & Stoyva, J. Biofeedback techniques in behavior therapy. In D. Shapiro, T.X. Barber, L.V. DiCara, J. Kamiya, N.E. Miller, & J. Stoyva (Eds.) *Biofeedback and self-control 1972*. Chicago: Aldine, 1973.

Byassee, J., Farr, S., & Meyer, R. Progressive relaxation and autogenic training in the treatment of essential hypertension. Unpublished manuscript, 1976.

Datey, K.K., Deshmukh, S.N., Dalvi, C.P., & Vinekar, S.L. "Shavasan": A yogic exercise in the management of hypertension. *Angiology*, 1969, *20*, 325–333.

Deabler, H.L., Fidel, E., Dillenkoffer, R.L., & Elder, S.T. The use of relaxation and hypnosis in lowering high blood pressure. *The American Journal of Clinical Hypnosis*, 1973, *16*, 75–83.

DiCara, L.V., Barber, T.X., Kamiya, J., Miller, N.E., Shapiro, D., & Stoyva, J. (Eds.) *Biofeedback and self-control 1974*. Chicago: Aldine, 1975.

Elder, S.T., Ruiz, R., Deabler, H.L., & Dillenkoffer, R.L. Instrumental conditioning of diastolic blood pressure in essential hypertensive patients. *Journal of Applied Behavior Analysis*, 1973, *6*, 377–382.

Elder, S.T., Uftwich, D.A., & Welserson, L.A. The fole of systolic-versus diastolic-contingent feedback in blood pressure conditioning. *The Psychological Record*, 1974, 171–176.

Elder, S.T. & Eustis, W.K. Instrumental conditioning in out-patient hypertensives. *Behavior Research & Therapy*, 1975, *13*, 185–188.

Frederick, A.D., & Barber, T.X. Yoga, hypnosis, and self-control of cardiovascular functions. *Proceedings of the American Psychological Association*, 1972, *1*, 859–860.

Fries, E.D. The chemotherapy of hypertension. *Journal of American Medical Association*, 1971, 218, 7, 1009–1014.

Galton, L. *The silent disease: Hypertension.* New York: Crown, 1973.

Geiger, H.J., & Scotch, N.A. The epidemiology of essential hypertension: A review with special attention to psychologic and sociocultural factors. I. Biologic mechanisms and descriptive epidemiology. *Journal of Chronic Diseases*, 1963, *16*, 1151–1181.

Gifford, R.W. A practical guide to medical management. In Merck, Sharp & Dohme (Eds.), *The hypertension handbook.* West Point: Merck & Co., Inc. 1974.

Goldfried, M.R., & Trier, C.S. Effectiveness of relaxation as an active coping skill. *Journal of Abnormal Psychology*, 1974, *83*, 348–355.

Green, E.E., Green, A.M., & Walters, E.D. Voluntary control of internal states: Psychological and physiological. *Journal of Transpersonal Psychology*, 1970, *2*, 26–51.

Gressel, G.C. Personality factors in arterial hypertension. *Journal of the American Medical Association*, 1949, *140*, 60–72.

Gulledge, A.D. The psychological aftermath of a myocardial infarction. In W.D. Gentry, & R.B. Williams, Jr. (Eds.), *Psychological aspects of myocardial infarction and coronary care.* St. Louis: Mosby, 1975.

Guyton, A.C., Cowley, A.W., Jr., & Coleman, T.G. Interaction between the separate pressure control systems in normal arterial pressure regulation and in hypertension. In *Hypertension 1972.* New York: Springer, 1972.

Insel, P.M., & Moos, R.H. The social environment. In P.M. Insel & R.H. Moos (Eds.), *Health and the social environment.* Lexington: D.C. Heath and Co., 1974.

Jacobson, E. *Progressive relaxation.* Chicago: University of Chicago Press, 1938.

_____. Variations in blood pressure with skeletal muscle tension in man. *American Journal of Physiology*, 1939a, *126*, 546–547.

_____. Variation of blood pressure with skeletal muscle tension and relaxation. *Annals of Internal Medicine*, 1939b, *12*, 1194–1212.

_____. *Anxiety and tension control: A physiologic approach.* Philadelphia: Lippincott, 1964.

_____. *Modern treatment of tense patients.* Springfield, Illinois: Charles C. Thomas, 1970.

Kalis, B.L. Response to psychological stress in patients with essential hypertension. *American Heart Journal*, 1957, 53, 572–578.

Klumbies, G., & Eberhardt, G. Results of autogenic training in the treatment of hypertension. In J.J. Lopez Ibor (Ed.), *IV world congress of psychiatry, Madrid, 5.–11. IX. 1966.* International Congress Series No. 117, 46–47. Amsterdam: Excerpta Medica Foundation, 1966.

Kanfer, F.H. Self-regulation: Research, issues and speculations. In M.R. Goldfried & M. Merbaum (Eds.), *Behavior change through self-control.* New York: Holt, Rinehart & Winston, 1973.

Lachman, S.J. *Psychosomatic disorders: A behavioristic interpretation.* New York: Wiley, 1972.

Lazarus, A.A. *Behavior therapy and beyond.* New York: McGraw-Hill, 1971.

Ledingham, J.M. The etiology of hypertension. *The Practitioner*, 1971, *207*, 5–19.

London, H., Schubert, S.P., & Washburn, D. Increased autonomic arousal by boredom. *Journal of Abnormal Psychology*, 1972, *80*, 29–36.

Love, W.A. Problems in therapeutic application of EMG feedback. Paper presented to the Biofeedback Research Society, Boston, November, 1972.

Love, W.A., Montgomery, D.D., & Moeller, T.A. Working paper number one. Unpublished research report. Nova University, 1973.

Luthe, W., & Schultz, J.H. *Autogenic therapy, volume III, applications in psychotherapy*. New York: Grune & Stratton, 1969.

Luthe, W. *Autogenic therapy, volume IV, research and theory*. New York: Grune & Stratton, 1970.

Luthe, W., & Schultz, J.H. *Autogenic therapy, volume II medical applications*. New York: Grune & Stratton, 1970.

Meyer, R.G., & Tilker, H. The clinical use of direct hypnotic suggestion: A traditional technique in light of current approaches. *International Journal of Clinical and Experimental Hypnosis*, 1969, *17*, 81–88.

Miall, W.E. Heredity and hypertension. *The Practitioner*, 1971, *207*, 20–27.

Miller, N.E. A psychologist's perspective on neural and psychological mechanisms in cardiovascular disease. In *Proceedings of the symposium on neural and psychological mechanisms in cardiovascular disease*. Stresa, 1971, in press, 1972b.

———. Learning of glandular and visceral responses: Postscript. In D. Singh, & C.T. Morgan (Eds.), *Current status of physiological psychology: Readings*. Monterey: Brooks-Cole, 1972a.

Miller, N.E., Barber, T.X., DiCara, L., Kamiya, J., Shapiro, D., & Stoyva, J. (Eds.) *Biofeedback and self-control 1973*. Chicago: Aldine, 1974.

Miller, N.E. Introduction: Current issues and key problems. In N.E. Miller, T.X. Barber, L.V. DiCara, J. Kamiya, D. Shapiro, & J. Stoyva (Eds.), *Biofeedback and self-control 1973*. Chicago: Aldine, 1974.

Moeller, T.A., & Love, W.A. A method to reduce arterial hypertension through muscular relaxation. *Journal of Biofeedback*, 1973, *1*, 38–44.

Montgomery, D.D., Love, W.A., & Moeller, T.A. Work paper number two. Unpublished research report. Nova University, 1974.

National Center for Health Statistics. *Blood pressure of adults by age and sex, United States 1960–1962*. U.S. Department of Health, Education, and Welfare, Vital and Health Statistics Series 11, No. 4 Washington: U.S. Government Printing Office, 1969.

Patel, C.H. Yoga and biofeedback in the management of hypertension. *The Lancet*, 1973, 1053–1055.

Paul, G.L. Outcome of systematic desensitization. I: Background, procedures, and uncontrolled reports of individual treatment. In C.M. Franks (Ed.), *Behavior therapy: Appraisal and status*. New York: McGraw-Hill, 1969a.

———. Outcome of systematic desensitization. II: Controlled investigations of individual treatment technique variations, and current status. In C.M. Franks (Ed.), *Behavior therapy: Appraisal and status*. New York: McGraw-Hill, 1969b.

Paul, G.L., & Trimble, R.W. Recorded vs. "live" relaxation training and hypnotic suggestion: Comparative effectiveness for reducing physiological arousal and inhibiting stress response. *Behavior Therapy*, 1970, *1*, 285–302.

Pickering, G.W. *High blood pressure*. London: Churchill, 1968.

Platt, R. The nature of essential hypertension. *The Lancet*, 1959, *2*, 55–57.

———. Heredity in hypertension. *The Lancet*, 1963, *1*, 899–904.

———. The natural history and epidemiology of essential hypertension. *The Practitioner*, 1964, *193*, 5–13.

Raskin, M., Johnson, G., & Rondestvedt, J.W. Chronic anxiety treated by feedback-induced muscle relaxation. *Archives of General Psychiatry*, 1973, *28*, 263–267.

Riddick, C. The efficacy of automated relaxation training with response contingent feedback. Unpublished doctoral dissertation, University of Louisville, 1971.

Schultz, J.H., & Luthe, W. *Autogenic training: A psychophysiologic approach in psychotherapy*. New York: Grune & Stratton, 1959.

Schultz, J., & Luthe, W. *Autogenic therapy, volume I, autogenic methods.* New York: Grune & Stratton, 1969.

Schwartz, G.E. Voluntary control of human cardiovascular integration and differentiation through feedback and reward. *Science*, 1972, *175*, 90–93.

Schwartz, G. Biofeedback as therapy: Some theoretical and practical issues. *American Psychologist*, 1973, *28*, 666–673.

Schwartz, G.E., & Shapiro, D. Biofeedback and essential hypertension. Current findings and theoretical concerns. *Seminars in Psychiatry*, 1973, *5*, 493–503.

Schwartz, G.E. Toward a theory of voluntary control of response patterns in the cardiovascular system. In P.A. Obrist, A.H. Black, & J. Brener (Eds.) *Cardiovascular Pyschophysiology*. Chicago: Aldine, 1974.

Shapiro, D., Myers, T., Reiser, M.D., & Ferris, E.B., Jr. Blood pressure response to veratrum and doctor. *Psychosomatic Medicine*, 1954, *16*, 478.

Shapiro, D., Tursky, B., Gershon, E., & Stern, M. Effects of feedback and reinforcement on the control of human systolic blood pressure. *Science*, 1969, *163*, 588–589.

Shapiro, D., Tursky, B., & Schwartz, G.E. Control of blood pressure in man by operant conditioning. *Circulation Research*, 1970a, *26 (Suppl. 1)*, *27*, 1227–I–32.

———. Differentiation of heart rate and blood pressure in man by operant conditioning. *Psychosomatic Medicine*, 1970b, *32*, 417–423.

———. Control of diastolic blood pressure in man by feedback and reinforcement. *Psychophysiology*, 1972, *9*, 296–304.

Shapiro, D., Barber, T.X., DiCara, L.V., Kamiya, J., Miller, N.E., & Stoyva, J. (Eds.) *Biofeedback and self-control 1972*. Chicago: Aldine, 1973.

Shapiro, A.K. Contributions to a history of the placebo effect. In N.E. Miller, T.X. Barber, L.V. DiCara, J. Kamiya, D. Shapiro, & J. Stoyva (Eds.), *Biofeedback and self-control 1973*. Chicago: Aldine, 1974.

Shoemaker, J.E., & Tasto, D.L. The effects of muscle relaxation on blood pressure of essential hypertensives. *Behavior Research & Therapy*, 1975, *13*, 29–43.

Sleight, P. The diagnosis of hypertension. *The Practitioner*, 1971, *207*, 36–42.

Steinhaus, A.H., & Norris, J.E. *Teaching neuromuscular relaxation*. U.S. Office of Education, Cooperative research project No. 1529, George Williams College, 1964.

Stoyva, J., Barber, T., DiCara, L., Kamiya, J., Miller, N.E., & Shapiro, D. (Eds.) *Biofeedback and self-control 1971*. Chicago: Aldine, 1972.

Suinn, R.M. Behavior therapy for cardiac patients. *Behavior Therapy*, 1974, *5*, 569–571.

Wallace, R.K., & Benson, H. The physiology of meditation. *Scientific American*, 1972, *226*, 84–90.

Wenger, M.A., Bagchi, B.K., Anand, B.K. Experiments in India on "voluntary" control of the heart and pulse. *Circulation*, 1961, *24*, 1319–1325.

Wilkins, W. Expectancy of therapeutic gain: An empirical and conceptual critique. *Journal of Consulting and Clinical Pyschology*, 1973, *40*, 69–77.

Wolpe, J. *Psychotherapy by reciprocal inhibition*. Stanford: Stanford University Press, 1958.

Wolpe, J., & Lazarus, A.A. *Behavior therapy techniques*. New York: Pergamon, 1966.

Wolpe, J. *The practice of behavior therapy*. New York: Pergamon, 1969.

Chapter 10

Urinary Disorders

*E. Wayne Sloop**

Historically a urinary disorder, nocturnal enuresis, was one of the first problems to which behavioral or conditioning methods were applied. Mowrer and Mowrer (1938) introduced a method, accidentally discovered by Pfaundler (1904), into the United States when they reported the successful treatment of 30 nocturnal enuretics. Since that time, a multitude of investigators have sought to discover the mechanism underlying this very successful method, improve on the initial success rate it achieves, reduce the relapse rate after successful conditioning, invent more efficient, dependable, and safer apparatus, and apply the method to children and adults outside the "normal" population. Recent attention has been devoted to the formulation of daytime treatment procedures which will solve the problem without the necessity of nighttime routines which disrupt the sleep of the enuretic, his parents, and others in the family. This chapter will briefly summarize most of the research on the treatment of nocturnal enuresis and then present a procedure, used by the author for the past 10 years, which can easily be adopted by the pediatrician, general practitioner, family physician, or clinical psychologist in treating this disorder.

In addition to nocturnal enuresis, a "new" process of toilet training the normal child, which has recently been presented by Azrin and Foxx (1974), will be discussed and its application by the physician to toilet training problems will be considered.

*Lynchburg Training School and Hospital, Lynchburg, Virginia.

NOCTURNAL ENURESIS

Nocturnal enuresis is usually defined as the involuntary discharge of urine during sleep after the age of 3 to 4 years in the absence of demonstrable organic pathology. Glicklich (1951) gives evidence to show that the problem has been recognized since ancient times and that a variety of remedies, some of which survive today, have been applied to its solution. Folk remedies have included such procedures as raising the foot of the bed, sleeping on the back, sleeping on a hard surface, and consumption of numerous potions (like cypress, juniper berries, and beer), restricting liquids, and setting alarm clocks to permit regular "potting." Often the bedwetter and his parents are told, "Don't worry about it, he'll 'grow' out of it." The problem is often hidden because of the embarrassment of the bedwetter and his family. Often punishment, spanking or the restriction of privileges, and the offering of rewards ("If you are dry for a month, we'll get you a bike") are used with very little success.

Etiological Theories

Perhaps the multiple number of theories proposed to explain enuresis have arisen because the processes underlying the voluntary control of urination while awake are complex and multifaceted. Add to this the factor of sleep and the whole situation is further complicated. In the infant, micturition is an automatic reflex to bladder distension stimulation, but the normal child or adult is able to inhibit this reflex beyond the point of the first sensations of urgency and also to initiate urination at low bladder volumes. While there is some controversy as to how this degree of control develops, it is probable that, as a consequence the detrusor muscle in the bladder wall is brought under inhibitory influence from the cortex. Normally, the inhibitory control transfers to the sleeping state and this, along with an increased bladder capacity occurring with maturation together with the reduced level of diuresis during sleep, usually enables the nonbedwetter to sleep through the night without voiding or to be able to respond to internal bodily cues and awaken to void appropriately. For some reason, this process breaks down, or does not occur, in some individuals and the problem of bedwetting results.

Until recently the psychoanalytic theory of enuresis has enjoyed the greatest popularity among psychiatrists and pediatricians. This theory postulates that enuresis represents an emotional disturbance arising from intense anxiety over the suppression of sexual impulses, primarily related to masturbation. Enuresis is considered to be a masturbatory equivalent in children and thus is seen a form of sexual discharge. In this framework, enuresis represents a substitute and equivalent of suppressed masturbation. The empirical evidence for this interpretation of enuresis is practically nonexistent and its popularity has given way in recent years to other, better substantiated etiological theories.

Investigators and practitioners who have utilized the conditioning approach in treating enuresis have generally adopted all, or major parts of, the "habit-deficiency" theory proposed by Mowrer and Mowrer (1938). The Mowrers believed that faulty habit training was the predominant, perhaps exclusive, causal factor in enuresis. The theory proposes that the ordinary "potting" procedure, whereby children are aroused at night to urinate, commonly employed in Western cultures is an inefficient method of conditioning nighttime bladder control since it may condition the child to void when the bladder is only partly filled. If this be true, and if the awakening response is not adequately associated with the stimuli arising from a partly filled bladder, then the child will void without awakening and enuresis will result. The form of treatment devised by the Mowrers was aimed at having arousal occur when bladder stimulation was at a maximal level which exists when urination occurs.

A number of writers base their etiological theories on the hypothesis that enuresis results because of the slowed maturation or development of certain cerebral "centers" or "mechanisms." This view holds that higher cerebral centers, which control urination while awake, do not exert this control during sleep and that areas in the lower brain, which are hypothesized to exert nighttime control, do not function adequately because of maturational delay. For example, Van Wagenen (1968) cites Meullener (1960) who concluded, after studying urination in 1000 children, that control of the micturition reflex is self-learned and is not effected by training as providing support for the conception that enuresis is due to slowed development of neural mechanisms. Gillison and Skinner (1958) feel that enuresis represents "a failure . . . to substitute cerebral control for the spinal control of infancy" (p. 1271). They add that a likely explanation is that in the enuretic child bladder sensations are not adequately perceived at the cerebral level during sleep, consequently the impulses which would inhibit voiding do not occur in the enuretic. The delayed cerebral maturity viewpoint has been criticized (cf. Baller, 1975, p. 10) because of the ambiguity which attaches to the concept of maturity and because it does not explain the phenomenon of secondary enuresis in which a child achieves dryness for up to 1 year but reverts to a pattern of nighttime wetting, or the more usual circumstance in which a betwetter will often experience periods of dryness over several nights or weeks between wetting episodes. The delayed cerebral maturity hypothesis is an intriguing idea but at present it must be considered very tentative since there is little substantive research evidence to support it.

Perhaps the most widely accepted ètiological theory among professionals and laymen alike is that a child is enuretic because of abnormally deep sleep which prevents awakening or tightening of the external sphincter to prevent voiding. The studies which have pointed to depth of sleep as a causative factor in enuresis have generally relied on parental reports or subjective judgments, rather than experimental data, in their attribution of a causative relationship between depth of sleep and enuresis. Helsborg (1950), in a series of EEG studies obtained at the moment of bedwetting, concluded that his data did not substantiate the notion that nocturnal enuresis occurs during unusually deep sleep and Bental (1961), in a study of enuretic twins, reached a similar conclusion. Forrester, Stein, and Susser (1964) obtained ratings from parents on the depth of sleep of their enuretic and nonenuretic children and, on this somewhat crude measure, reported that the sleep of enuretic children was judged to be no deeper than that of their nonenuretic siblings. After studying continuous nocturnal EEGs on 25 randomly selected subjects, Ditman and Blinn (1955) concluded that "functional nocturnal enuresis is not due to excessively sound sleeping" (p. 919). Boyd (1960) compared 100 enuretics, age 5 to 15 years, with 100 nonenuretic controls on depth of sleep. Using rapidity of awakening by an adult as the dependent measure, it was concluded that there was no difference in depth of sleep between enuretic and nonenuretic children. Support for deep sleep as a causitive factor in enuresis is unimpressive as the majority of the experimental evidence casts serious doubt on the utility of this theory. Therefore, the burden of proof for this conception awaits evidence which will negate the negative results found in recent experimental studies.

Hereditory factors have also been given important attention in accounting for enuresis. Early writers reported that 60 percent or more of the bedwetters in their studies had parents with a history of enuresis (cf. Baller, 1975, p. 13). A majority of the studies which have examined hereditory factors in bedwetting show that the estimates of a family history of enuresis fall in the range from 40 to 55 percent. An accurate determination of a familial history of enuresis among enuretics, while likely to be high, is difficult as tracing and interviewing relatives is often impossible and the memories of parents are often unreliable. One important fact about hereditary factors in the problem of enuresis is that the belief in such factors is often accompanied by the rather fatalistic view that since the problem is inherited there is no use in trying to correct it. Such a view is most unfortunate as our consideration of treatment techniques will show.

Incidence of Enuresis

Professional experience with nocturnal enuresis is probably sufficient to convince most physicians and psychologists that the problem is fairly common among children and that there are a large number of bedwetters in a country as large as the United States. Estimates of the incidence of enuresis are obtainable from many sources but perhaps the best data are to be found in three surveys by Bransby, Bloomfield, and Douglas (1955) who obtained data on the prevalence of bedwetting: (1) from the parents of 1648 children who underwent routine physical exams in Birmingham, England; (2) determined the incidence of enuresis among all legitimate single born children born in the first week of March 1946 in all parts of Britain; (3) asked all mothers of children with surnames beginning with "D" for whom there was a school medical card for information on bedwetting for all their children above three years of age. Weighted averages from these three surveys were smoothed and extrapolated by Lovibond (1964) to provide the estimated age-incidence curve shown in Figure 10–1. This curve suggests that approximately one child in five is enuretic at age three. As age increases the proportion of bedwetters decreases until, at age 14, the proportion of enuretics is about 1 in 35. Using this curve, Baller (1975) estimates that there are over four million enuretic children between 3½ and 17 in the United States. Surveys have generally found the number of male enuretics to be

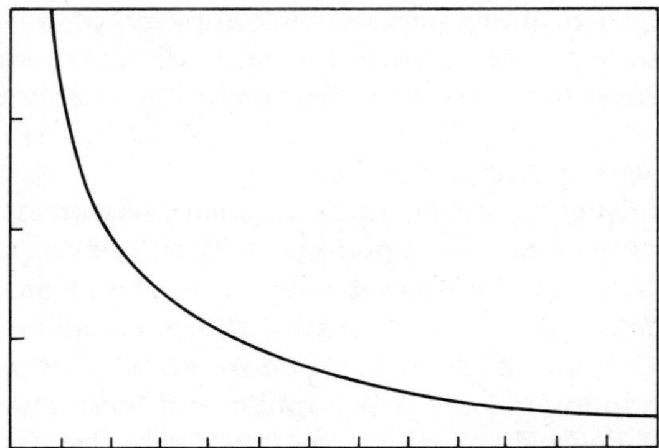

Figure 10–1. Bedwetting incidence at different ages estimated from data in Bransby et al. (1955). Curve constructed by Lovibond (1964). Reproduced from S.H. Lovibond. *Conditioning and enuresis*. Pergamon Press, Oxford, 1964 with permission.

higher than female enuretics. Baller concludes that "the ratio of males to females throughout childhood and adolescence is approximately three to two" (p. 20). By even a conservative estimate, nocturnal enuresis represents a significant childhood problem.

The fact that the prevalence of enuresis declines with increasing age may account for the widely held belief among professionals that bedwetters outgrow the "habit." Even though this is true in most cases, the odds are not as great as might be expected. If we compare the percentage figure for age 10 years with that for 14 years, the conclusion would be that a 10-year-old has approximately a 25 percent chance of becoming dry "on his own" by age 14. In my opinion, these are not great odds particularly when compared to the chances for correction of the problem by appropriate treatment.

Waiting for an individual child to "outgrow" his or her enuresis is undesirable from another standpoint: the sometimes serious psychological and emotional disruptions caused by continued bedwetting. For the bedwetter who is shamed and criticized by his parents, siblings, and peers, who is unable to go to camp or "spend the night," and who often believes that there is something "wrong" with him, betting on 25 percent odds seems to be a pretty poor chance to take. Considerable evidence exists, and is well reviewed by Baller (1975), that the bedwetter often manifests various emotional problems: poor school performance, inattentiveness, withdrawal from interpersonal relationships, lowered "self-concept," tension and anxiety, a feeling of being "odd," and a personal sense of shame and embarrassment. These difficulties most often follow persistent bedwetting and are secondary to it. Forgetting for a moment the bother of daily changing and washing bed linens and sleeping apparel, of no small matter to the bedwetter's parents, these emotional difficulties alone justify a continuing search for more effective treatment techniques.

Drug Treatment of Nocturnal Enuresis

A variety of drugs have been used to treat bedwetting but, by and large, the effects have been disappointing (Braithwaite, 1955). Brown and Ford-Smith (1941) compared a dozen different medications, including belladonna, barbital derivatives, diuretics, and ephedrine sulfate, and found none of them to be more effective than a placebo. In the 1950s amphetamines were popular and were given to combat the abnormally deep sleep which, as previously discussed, has been poisted as an important causative factor.

The relative ineffectiveness of the amphetamines was followed by the increasing popularity of imipramine (Tofranil) which occurred in the 1960s. Poussaint and Ditman (1965) conducted a placebo-controlled study of imipramine in the treatment of 47 subjects representative of enuretics typically seen by family physicians and pediatricians. A higher than usual dosage was used and the drug was gradually, rather than suddenly, withdrawn. At the end of 8 weeks, imipramine had produced a significantly greater reduction in wetting than the placebo. At this stage the dosage was increased, and the treatment response markedly improved. Eleven children (24 percent) became completely dry, and remained so when the drug was gradually withdrawn over a period of 4 to 6 weeks. Only 7 children (15 percent) showed no improvement when the drug was raised to maximum levels. Similar results were reported, again with imipramine, by Kardash, Hillman, and Werry (1968).

Generally researchers and practitioners using drugs as the sole treatment agent analyze their results in terms of a reduction in the number, or frequency, of wettings. On the other hand, workers employing conditioning treatment generally discuss their results from the standpoint of achieved cures, defined as the absence of bedwetting, and not in terms of a reduction in number of nocturnal wettings. Since the goals of those employing the two techniques seem to be different, it may not be appropriate to directly compare the two treatment procedures. However, this much seems certain—conditioning treatment has produced better results in the one study in which it has been directly compared with drugs (Forrester et al., 1964) and in general the number of cures is much higher with conditioning treatment than the usual 30 to 40 percent rate found with drug treatment.

Another problem with drug treatment is that there is usually a return of bedwetting after the medication is withdrawn (Baller, 1975). If the goal of treatment is a lasting correction, then it must be concluded that drugs have failed to successfully combat the problem of nocturnal enuresis.

In a recent discussion of 3 methods of treating bedwetting, advice and encouragement, prescribing antidepressants, and conditioning treatment, Stewart (1975) mentions the unfortunate psychological side effects of antidepressant treatment (e.g., imipramine) and the available evidence which suggests no carry over of improvement when the drug is withdrawn and concludes that caution should be exercised in using this method with children. The use of systematic advice and encouragement is recommended as the first course of action to be followed, when unsuccessful, by conditioning treatment. Stewart's position may lead to a reduction in the use of antidepressants in enuresis treatment; at least it suggests careful consideration should be given before antidepressant drugs are used.

Psychotherapeutic Treatment of Nocturnal Enuresis

Psychotherapeutic methods of treatment rely upon verbal psychotherapy with hypnosis occasionally being used as an adjunct. When psychotherapy is used, it is usually based upon the belief that enuresis is a symptom of some underlying emotional problem(s). Efforts at correction must, therefore, be aimed at locating and alleviating the problem(s), by helping the patient gain insight, rather than by direct treatment of the symptom. Both Lovibond (1964) and Baller (1975), in their important works on enuresis, conclude that the results with psychotherapy have been discouraging with the correction rate achieved by psychotherapy to be far below that obtained by conditioning treatment.

Two studies in the mid-1960s (Werry and Cohrssen, 1965; DeLeon and Mandell, 1966) made a comparison of conditioning treatment and psychotherapy in the treatment of enuresis. Werry and Cohrssen used subjects referred to an enuresis clinic who had never been dry for more than three months and who exhibited a wetting frequency of, at least, once per week. A no-treatment group was told that mothers would be contacted after four months to check on the child's progress. A brief psychotherapy group received six to eight sessions of psychodynamically oriented supportive psychotherapy while a conditioning group was treated by a buzzer apparatus in their homes. The results showed significantly greater improvement for the conditioning group with 17 of 21 subjects (81 percent) rated "improved," "greatly improved," or "cured" while only 7 of 21 (33 percent) subjects in the brief psychotherapy group were correspondingly rated.

In the DeLeon and Mandell study, the subjects were 85 children of both sexes, aged 5 to 14, who were referred to a mental health center with a diagnosis of functional enuresis. Three groups were used: conditioning treatment, psychotherapy-counseling, and a control group. The conditioning group received treatment in their homes while the psychotherapy-counseling group were seen for 12 sessions on a weekly basis with 40 minutes of each session with the child alone and 20 minutes with the mother alone. The percentage of subjects reaching the success criterion (13 successive dry nights) in the three groups was as follows: conditioning—86.3, psychotherapy-counseling—18.2, and control—11.1.

While the results of these two studies do not permit the conclusion that psychotherapy per se is ineffective in treating enuresis, they do suggest that those who regard psychotherapy as the treatment of choice for enuresis might wish to rethink their position. It would seem unwise to prefer, as the treatment of choice, a method that produces success in only about 10 to 35 percent of cases while a method that produces a success figure of over 80 percent is available.

Conditioning Treatment of Nocturnal Enuresis

Conditioning treatment of nocturnal enuresis began in 1938 when Mowrer and Mowrer improved upon the apparatus and procedure reported by Pfaundler (1904). After a decade of inattention, interest in the conditioning technique was revived in the 1950s and since that time a large number of investigations have been reported which have sought to improve the procedure and to increase the success rate when it is used. It is possible to group the chief contributions of these investigations into the following categories:

1. Interested in improving the technological aspects of the treatment, especially in improving the pad design (Coote, 1965; Davidson and Douglas, 1950; Seiger, 1952).
2. Interested in seeing the technique more widely used (Baller, 1975; Geppert, 1953; Lovibond, 1964).
3. Called for close supervision of the apparatus user during treatment (Baller and Schalock, 1956; Baller, 1975; Lovibond, 1964; Yates, 1975).
4. Collected questionnaire data on the success of treatment by parents who used a commercially sold conditioning device (Martin and Kubly, 1955).
5. Proposed a reformulation of the theoretical basis of conditioning treatment (Crosby, 1950; Lovibond, 1964; Yates, 1975).
6. Interested in decreasing the amount of time required for successful conditioning (Azrin, Sneed, and Foxx, 1974; Kennedy and Sloop, 1968; Lovibond, 1964; Young and Turner, 1965).
7. Extended the technique to the institutionalized mentally retarded (Deacon, 1939; Sloop and Kennedy, 1973).
8. Extended the technique to the treatment of adults (Turner and Taylor, 1974).
9. Attempted to reduce the relapse rate (Baller, 1975; Finley et al., 1973; Lovibond, 1964; Turner, Young, and Rachman, 1970).
10. Compared conditioning treatment to other treatment techniques (DeLeon and Mandell, 1966; Forrester, Stein, and Susser, 1964; Werry and Cohrssen, 1965).
11. Determined if conditioning treatment led to "symptom substitution" (Baker, 1969; Baller, 1975; Lovibond, 1964).
12. Compared the response of "primary" and "secondary" enuretics to conditioning treatment (Sacks and DeLeon, 1973).

A detailed review of each of the studies in these categories is well beyond the scope of this chapter and the interested reader is referred to Baller (1975), Lovibond (1964), Lovibond and Coote (1970), and Yates (1970, 1975) for a more in-depth discussion of the issues raised in these studies.

Table 10–1 presents a compilation of 25 studies published since 1938 which have reported the results of conditioning treatment of nocturnal enuresis. These studies indicate an initial arrest of the problem of enuresis in slightly more than 80 percent of the children to which it has been applied and an initial failure rate of slightly more than 19 percent. These results have been obtained by investigators with different goals in studying conditioning treatment, with a wide variety of children, including the institutionalized mentally retarded, and with varying criterion for arrest of nighttime bedwetting. Taken as a group, they suggest very clearly that conditioning treatment is highly successful in correcting the problem of enuresis since all of these studies used a criterion of complete remission of the habit rather than a reduction in the frequency of wetting as is often true when drug therapy or psychotherapy is used. It would appear safe to conclude, then, that conditioning treatment is the treatment of choice for nocturnal enuresis as no other well-studied technique has thus far produced comparable results.

The relapse rate, of approximately 25 percent, has, as noted earlier, occupied the attention of several researchers. Although various criteria for determining relapse have been used, there seems to be a tendency among workers in the field to define a subject as having relapsed if he returns to the pretreatment level of wetting or if he consistently wets the bed more than one night per week. Despite several efforts to reduce the relapse rate (Baller, 1975; Lovibond, 1964; Turner, Young, and Rachman, 1970) it still remains one of the perplexing aspects of this form of treatment. Considering the relapse rate, it can be concluded from the studies in Table 10–1 that conditioning treatment resulted in a more or less complete "cure" in approximately 55 percent of the nocturnal enuretics with which it has been used with the possible exception of the institutionalized mentally retarded (Sloop and Kennedy, 1973). Even after the relapse rate is considered, this form of treatment appears to result in a relatively permanent "cure" in 55 percent of the cases which is still vastly superior to the results obtained with other treatment modalities.

Baller (1975) reports a 12 year follow-up study of 55 subjects originally treated by Baller and Schalock (1956). He found that approximately 45 percent of the subjects who attained the initial criterion of dryness (14 consecutive dry nights) sustained the correction

Table 10–1. Results of Conditioning Treatment of Enuresis

Investigator	*N*	*% Initial Arrest*	*% Initial Failure*	*% Relapses*	*Follow-up in Months*
Baller and Schalock (1956)	55	98	2	48	24–40
Behrle et al. (1956)	19	100	0	32	18–39
Biering and Jespersen (1959)	21	71?	29?	20?	6– ?
Bostock (1954)	11	82	18	11	1–20
Coote (1962)[a]	216	98	2	20	1– 6
Crosby (1950)	58	90	10	8?	6–30
Davidson and Douglas (1950)	20	75	25	13	5– 9
Deacon (1939)[b]	7	85	15	---	-----
DeLeon and Mandell (1966)	56	86	14	79.6[c]	1–22
Dibden and Holmes (1955)	26	88	12	52	9–54
Forrester et al. (1964)	16	62	38	---	-----
Freyman (1963)	71	65	35	35	12?
Geppert (1953)	42	90	10	13	?
Gillison & Skinner (1958)	100	90	10	14	4–12
Kahane (1955)	21	100	0	62	1– 7
Lowe (1960)[d]	769	87	13	---	-----
Martin and Kubly (1955)	118	56	44?	---	-----
Morgan and Witmer (1939)	5	80	20	---	-----
Mowrer and Mowrer (1938)	30	100	0	---	-----
Murray (1960)[d]	33	75	25	---	-----
Seiger (1952)	108	93	7	9?	2–36
Sloop and Kennedy (1973)[b]	21	52	48	36	7–12
Taylor (1963)	100	64	36	---	6– ?
Young and Turner (1965)	105	63	35	12	12
Wickes (1958)	100	65	35	14	?
Conditioning Means[e]		80.3	19.5	24.9	6–24

[a]Personal communication to Lovibond (1964, p. 56).
[b]Used institutionalized mentally retarded subjects.
[c]Used a single wet night as a relapse criterion.
[d]Personal communication to Jones (1960, p. 400).
[e]Does not include numbers from DeLeon and Mandell (1966).

throughout the entire 12 year period. There were 13 subjects who repeated conditioning treatment once, after which they remained dry for six or more years. When these 13 subjects are combined with the group who remained continuously dry, the percentage of long-term dryness is approximately 78 percent. Baller recommends that the possibility of relapse be considered when initiating conditioning treatment and advises that the patient and his parents be told that two trials of conditioning treatment may be required to correct the habit. Even though the response of relapsed subjects is somewhat variable, it would appear that slightly more than 50 percent of relapsed patients who are retreated will achieve consistent dryness (Baller, 1975; Freyman, 1963; Lovibond, 1964).

His study of the relapse problem has led Baller (1975) to conclude that there are two broad categories, patient-environment factors and placement and supervision factors, that contribute to relapses. The following are listed as patient-environment factors that contribute to a relapse:

1. Persistent *blame* on the part of parents and/or other adults directed toward the bedwetter.
2. Continuing threats of *rejection* if the bedwetter does not respond promptly to treatment.
3. *Ridicule.*
4. Poorly hidden *skepticism* on the part of the family that correction will be achieved and endure.
5. *Neglect* on the part of parents in assisting and supervising the use of the conditioning equipment.
6. *Carelessness* in observing a regular bedtime leading to fatigue.
7. *Nonavoidance of emotionally disturbing or stressful experiences.*
8. *Excessive demands* imposed by the school or apparent rejection and/or ridicule by the teacher.
9. *Limited cooperation* with the professional supervising the treatment.
10. *Organic ailment* not accurately diagnosed by the physician.

Placement and supervision errors by the professional supervising the treatment are listed as follows:

1. Ineffective presentation of the method by using language not understood by the patient and his family, failure to have all family members present when the treatment program is discussed, and inadequate demonstration of how the equipment works.
2. Failure to communicate to the patient that the supervisor or counselor is concerned about him and wishes him to succeed.

3. Failure to provide conscientious, systematic follow-up of the treatment program.
4. Exaggerated claims for the chances of success.
5. Overemphasis on the speed with which a patient can achieve dryness.
6. Exaggerated praise given to a patient before the dryness criterion is reached.

The presence of these factors can add to the likelihood of relapse and the professional supervising the treatment must be aware of their negative influence and attempt to prevent their occurrence.

Apparatus. There are two basic types of apparatus, the so-called "Mowrer" type which consists of either a "sandwich" arrangement of two foil pads (as in the units sold commercially by Sears and Montgomery-Ward) separated by a sheet of some type of thin, absorbent material and a flexible, usually rubber or molded neoprene, pad which has the electrode wire bonded to the pad, as in the Seiger (1952) structure, or recessed into the material, as in the pad designed by Coote (1965). The pads are connected to a buzzer or bell box by lead wires and electrical power to operate the unit comes from either a dry cell battery, contained in the box containing the bell or buzzer, or from ordinary household current. In the Mowrer, or sandwich, type of pad arrangement, the circuit is completed when urine passes through the top foil pad and soaks the thin separating sheet. In the Seiger-type device, the circuit is completed when urine contacts adjacent wire filaments. Although superiority is claimed for each type of apparatus, the most important characteristics are reliability, durability, and safety. The Seiger-type pad arrangement is probably more durable but no more reliable than the sandwich type and may be less safe as it can produce electrode burns if the subject's bare skin comes in contact with the wire filaments. The Coote pad overcomes this danger with recessed electrodes without sacrificing durability and reliability. Generally, the sandwich-type apparatus is less expensive than the Seiger type and is sometimes preferred for that reason.

Conducting Conditioning Treatment of Nocturnal Enuresis

The author has always been impressed with the reluctance shown by many in his own profession and those in medicine to become involved in the supervision of the conditioning treatment of nocturnal enuresis. Following is an overview of the strategy that I have followed, over the past 10 years, in treating hundreds of bedwetters.

Hopefully, the reader will consider the procedure both appropriately simple and systematic, and will venture into the conduct of this very successful treatment regimen.

Physical Examination. An adequate physical examination is a prerequisite for any treatment using a conditioning device. Nonmedical practitioners are especially cautioned not to proceed with treatment until they are assured that no organic cause of the enuresis exists.

Session 1. The bedwetter and his parents are seen *together* at the first session. Often siblings are included but a decision about their involvement must be made on the basis of some understanding about the workings of the family. A detailed history of the problem is taken along with an estimate of the number of nights per week bedwetting occurs. The methods of dealing with the problem which have been previously tried are discussed. At this point in the interview, the child is directly addressed and is asked for his opinion about the problem. This is done to impress upon both the child and his parents that he is the central figure in what is to happen. I usually indicate, at this point, that approximately 10 percent of children between the ages of 4 and 14 are bedwetters with the number of boys slightly higher than that of girls. It is also mentioned that the bedwetting is not being done intentionally but is a "habit" that the bedwetter has not been able to break but that there is a device that can "teach" the bedwetter to break the habit. At this point, the conditioning device is shown to the child and his parents and its use is demonstrated.[1] The device is set up and a drop of saline solution is used to trigger the alarm. The child and his parents are asked to repeat this step while placing one hand on the pad to assure them that there is no danger of shock from the device. The steps necessary to reset the device after a wetting episode are then fully and carefully discussed along with the necessity of the bedwetter going to the toilet to finish urinating after a buzzer activation. With children of nine or older, or younger children who are quite mature, it is emphasized that the child should assume responsibility for his own treatment with the parents serving in a monitoring or supervising role. The importance of the parents role is emphasized to them and it is freely acknowledged that one or both will have to endure a period of sleep disruption if the program is to be successful.

1. A list of suppliers of conditioning devices is available by writing the author, E. Wayne Sloop, Lynchburg Training School & Hospital, P.O. Box 1098, Lynchburg, Virginia 24505.

Data sheets are then provided to the child and his parents and the correct way of filling them out is explained. Figure 10–2 shows the data sheet that we have found to be useful in collecting the information necessary to supervise the treatment program. The importance of record keeping is explained to both the child and his parents and they are told that the data are to be brought in at each subsequent visit.

The success of this method of treatment is discussed with parents and child being told that 80 percent of the children who are treated by this method are able to reach a criterion of 14 successive dry nights. The possibility of a relapse, i.e., a return to a pattern of wetting the bed at least once per week, is discussed and it is emphasized that two conditioning periods may be necessary to determine if the treatment will have a lasting success.

The child and his parents are then told that the usual treatment period is from 8 to 12 weeks and that the program can be expected to last that long. Three signs of success are then described: (1) decreasing size of the wet spot (size of wet spot is estimated as follows: large = 12 inches or more in diameter; medium = 6 inches to 12 inches in diameter; small = less than 3 to 6 inches in diameter); (2) progressively later times of the wetting episodes; (3) the tendency of the child to awaken to void without wetting the bed. Awakening to void is defined as a "success" as is sleeping through the night without voiding. Fluid restriction, if it is being practiced is discontinued, and, in fact, the child is encouraged to drink fluids before bed in order to maximize the number of buzzer activations. The child is asked to sleep without pajama bottoms while the program is in effect.

After answering any questions presented by either the child or his parents, an appointment for a second session, preferably in one week's time, is made. The child-patient and his parents are encouraged to telephone, or come by for a visit, if problems develop in the interim.

Session 2. Usually a brief session is held a week to ten days after the initial session. The data sheets are brought in and reviewed for accuracy and errors in data recording are cleared up. If, during the first week, the child has had only one bedwetting episode, it is noted that he is not a particularly "good" bedwetter and that the treatment might take slightly longer than usual. Problems with the apparatus, such as "false alarms" (buzzer activations in the absence of urination) are discussed and suggestions for their solution are made. The individual assuming major responsibility for the treatment program, either the child or one of his parents, is asked to call in one week to

Subject ______________________ Age ______________

Date	Dry Night	Spot Size			Time	Ease of Awakening		
Mo / Day	XXXXXXXXXX	L	M	S	XXXX	Bell Awake	Easy Awake	Hard Awake

Figure 10−2. Enuresis data sheets used in conducting conditioning treatment of enuresis.

report the data recorded and a follow-up session is scheduled in two weeks.

Session 3. By the time of the third appointment, the program will have been in effect for three weeks, or slightly longer, and there should be indications of the likely response. A number of dry nights should have been observed, even in a frequent bedwetter, the time of wetting should be getting slightly later, and the amount of urine voided in each episode, indicated indirectly by the size of wet spot, should be decreasing. Session 3, and subsequent sessions, are usually fairly short and consist of data sheet analysis and encouragement to the child and his parents that the program is going according to schedule. A session is scheduled for one month's time and, in the interim, weekly calls, to indicate the data sheet recordings, are arranged.

Session 4 or Final Session. Session 4 is held seven weeks after initiation of the program and many patients will have reached the 14 successive dry nights criterion by this time or will be making steady progress toward it. The child and his parents are asked to continue weekly telephone contact and to be sure to let me know when the dryness criterion is reached. I customarily schedule a child for a visit within a few days of his reaching dryness and encourage the parents to "celebrate" this event with the child. The possibility of relapse, which is defined as a return to the prior level of wetting or to wetting at least once per week, is thoroughly explained and arrangements are made for a second course of treatment. The occurrence of occasional wet nights due to stress, fatigue, or a change in family routine is clearly pointed out so that the child-patient and his parents will not be unduly concerned if these occur. The child and his parents are instructed to contact me as soon as they feel a relapse is occurring so that plans can be made to deal with it.

A decade of following the format just outlined has led to success with approximately 90 percent of the enuretic children with whom I have worked. It can be seen that the entire treatment program is carefully supervised as is clearly recommended by Baller (1975) and Lovibond and Coote (1970). *Careful supervision is a must in order to maximize the chances for success with this program.* I would judge that relapses have been experienced in approximately 25 percent of the cases and that most of these, if they chose a second course of treatment, have been successfully corrected after a second trial. I would encourage those who work with enuretic children to seriously consider becoming involved in this highly successful and rewarding type of treatment program.

A Word About Symptom Substitution

As noted in an earlier section, practitioners influenced by a psychodynamic view will often oppose conditioning treatment on the basis that it represents a treatment of the symptom only and does not attack the underlying cause of the bedwetting problem. For example, Sperling (1965) states, "The removal of the symptom of enuresis without providing other outlets for the child, leads to a replacement by other symptoms. . . ." (p. 30). The evidence presented by various investigators (Baker, 1969; Baller, 1975; Baller and Schalock, 1956; Lovibond, 1964; Lovibond and Coote, 1970; Werry and Cohrssen, 1965) argues strongly against this belief. In fact, I have not found a single documented report of the occurrence of symptom substitution when enuresis is treated by the conditioning method.

Baker (1969) has recently conducted a controlled investigation which assessed the adjustment of enuretic children immediately after removal of the symptom by conditioning treatment. Several indices of patient adjustment were used including: *parent* measures (composed of an Adjective Check List and Behavior Problem Record); *teacher*'s ratings (composed of 67 items) which were completed just before treatment began for the enuretic subjects, 10 weeks after treatment began, and 22 weeks after treatment began; and *child* measures (a test battery including the DAP, Draw Your Family, a Self-Image questionnaire designed by the author, and the Neurotic Inventory devised and employed with enuretics by Lovibond [1964]). Control procedures were employed to disguise the purpose of the various measures from parents, teachers, and children. The enuretic and control subjects did not differ significantly on any of the pretreatment measures. Subsequent to treatment, test measures did not indicate a worsening in adjustment for enuretic subjects treated by conditioning as would be expected following the symptom substitution hypothesis. In fact on parent measures, some aspects of teacher's ratings, and on the Self-Image questionnaire and the Neurotic Inventory, cured enuretics showed significantly greater improvement than their controls. Finally, the drawings showed a pronounced improvement in the "self-image" of the cured enuretic child.

In summary, it may be said that no case of symptom substitution has yet been reported and almost all investigators report that a number of their subjects have exhibited favorable personality changes as the result of conditioning treatment. In light of this fact it would seem that the symptom substitution hypothesis, long used as an argument against the conditioning treatment of enuresis, is untenable. In any case, the burden of proof would now seem to rest with the proponents of the symptom substitution hypothesis.

Diurnal Bladder Tolerance Training as a Treatment for Enuresis

Kimmel and Kimmel (1970) presented an "instrumental" method for treating enuresis which is similar to the procedure proposed by Muellner (1960). In Muellner's technique bedwetters are required to practice the "holding" of urine after the ingestion of increased quantities of fluid during the daytime. The purpose of this regime is to increase the functional capacity of the bladder, a deficiency which is seen by Muellner as the essential cause of enuresis. Kimmel and Kimmel, without citing Muellner, expanded upon this technique by involving the child's parents who are told by the child when the urge to urinate occurs. The parent then instructs the child to "hold it in" for a short period of time, say five minutes. The child is promised a reward if this is done. When the time expires, the child is rewarded and permitted to urinate. The time is gradually increased up to as much as 30 minutes. In the original report, the successful treatment of three females within seven days is described. In a later report, Paschalis, Kimmel, and Kimmel (1972) describe the treatment of 31 enuretic children with a more systematic 45 minute delay of urination being used. Training took 20 days and 15 of the children were completely free of enuresis and 8 more showed significant improvement at a three month follow-up. Stedman (1972) applied the Kimmel technique with a 13-year-old girl whom he asked to self-record her frequency of daytime urination and nighttime wettings and to delay urination during the day for up to 30 minutes. Stedman used only social reinforcement (praise) and informational feedback from her own record keeping as rewards for his patient rather than tangible rewards used by Kimmel and Kimmel and Paschalis et al. Nocturnal enuresis was eliminated after a 12-week training period and only four instances of wetting occurred during a 3-month follow-up. Miller (1973) applied the Kimmel technique, which he modified and renamed "Retention Control Training," to two institutionalized enuretics with complete success after 14 weeks with a 13-year-old male and 16 weeks with a 14-year-old female.

Yates (1975) in his recent discussion of enuresis treatment concludes that both the Kimmel technique and the nighttime conditioning treatment technique are successful because they increase the functional bladder capacity of the enuretic. He cites Starfield and Mellits' (1968) work as evidence that enuresis results from a bladder of functionally small capacity in which there is a failure of the detrusor muscle to adapt to increasing bladder volumes and pressures and in which the detrusor muscle triggers off reflex urination at low volumes and pressures. Yates believes, then, that for nocturnal enuresis to be successfully overcome the functional capacity of the bladder must be trained to adapt to increasing volumes and pressures of urine. The Kimmel technique accomplishes this to some extent, as shown in a recent study with a 3½-year-old female (Doleys and Wells, 1975), although it would be somewhat surprising, according to Yates, if completely satisfactory results were obtained since this technique relies on a "carry-over" from daytime training to nighttime control. Yates concludes that the conditioning technique has an advantage, over the Kimmel technique, since it operates directly on the events occurring during sleep by producing direct inhibition of detrusor muscle activity at the moment of wetting and then relying on this inhibition to generalize to earlier stages of detrusor muscle activity. "In other words, the Mowrer technique [conditioning treatment] directly trains the detrusor muscle activity to induce sphincter contraction rather than sphincter relaxation, and achievement of this latter state of affairs automatically guarantees dryness" (Yates, 1975, p. 85).

While the results with the Kimmel technique are impressive, its effectiveness remains to be demonstrated with large numbers of enuretic children as has been done with conditioning treatment. An interesting, and valuable, research program would involve the combination of these two procedures with perhaps improved results. Until further research is conducted with the Kimmel technique, it must be concluded that conditioning treatment, when only a single treatment program is to be used, should be the treatment of choice.

TOILET TRAINING THE "NORMAL" CHILD

Toilet training is given considerable attention in our society by both parents and professionals who deal with children. Until very recently, practitioners of behavior modification or behavior therapy had neglected this area of child development. Nathan Azrin and Richard Foxx, at the Behavior Research Laboratory at Anna State Hospital in Illinois, reported the development of a technique for a rapid toilet training of the institutionalized mentally retarded in 1971 (Azrin and Foxx, 1971) which proved capable of teaching appropriate toileting behavior in three or four days rather than months or years as had formerly been true. This technique has been modified to produce the set of procedures for normal or slightly retarded children which are described in *Toilet Training in Less Than a Day* (Azrin and Foxx, 1974). Our discussion in this section will summarize these procedures and explore their possible use by the physician and psychologist who may be confronted with the problem of toilet training in their clinical practice.

Historically, the attempt to apply behavioral techniques to the toilet training of "normal" children began in 1965 in studies reported by Madsen (1965) and Pumroy and Pumroy (1965) even though such procedures had been used with the institutionalized mentally retarded a year before (Dayan, 1964). Madsen described the use of positive reinforcement, consisting of candy and praise, verbal instruction by the parents, and report by the child of her need to urinate in toilet training a 19-month-old girl in 12 days. Pumroy and Pumroy used similar procedures in training their own children, a 26-month-old male and a 29-month-old female, in about four months.

Madsen and his colleagues (Madsen, Hoffman, Thomas, Koropsak, and Madsen, 1969), compared reinforcement techniques, transistorized buzzer pants, buzzer pants plus reinforcement techniques, and "parents methods" in a systematic study and found that the parents using reinforcement (treats plus praise) and reinforcement plus buzzer pants were more successful over a four week period in reducing accidents and in increasing successes than were parents in the other groups. Mahoney, Van Wagenen, and Meyerson (1971) reported the successful training of seven children, three of normal intelligence and four retarded children, by using a urine sensing device to provide auditory feedback to the subjects when wetting occurred. They also broke the chain of behaviors required in appropriate toileting into five components: walking to the commode, lowering pants, sitting or standing properly at the commode, eliminating in the commode, and pulling up pants. No additional reports of the application of behavioral approaches to toilet training normal children appeared until Foxx and Azrin (1973) reported on their "Dry Pants" method.

The "Dry Pants" method represents a preliminary version of the expanded program described in *Toilet Training in Less Than a Day.* In this report, 34 children were trained by two female trainers in their own homes. The children, 22 boys and 12 girls, averaged 25 months of age (range = 20–36 months) and all were trained to self-initiate appropriate toileting behavior; i.e., to toilet themselves completely without being prompted by the trainer, in an average of 3.9 hours. Prior to training, the children averaged about six accidents per day per child but after the first week of training, accidents had decreased by 97 percent (0.2 accidents per day per child) according to data kept by their parents. This near-zero level of accidents was maintained during a four month follow-up. The older children in the study, aged 26–36 months, were trained in a total training time of about 2¼ hours while the 20–25-month-old group took about 5 hours to train. Girls were observed to train somewhat faster than boys.

The procedures followed in the Foxx and Azrin (1973) study are described in more detail, and also in simpler terms, and constitute the central content of *Toilet Training in Less Than a Day.* Let us now turn to a summarization of the major strategies described in this book.

The overall objective is to teach the child to independently toilet himself. Several teaching aids are obtained prior to beginning. These include: a hollow doll that wets, a well-designed potty chair with a pot that is removed from the top rather than from the back, tasty drinks, candies and other treats, and several pairs of loosely fitting training pants. The following twelve procedures are then presented for the parent-trainer:

1. Give the child all he wants to drink in order to increase the number of urinations during training.
2. Conduct the training in a distraction-free part of the home.
3. Have the child practice walking to the potty chair and practice raising and lowering his pants himself.
4. Teach the child to sit quietly while on the chair.
5. Give very brief and simple instructions.
6. Use the doll that wets to teach by imitation by demonstrating how the doll potties herself correctly.
7. Have the child teach the doll how to potty.
8. Use gentle manual guidance when the child does not respond to an instruction.
9. To motivate the child to potty correctly, show approval by praising, hugging, and giving edible rewards.
10. Teach the child that others important to him will give approval for correct pottying.
11. Continually communicate pleasure to the child for his dry, i.e., "clean," state.
12. Show disapproval when an accident occurs, either during or after training, require the child to change his wet clothing, and have him practice the various pottying actions.

These 12 procedures are the crucial aspects of the program and the rationale behind them is given.

Azrin and Foxx note that several conditions must exist before a child is likely to respond favorably to the training procedure. They suggest that children less than 20 months of age are probably too young for training since youngsters below this age are probably not physiologically and psychologically "ready" for toilet training. Of course, medical advice is to be sought if the parent suspects any physical problem that might affect the child's ability to be trained. An Instructional Readiness test, consisting of 10 simple actions (e.g., point to your nose, sit down on a chair), is given to determine if the child has sufficient social responsiveness, understanding, and adequate language development to respond to training. If the child fails more than 2 of the 10 tasks on the Instructional Readiness test, training should be postponed.

The entire sequence of steps, along with detailed instructions for the parent-trainer, are then given and will not be repeated here. In general though, the procedure begins by using the doll and, after the doll wets, the parent demonstrates correct pottying actions and then has the child teach the doll. The doll is generally used for about one hour, during which time the child is taught to empty the pot in the toilet and to flush it, and then the parent begins "Dry-Pants" inspections every few minutes. The child is required to feel his pants to determine if they are dry and, if so, a drink and/or a treat are given. Dry-Pants inspections are continued every three to five minutes whenever other instructions are not being given. Throughout the procedure, as much of the different beverages are given as the child wants in order to create the desire to urinate.

Following the beginning of Dry-Pants inspections, prompted potty trials, during which all necessary pottying actions are performed, are given about 15 minutes until the child is not having difficulty with any of the pottying actions. The child should remain seated on the potty chair for about 10 minutes for the first few prompted potty trials. Between potty trials, the parent-trainer should observe carefully in order to detect any signs of the desire to urinate. When these signs occur, the child should be immediately prompted to potty. During this process it is very important for the parent-trainer to detect urinations in the potty so that they may be immediately reinforced and suggestions to aid in detecting urinations in the potty are given.

During prompted potty trials, two other procedures. "Friends-Who-Care" (like father, brother, grandparents) and a great deal of verbal rehearsal (going over verbally all aspects of pottying) are used. The prompted potty trials continue until the child responds by going to the potty when general questions like "Billy, are your pants dry?" are asked. Termination of approval for pottying occurs when the child has urinated appropriately, pulled up his pants, emptied the potty, flushed the toilet, and returned the potty to the training area. Thereafter approval is given only for dry pants.

When accidents occur during training a verbal reprimand is given, expressing the parent-trainer's displeasure, followed by 10 Positive Practice trials in which the child goes to the potty, lowers his pants, sits for only a second or two, arises, pulls up his pants and goes to another location in the house to repeat the sequence. Immediately after the Positive Practice trials, at least 10 pants inspections are performed by the child at the instruction of the parent-trainer. After the last wet-pants inspection the child is required to change into clean dry pants.

The procedures briefly described above are the essential aspects of the training program and a child is considered trained when he walks to the potty chair for the first time without a reminder and completes the entire toileting experience without the need for instructions or guidance. After training six to seven pants inspections are made daily and "dry" pants receive praise but not snacks, treats, or drink. The pants inspections are discontinued after one week with no accidents.

The Azrin-Foxx procedure maximizes the conditions for the learning of toileting skills and, no doubt, will achieve a high degree of success if correctly applied. However, as Kimmel (1974) has pointed out, parts of the procedure are subtle, and many parents may lack the requisite self control required for successful training. In addition, it would seem that at least a high school reading level would be needed to adequately understand the book. I would also expect that most parents would need to read the book several times, and actively study it, in order to conduct the training smoothly and to avoid errors in following the procedures. My impression, gained by talking with about a dozen parents who have used the book, is that approximately 50 percent of parents are successful using just the book.

Thus far only one study (Butler, 1976) has appeared which attempts to evaluate the success of parents using the book with only very minimal supervision. Butler offered three classes, one a week for three weeks, to parents of 49 children who used the book in training their children. The first class focused on the necessary pretraining activities needed for toilet training (Azrin and Foxx, 1974, pp. 17–48), the second on the toilet training procedures themselves (pp. 49–97), and the third, a review of the training day procedures and after training procedures. During the last class, parents selected a training date and those who requested being able to call daily for two weeks after training and for eight weeks of follow-up were requested to keep certain records during and after training. Butler provided a written form outlining the training day procedures, after training procedures, and the records to be kept during and after training to be used by the parents along with the book. Butler found that 77 percent of the parents were able to successfully train their children, and to maintain the training over a two-month follow-up, using only the book, the written information he provided, and the three classes. Foxx and Azrin (1973) found the average time for training was about 4 hours with girls training slightly faster than boys. Butler found that the parents in his study required about 4½ hours (range = 1¼ to 10 hours) to complete training with boys training slightly faster than girls. In Butler's study, children over 25 months trained in about 4 hours while those under 25 months required about 5¼ hours which is consistent with the findings of Foxx and Azrin (1973). Butler's findings are quite impressive for a procedure that was learned through reading the book, attending three lectures, and using some additional written materials provided by him.

The effectiveness of the Azrin-Foxx method of toilet training normal children is yet to be determined with a large number of children. Obviously, the method can be highly successful when carried out by experienced trainers (Foxx and Azrin, 1973) and appears to be very successful when parents are given only minimal assistance by a professional (Butler, 1976).

REFERENCES

Azrin, N.H., & Foxx, R.M. A rapid method of toilet training the institutionalized retarded. *Journal of Applied Behavior Analysis*, 1971, *4*, 89–99.

Azrin, N.H., & Foxx, R.M. *Toilet training in less than a day.* New York: Simon and Schuster, 1974.

Azrin, N.H., Sneed, T.J., & Foxx, R.M. Dry-bed training: Rapid elimination of childhood enuresis. *Behaviour Research and Therapy*, 1974, *12*, 147–156.

Baker, B.L. Symptom treatment and symptom substitution in enuresis. *Journal of Abnormal Psychology*, 1969, *74*, 42–49.

Baller, W.R. *Bed-wetting: Origins and treatment.* New York: Pergamon, 1975.

Baller, W.R., & Schalock, H.D. Conditioned response treatment of enuresis. *Exceptional Children*, 1957, *22*, 233–236.

Behrle, F.C., Elkin, M.T., & Laybourne, P.C. Evaluation of a conditioning device in the treatment of nocturnal enuresis. *Pediatrics*, 1956, *17*, 849–855.

Bental, E. Dissociation of behavioral and electroencephalic sleep in two brothers with *enuresis nocturna. Journal of Psychosomatic Research*, 1961, *5*, 116–119.

Biering, A., & Jespersen, I. The treatment of enuresis nocturna with conditioning devices. *Acta Pediatrica*, 1959, *48*, Suppl. 118, 152–153.

Bostock, J. Use of Watvic machine in enuresis. Report of cases. *Medical Journal of Australia*, 1954 2, 141–143.

Boyd, M.M.M. The depth of sleep in enuretic school children and in non-enuretic controls. *Journal of Psychosomatic Research*, 1960, *4*, 274–281.

Braithwaite, J.V. Some problems connected with enuresis. *Proceedings, Royal Society of Medicine*, 1955, *49*, 33–38.

Bransby, E.R., Blomfield, J.M., & Douglas, J.W.B. The prevalence of bed-wetting. *Medical Officer*, 1955, *94*, 5–7.

Brown, R.C., & Ford-Smith, A. Enuresis in adolescents. *British Medical Journal*, 1941, *2*, 803–805.

Butler, J.R. The toilet training success of parents after reading *Toilet training in less than a day*. *Behavior Therapy*, 1976, *7*, 185–191.

Coote, M.A. Apparatus for conditioning treatment of enuresis. *Behaviour Research & Therapy*, 1965, *2*, 233–238.

Crosby, N.D. Essential enuresis: Successful treatment based on physiological concepts. *Medical Journal of Australia*, 1950, *2*, 533–543.

Davidson, J.R., & Douglas, E. Nocturnal enuresis: A special approach to treatment. *British Medical Journal*, 1950, *1*, 1345–1347.

Dayan, M. Toilet training retarded children in the state residential institution. *Mental Retardation*, 1964, *2*, 116–117.

Deacon, J.R. The conditioned habit treatment of nocturnal enuretics. *Proceedings, American Association of Mental Deficiency*, 1939, *44*, 133–138.

DeLeon, G., & Mandell, W. The treatment of functional enuresis. *Journal of Clinical Psychology*, 1966, *22*, 326–330.

Dibden, W.A., & Holmes, M.A. Enuresis: A survey of its treatment by the "Dri-Nite" apparatus. *Clinical Reports, Adelaide Children's Hospital*, 1955, *2*, 247–255.

Ditman, K.S., & Blinn, K.A. Sleep levels in enuresis. *American Journal of Psychiatry*, 1955, *11*, 913–920.

Doleys, D.M., & Wells, K.C. Changes in functional bladder capacity and bed-wetting during and after retention control training: A case study. *Behavior Therapy*, 1975, *6*, 685–688.

Finley, W.W., Besserman, R.L., Bennett, F.L., Clapp, R.K., & Finley, P.K. The effect of continuous, intermittent, and "placebo" reinforcement on the effectiveness of the conditioning treatment for enuresis nocturna. *Behaviour Research and Therapy*, 1973, *11*, 289–297.

Forrester, R.M., Stein, A., & Susser, H.W. A trial of conditioning therapy in nocturnal enuresis. *Developmental Medicine and Child Neurology*, 1964, *6*, 158–166.

Foxx, R.M., & Azrin, N.H. Dry pants: A rapid method of toilet training children. *Behaviour Research and Therapy*, 1973, *11*, 435–442.

Freyman, R. Follow-up study of enuresis treated with a bell apparatus. *Journal of Child Psychology and Psychiatry*, 1963, *4*, 199–206.

Geppert, T.V. Management of nocturnal enuresis by conditioned response. *Journal of the American Medical Association*, 1953, *152*, 381–383.

Gillison, T.H., & Skinner, J.L. Treatment of nocturnal enuresis by the electric alarm. *British Medical Journal*, 1958, *2*, 1268–1272.

Glicklich, L.B. An historical account of enuresis. *Pediatrics*, 1951, *8*, 859.

Helsborg, H.C. Studies on hereditary and electroencephalographic pattern in enuresis. *Uresk Laeger*, 1950, *112*, 256.

Jones, H.G. The behavioral treatment of enuresis nocturna. In H.J. Eysenck (Ed.), *Behaviour therapy and the neuroses.* Oxford: Pergamon, 1960.

Kahane, M. An experimental investigation of a conditioning treatment and a preliminary study of the psychoanalytic theory of the etiology of nocturnal enuresis. *American Psychologist*, 1955, *10*, 369–370. (Abstract).

Kardash, S., Hillman, E.S., & Werry, J. Efficacy of imipramine in childhood enuresis: A double-blind control study with placebo. *Canadian Medical Association Journal*, 1968, *99*, 263–266.

Kennedy, W.A., & Sloop, E.W. Methedrine as an adjunct to conditioning treatment of nocturnal enuresis in normal and institutionalized retarded subjects. *Psychological Reports*, 1968, *22*, 997–1000.

Kimmel, H.D. Review of "Toilet training in less than a day." *Journal of Behavior Therapy and Experimental Psychiatry*, 1974, *5*, 113–114.

Kimmel, H.D., & Kimmel, E. An instrumental conditioning method for the treatment of enuresis. *Journal of Behavior Therapy and Experimental Psychiatry*, 1970, *1*, 121–123.

Lovibond, S.H. *Conditioning and enuresis.* New York: Macmillan, 1964.

Lovibond, S.H., & Coote, M.A. Enuresis. In C.G. Costello (Ed.), *Symptoms of psychopathology.* New York: John Wiley, 1970.

Madsen, C.H., Jr. Positive reinforcement in the toilet training of a normal child: A case report. In L.P. Ullman and L. Krasner (Eds.), *Case studies in behavior modification.* New York: Holt, Rinehart and Winston, 1965.

Madsen, C.H., Jr., Hoffman, M., Thomas, D.R., Koropsak, E., & Madsen, C.K. Comparisons of toilet training techniques. In D.M. Gelfand (Ed.), *Social learning in childhood: Readings in theory and application.* Belmont, California: Brooks/Cole, 1969.

Mahoney, K., Van Wagenen, R.K., & Meyerson, L. Toilet training of normal and retarded children. *Journal of Applied Behavior Analysis*, 1971, *4*, 173–181.

Martin, B., & Kubly, D. Results of treatment of enuresis by a conditioned response method. *Journal of Consulting Psychology*, 1955, *19*, 71–73.

Miller, P.M. An experimental analysis of retention control training in the treatment of nocturnal enuresis in two institutionalized adolescents. *Behavior Therapy*, 1973, *4*, 288–294.

Morgan, J.J.B., & Witmer, F.J. The treatment of enuresis by the conditioned reaction technique. *Journal of Genetic Psychology*, 1939, *55*, 59–65.

Mowrer, O.H., & Mowrer, W.M. Enuresis: A method for its study and treatment. *American Journal of Orthopsychiatry*, 1938, *8*, 436–459.

Muellner, S.R. Development of urinary control in children. *Journal of the American Medical Association*, 1960, *172*, 1256–1261.

Paschalis, A. Ph., Kimmel, H.D., & Kimmel, E. Further study of diurnal instrumental conditioning in the treatment of enuresis nocturna. *Journal of Behavior Therapy and Experimental Psychiatry*, 1972, *3*, 253–256.

Pfaundler, M. Demonstration eines Apparates zur silbstatigen Segnalisierung stattgehabter Bettnassung. *Verhand. Ges. Kinderheilk*, 1904, *21*, 219–220.

Poussaint, A.F., & Ditman, K.S. A controlled study of imipramine (Tofranil) in the treatment of childhood enuresis. *Journal of Pediatrics*, 1965, *67*, 283–290.

Pumroy, D.K., & Pumroy, S.S. Systematic observation and reinforcement techniques in toilet training. *Psychological Reports*, 1965, *16*, 467–471.

Sacks, S., & DeLeon, G. Conditioning two types of enuretics. *Behaviour Research and Therapy*, 1973, *11*, 653–654.

Seiger, H.W. Treatment of essential nocturnal enuresis. *Journal of Pediatrics*, 1952, *40*, 738–749.

Sloop, E.W., & Kennedy, W.A. Institutionalized retarded nocturnal enuretics treated by a conditioning technique. *American Journal of Mental Deficiency*, 1973, *77*, 717–721.

Sperling, M. Dynamic considerations and treatment of enuresis. *Journal of the American Academy of Child Psychiatry*, 1965, *4*, 19–31.

Starfield, B., & Mellits, E.D. Increase in functional bladder capacity and improvements in enuresis. *Journal of Pediatrics*, 1968, *72*, 483–487.

Stedman, J.M. An extension of the Kimmel treatment method for enuresis to an adolescent: A case report. *Journal of Behavior Therapy and Experimental Psychiatry*, 1972, *3*, 307–309.

Stewart, M.A. Treatment of bedwetting. *Journal of the American Medical Association*, 1975, *232*, 281–283.

Taylor, I.O. A scheme for the treatment of enuresis by electric buzzer apparatus. *Medical Officer*, 1963, *110*, 130–140.

Turner, R.K., & Taylor, P.D. Conditioning treatment of nocturnal enuresis in adults: Preliminary findings. *Behaviour Research and Therapy*, 1974, *12*, 41–52.

Turner, R.K., Young, G.C., & Rachman, S. Treatment of nocturnal enuresis by conditioning techniques. *Behaviour Research and Therapy*, 1970, *8*, 367–381.

Van Wagenen, R.K. Bed-wetting and the development of nocturnal urinary continence. Paper presented at the Western Psychological Association, March 1968.

Werry, J.S., & Cohrssen, J. Enuresis—An etiologic and therapeutic study. *Journal of Pediatrics*, 1965, *67*, 423–431.

Wickes, I.G. Treatment of persistent enuresis with an electric buzzer. *Archives of Disease in Childhood*, 1958, *33*, 160–164.

Yates, A.J. *Behavior therapy*. New Tork: John Wiley, 1970.

Yates, A.J. *Theory and practice in behavior therapy*. New York: John Wiley, 1975.

Young, G.C., & Turner, R.K. CNS stimulant drugs and conditioning treatment of nocturnal enuresis. *Behaviour Research and Therapy*, 1965, *3*, 93–101.

Chapter 11

Fecal Incontinence

*Bernard T. Engel**

It has been known since the nineteenth century that distension of the rectum will cause a reflex relaxation of the internal anal sphincter (Gowers, 1877). However, the physiological and clinical significance of the anal sphincteric reflexes has only recently been elucidated (Schuster, Hendrix, and Mendeloff, 1963; Schuster et al., 1965). In general, abnormalities in response of the external anal sphincter are associated with disorders of continence, i.e., retention of solid stool; and abnormalities in response of the internal anal sphincter are associated with disorders of stool formation or with disorders of defecation (Schuster, 1968; Christensen, 1971). Figure 11–1 illustrates the apparatus we used to record the recto-sphincteric reflexes, and it also shows the response of a normal subject to rectal distension. There are two features of this reflex which are important to note: First, the external sphincteric response is brief as one might expect from striate muscle, and the internal sphincteric response is prolonged as one might expect from smooth muscle; Second, the reflexes are highly synchronized with external sphincteric contraction occurring just prior to or synchronous with the onset of internal sphincter relaxation. The timing of the reflexes is critical since any significant temporal deviation of the external sphincteric response could result in stool expulsion at inappropriate times. There are two, additional features of the recto-sphincteric reflexes which are not shown in Figure 11–1 but, which have been

*Gerontology Research Center (Baltimore), National Institute on Aging, National Institutes of Health, PHS, U.S. Department of Health, Education, and Welfare, Bethesda, and the Baltimore City Hospitals, Baltimore, Maryland 21224.

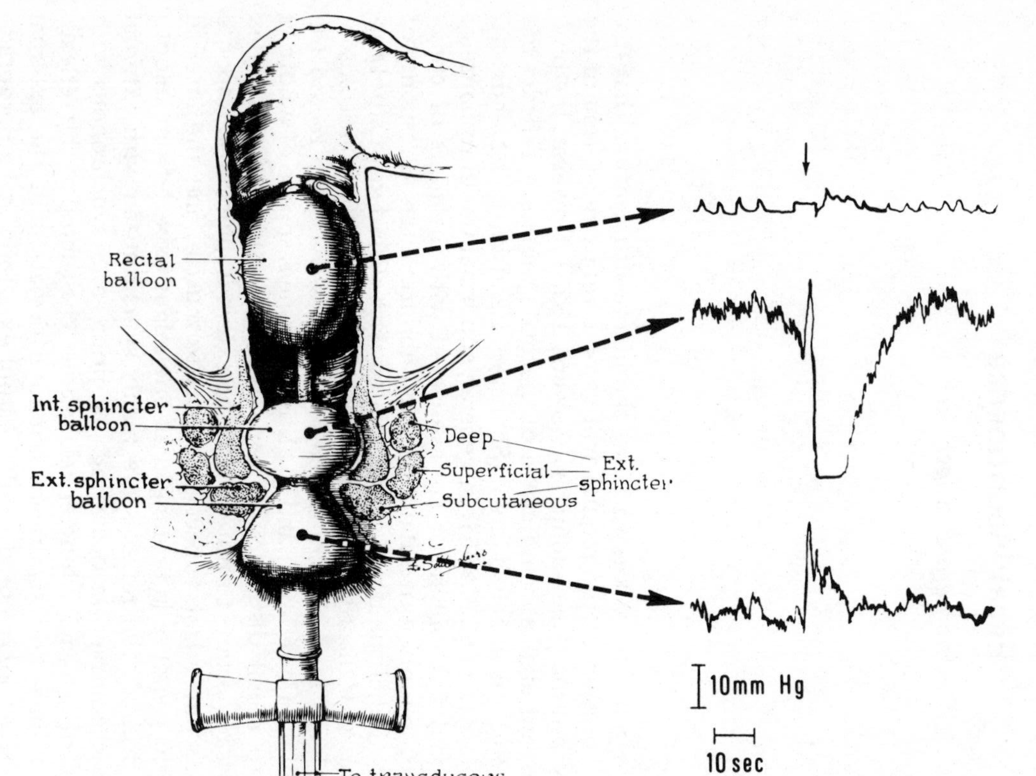

Figure 11–1. Schematic diagram of recording technique. Rectal balloon is shown in distended state used for stimulating changes in sphincter tone. (Reprinted, by permission, from the Bulletin of the Johns Hopkins Hospital, *116*: 81, 1965.)

reported elsewhere (Schuster, et al., 1965). The first is that the amplitude of response of each sphincter is dependent, in part, on the degree of rectal distension. This "dose" dependent effect permits one to carry out threshold studies of each sphincter. The second feature of the recto-sphincteric reflexes is that they do not habituate. Thus, it is possible to elicit the reflex repeatedly such as one would need to do to carry out a conditioning study.

In 1974 (Engel, Nikoomanesh, and Schuster) we reported on a series of six patients, whom we trained to produce synchronized, external sphincteric responses to rectal distension. All of these patients had histories of chronic, severe fecal incontinence of solid stool (five soiled daily, one soiled episodically). In all but one case, the incontinence could be related to an organic cause. All patients participated in a triphasic study. Phase 1 was a diagnostic study during which the degree of impairment of the recto-sphincteric reflexes was determined objectively. The second and third phases of the study were training phases during which the patient was operantly conditioned to control his recto-sphincteric reflexes. The differences between these phases will be described below.

During phase 1, in all six patients it was noted that the external sphincter response either was diminished or absent. After these diagnostic studies were completed and before training began, we explained in detail to each patient the nature and function of the recto-sphincteric reflexes, and we showed him how his response differed from normal. After it was clear that the patient understood, we began the training phases. During phase 2 we elicited sphincteric reflexes using a stimulation volume which was below threshold for that patient. The patient observed the polygraph tracings of his sphincteric responses, and after each stimulation he attempted to emit external sphincteric responses which were sufficient in amplitude and which were synchronized properly with respect to the internal sphincter response. During each trial—i.e., following each distension—we reinforced the subject verbally by telling him whether his responses met the amplitude and synchrony criteria. We encouraged him when his behavior approached criteria, and we advised him when his responses fell below criteria. As it became clear that the patient was gaining control of his responses, we reduced our verbal behavior.

Once the patient became consistent in emitting appropriate sphincteric responses, he entered into the third and last phase of the study. During this phase we withheld visual feedback during progressively greater numbers of trials while the patient continued to attempt to control his responses. This phase of the study had two goals: First, we wanted to wean the patient from any dependence on the apparatus; and second, we wanted to use these transfer trials to help the patient to refine his control. The need for refinement became clear since all patients showed a strong tendency to emit greater responses than necessary during the early transfer trials.

Figure 11–2 shows a study with a typical patient. Figure 11–2A was taken during phase 1, Figure 11–2B is from phase 2; and Figure 11–2C is from phase 3. It should be noted here that many of the patients were able to complete the three phases of study during a single, 2 hour session during which there were about 50 training trials. Many patients returned for one or two additional sessions. These subsequent sessions were scheduled at 3–4 week intervals to enable the patient to evaluate his performance under natural circumstances.

Since our first report a total of 40 patients have been treated (Cerulli, Nikoomanesh, and Schuster, 1976). These patients ranged in age from 6 to 96 years, and were incontinent for periods ranging from 1 to 38 years. Thirty were women and ten were men. Incontinence in these patients was associated with prior ano-rectal surgery, laminectomy, or a variety of medical problems such as irritable bowel syndrome, diabetes, rectal prolapse or myelomeningocele. Twenty eight of the patients (70 percent) have responded well to biofeedback treatment as evidenced by disappearance of incontinence or by decrease in frequency of incontinence of at least 90 percent. These patients have been followed for periods ranging from four months to eight years during which time they have continued to be continent suggesting strongly that the improvement obtained by biofeedback treatment may be permanent.

In reviewing these studies four factors emerge as significant determinants of clinical success. One is the identification of a well-defined, readily measurable response, contraction of the external anal sphincter. The second is presence of response variability, synchronization of the sphincteric responses. It appears that the patient learns both to emit the appropriate response, and to coordinate that response into an integrated pattern. The third factor which seems to be important in learning is the ability of the patient to perceive the appropriate stimuli which enable him to emit the sphincteric responses under natural conditions. In this case the cue is rectal distension which subjects readily sense. The last factor which seems important in determining a successful outcome is the patient's motivation. The social disruptiveness of fecal incontinence is so severe that the patients are strongly driven to practice the response control which they learned in the laboratory. The speed with which the patients learn such control very likely is a result of their high degree of motivation.

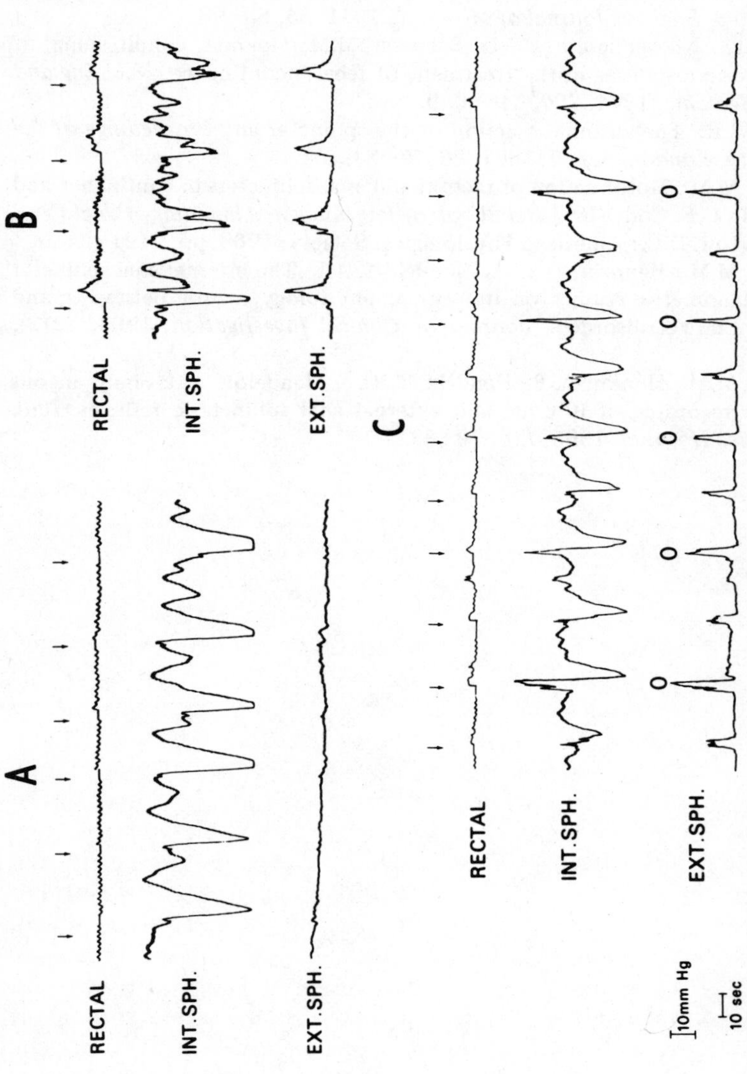

Figure 11–2. Sphincteric responses to rectal distention (↓) in a representative patient showing the response to 25–M1 distention before training (A), responses to 20–M1 distention during early training (B) and responses to 20–M1 distention (C) with and without (0) feedback. Note the tendency to overrespond during trials when feedback is withheld. (Reprinted, by permission, from the New England Journal of Medicine, *290*: 648, 1974.)

REFERENCES

Cerulli, M., Nikoomanesh, P., & Schuster, M.M. Progress in biofeedback treatment of fecal incontinence. *Gastroenterology*, 1976, *70*(5), part 2, A–11/869.

Christensen, J. The controls of gastrointestinal movements: Some old and new views. *New England Journal of Medicine*, 1971, *85*, 85–98.

Engel, B.T., Nikoomanesh, P., & Schuster, M.M. Operant conditioning of rectosphincteric responses in the treatment of fecal incontinence. *New England Journal of Medicine*, 1974, *290*, 646–649.

Gowers, W.R. The automatic action of the sphincter ani. *Proceedings of the Royal Society, London, Ser. B.* 1877, *26*, 77–84.

Schuster, M.M. Motor action of rectum and anal sphincters in continence and defecation. In C.F. Code (Ed.) *Handbook of Physiology—Alimentary Canal* (Vol. IV). Washington, D.C.: American Physiological Society, 1968, pp. 2121–2146.

Schuster, M.M., Hendrix, T.R., & Mendeloff, A.I. The internal anal sphincter response: Manometric studies on its normal physiology, neural pathways, and alteration in bowel disorders. *Journal of Clinical Investigation*, 1963, *42*(2), 196–207.

Schuster, M.M., Hookman, P., Hendrix, T.R., & Mendeloff, A.I. Simultaneous manometric recording of internal and external anal sphincteric reflexes. *Bull. Johns Hopkins Hospital*, 1965, *116*, 70–88.

Chapter 12

Chronic Pain

W. Doyle Gentry
*Guillermo A.A. Bernal**

Behavioral scientists have been utilizing behavioral treatment strategies in the treatment of chronic pain for almost a decade. Much of the published work in this area has been reported by Fordyce and coworkers (Fordyce, Fowler, and DeLateur, 1968; Fordyce et al., 1968) using an operant treatment model and more recently by Fowler (1975) using a respondent model employing biofeedback. This chapter reviews this literature, and presents as yet unpublished reports of successful treatment of chronic pain[1] using behavioral techniques.

OPERANT APPROACH

Most of the work previously reported on the behavioral treatment of chronic pain has utilized an *operant* model both in attempting to understand the factors which elicit and maintain the chronic pain syndrome and in attempting to intervene in this pattern of behavior. Basically, this model emphasizes the relationship between pain behavior (e.g., a grimace, moan, limp) and its consequences in the external environment. It does not deal directly with pain per se, which is regarded as a private, subjective experience which does not lend itself to objective measurement or control. Rather, it focuses on an individual's maladaptive pain behavior such as decreased activity in areas of work, sex, and social/recreational endeavors, complaining,

*Duke University Medical Center

1. Studies dealing with the behavioral treatment of headache pain are not covered in this chapter; see Chapter 4.

crying, and so forth as the target of diagnosis and treatment. These behaviors are referred to as operants in that they operate on the environment by producing either positive or negative consequences. The consequences are termed reinforcement and they in turn determine the probability that the behavior in question will be manifest by the individual in pain. For example, if a patient's verbal reports of pain (complaints) are immediately and consistently rewarded by attention from family members and/or health care personnel or the patient receives painkilling drugs every time he reports an increase in pain, the frequency, duration, and intensity of pain complaint is very likely to increase. On the other hand, if the patient's complaints are for the most part ignored and do not lead to immediate, predictable pain medication, they are likely to decrease in frequency, duration, and intensity.

Fordyce (1976) has indicated that operant pain behavior is acquired and maintained in three ways. First, pain behavior is often subject to direct, positive reinforcement. In childhood, for example, illness involving complaints of pain may elicit a nurturing, protective response from a parent which otherwise would not be forthcoming. In essence, the child learns to manifest pain behavior on a more and more frequent basis in order to receive special attention from parents, who may only show such attention during times of illness. Similarly, a husband may receive sympathy, affection, or a soothing back rub from his ordinarily "inattentive" spouse when he complains of chronic pain in his lower back and hobbles about the house. Financial compensation, attention from lawyers and physicians, and medication also serve as objective rewards for pain behavior. Second, pain behavior can be in evidence because it indirectly produces positive consequences by allowing the pained individual to avoid unpleasant experiences in everyday life, what is referred to as avoidance learning. Examples include a decrease in sexual activity (which is often not regarded as particularly pleasant), being excused from work, relinquishing of parental responsibilities, and a decrease in "nagging wife" behavior—all of which result from the individual's complaint of pain or certain motoric pain behaviors. Finally, pain behavior may result from a systematic nonreinforcement of "well behavior." That is, an individual with a history of little success in everyday life and notable deficits in social skills may derive undue reward from pain behavior accompanying illness either directly or indirectly as noted above. In most clinical cases, all three of these conditions for acquiring pain behavior are no doubt present to some degree.

The behavioral treatment of chronic pain using operant techniques simply entails a reversal of the maladaptive reinforcing relationships previously outlined. This can be nicely illustrated by a case report by Fordyce et al. (1968), which systematically manipulated pain medication, attention, and rest as positive reinforcers for nonpain behavior in a thirty-seven-year-old woman evidencing an eighteen-year history of debilitating back pain. At treatment onset, the patient complained of continuous pain, habitually took analgesic medication throughout the day, and was virtually unable to engage in any type of activity for more than twenty minutes without resting. The behavioral program consisted of: (a) providing medication on a time-contingent rather than pain-contingent basis (i.e., at specific time intervals, not when the patient experienced and/or complained of pain); (b) providing social reinforcement (staff or family attention and praise for improvement) for nonpain behavior, e.g., increased ward activity, and ignoring (extinction) pain behavior such as moaning, grimacing, and inactivity; (c) providing social reinforcement for increased walking; and (d) providing programmed rest periods as a reward for greater involvement in occupational therapy. After eight weeks of inpatient treatment and twenty-three weeks of outpatient treatment, the woman had changed dramatically with respect to her pain behavior. She could remain physically active for periods of up to two hours without complaining of pain or needing rest and was able to function without pain medication entirely. She could walk farther and faster than before and she was taking driving lessons so that she could resume an active, mobile life in the community.

Fordyce et al., (1973) have reported equally dramatic results for a large ($n = 36$) group of patients experiencing mechanical back pain who were followed after treatment for up to three years. To indicate the nature of the chronic pain syndromes characterizing their patients, the average time since onset of pain for the entire group of patients was 93 weeks, the average time since last fulltime employment was 41 weeks, and the average number of previous operations for pain was 2.69. Their medical diagnoses included: herniated disc, multiple sacral cysts, lumbosacral strain, compression fracture, and chronic low back and cervical pain. The behavioral treatment program was identical to that outlined above for the individual case and on the average lasted 7 weeks in the inpatient setting and another 3 weeks in outpatient clinic. The results indicate a 30 percent decrease in intensity of reported pain, a 40 percent decline in the degree to which pain tended to interfere in the patient's everyday living activities, a marked reduction in medication intake, and an increase in uptime (time out of bed) from an average of 10 hours/day on admission to 13 hours/day following discharge, all of which was maintained in follow-up over the subsequent 76 weeks.

RESPONDENT APPROACH

A second, and less applied, behavioral model for understanding and treating chronic pain is the *respondent* approach. Using this model, pain is viewed both as a response to and antecedent of physical tension, specifically muscular tension. That is, whenever there is an organic insult (injury) to the body, causing pain, the resulting physiological response may be one of immediate tensing of the muscles surrounding the injured area. Such tensing may in turn increase the subjective experience of pain, which leads to increased tension in neighboring muscle groups as a means of further immobilizing the injured site. In short, what is developed is a pain-tension-pain cycle.

Over time, the pain-tension cycle brings about many different behavioral responses from individuals, beginning with a generalized attempt to reduce pain through immobilization. This immobilization may be self-initiated or ordered by a physician and can include bed rest, use of crutches, braces, etc., all of which contribute to shortened muscle fibers or contractures. This will eventually lead to more pain. As time passes, there will also be problems involving fatigue, sleep abnormalities, increased use of and dependence on pain medications, and increased anxiety and agitation. These in turn can cause still further pain, tension, and so forth.

Physicians and physical therapists have known for years that muscle tension tends to increase pain and thus have used massage, heat, traction and ultra-sound to reduce the pain-tension cycle. All of these approaches, however, are *things done to the patient*, i.e., he is passive throughout, and they do not assist the patient in learning how to reduce tension-pain on his own. While such methods usually give the pained patient a certain amount of initial relief, the effects are generally not long lasting.

Biofeedback, on the other hand, is a treatment method by which the patient can learn to interrupt the pain-tension cycle, in which *he is the therapist*, and which the patient can carry with him outside of the doctor-patient situation. Biofeedback is simply a means of providing the patient with information about the status of a particular physiological system, in this case electrical activity in muscles effected by the pain, so that he can bring such systems into a normal range of functioning using one or another means of relaxation—a physiological state opposite to that of tension. The aim of biofeedback therapy is to teach the patient to monitor his level of tension in a particular physical system, as well as his body as a whole, and to learn to relax whenever he begins to feel tense so as to avoid or lessen the pain sensation.

In the Clinical Biofeedback Laboratory at Duke University Medical Center, we have for the past two years been utilizing biofeedback as one means of treating patients with chronic pain problems. We have found that the frontalis muscle is a good indicator of overall body tension and we have directed our efforts at training patients with chronic pain to decrease the level of tension in this site. We have done this by providing patients with feedback about the level of electrical activity in the frontalis muscle (EMG) both visually and audibly. For example, patients are seated in a sound-proof chamber and are given visual feedback of frontalis EMG activity on an oscilloscope screen; a moving dot appears, which signals increased tension when it moves up and decreased tension when it moves down. Similarly, the patients are provided with headphones which signal increased tension by an increase in the pitch of a tone and decreased tension by a decrease in same.

Electrodes are attached to the patient's forehead above each eyebrow and are spaced about four inches apart. A ground electrode is placed in the middle of the patient's forehead. Electrode resistances are maintained at less than ten thousand ohms and the EMG measures are calibrated at one hundred microvolts.

The treatment program itself consists of an initial evaluation of the patient's pain problem and an explanation of the biofeedback procedures. Patients are asked to rate the intensity of their pain on a 7-point scale (0–6) every two hours from ten o'clock in the morning until ten o'clock in the evening daily. The higher the rating, the more intense the level of pain experienced. On the first day of treatment, a ten minute baseline is obtained for frontalis EMG activity, after which the patient is allowed to explore his ability to change his tension level either up or down by attending to both the visual and auditory feedback and also is told to notice what seems to decrease his tension level. Patients are then told to imagine some anxiety-provoking situation (usually obtained from the initial interview) and to observe what effect this has on their EMG activity. It has been our experience that EMG activity usually rises dramatically during such imagery and this gives us a chance to illustrate for the patient the direct relationship between psychological tension and physical tension, and ultimately pain. The remainder of the initial treatment session is spent helping the patient evolve his own technique for lowering EMG activity. Patients are encouraged to try and come up with some type of relaxation technique themselves, but are provided with suggestions if they cannot. Common relaxation techniques include: making the mind a blank, focusing on breathing, covertly saying "relax" to oneself, and counting backwards from 300 and repeating the word "relax" after each number.

A computer provides us with 60-second readings of EMG levels plus a percentage decrease from baseline level every five minutes. The baseline average of EMG activity and the average of the first five minutes of biofeedback treatment are important since they reflect day-to-day changes in general tension level and also the effects of learned reduction of muscular tension. The final five minutes of each treatment session are equally important in that they reflect trends that occur within a treatment session.

Patients are encouraged to attend to the subjective feelings that they experience when the dot on the oscilloscope is down or the tone is low, indicating a low level of tension. Most of our patients report feelings of warmth, heaviness, of a floating sensation, or a tingling sensation. By identifying feelings that accompany low levels of tension in the treatment situation, patients are thus able to tell when they are relaxed outside of treatment, e.g., when they are practicing their relaxation exercises at home.

To help patients get a better idea of what deep relaxation feels like, a relaxation tape is played to them on their third or fourth session. The tape uses both autogenic phrases (Schultz and Luthe, 1969), e.g., "my arms and hands are quite warm and heavy," and instructions for progressive relaxation exercises (Jacobson, 1939). Throughout the treatment sessions, the patients are closely monitored and asked numerous specific questions concerning their subjective feelings, changes in EMG levels, etc.

The following two cases will illustrate the biofeedback treatment program as applied to patients with chronic pain disorders:

CASE 1

Mr. P was a 42-year-old male complaining of chronic low back pain secondary to an injury sustained while unloading a milk truck. He also complained of pain and numbness in both legs. He had had five prior operations, though none were for his back disorder. He described his pain as constant and indicated that it had interfered with all of his daily living activities including work, sex, and social/recreational activities. Initial psychological testing revealed that Mr. P had a tendency to develop somatic symptoms under stress, although he was not incapacitated by same, and that he could easily assume a passive, dependent, immature relationship with his environment secondary to his pain disorder.

Mr. P was asked to rate the intensity of his back pain for a two week period prior to biofeedback treatment. He reported that he experienced pain every day and that his average rating on the 0 (no pain) to 6 (very severe pain) scale was 4.82 indicating a moderately severe level of pain. His initial EMG reading during the baseline recording period was 7.0 microvolts, as compared to a level of 2.5 to 3.5 microvolts for individuals reporting little or no physical tension.

Each biofeedback session lasted approximately 25 minutes and the sessions were conducted daily. In the first treatment session, Mr. P showed little ability to reduce his EMG level after 25 minutes of feedback; in fact, his EMG reading for the last five minutes of this session was 7.6 microvolts, indicating a 15 percent increase in tension level above baseline. By the fifth session, however, Mr. P came in with a baseline reading of 5.9 microvolts and within the first five minutes of feedback was able to reduce his EMG activity by 19 percent. By the end of the fifth session, he was able to lower his EMG level to 3.7 microvolts which was a 37 percent decrease for that particular session. His self-report pain ratings also indicated that he was experiencing less back pain; the average rating reported at the fifth session was 3.85, suggesting a 20 percent reduction in perceived intensity of pain. His medication intake of Darvon had also decreased noticeably during this short period. By the tenth treatment session, Mr. P's resting EMG level in the frontalis muscle was 5.0 microvolts and with the first five minutes of biofeedback he could reduce it by 22 percent to a level of 4.1 microvolts. His average pain rating at this point had decreased still further to 3.62, which now described pain of moderate intensity. He also noted that there were many days when his pain was mild for several hours and much less disruptive with respect to activities of daily living.

Following the tenth biofeedback session, Mr. P began working with vocational rehabilitation with the idea of working toward starting his own upholstering business. At this time he was able to work for only about thirty minutes at a time before his pain became severe and caused him to stop. He was instructed to work for half an hour and then to practice his relaxation exercises for half an hour, rest for fifteen minutes, and then work half an hour. He was told to maintain this schedule for two weeks and each subsequent week he was to increase his working time by five minutes.

After three additional biofeedback treatment sessions, Mr. P terminated for reasons beyond our control. However, he was asked to return for follow-up evaluation six weeks later and he did. At this time, Mr. P reported that he was now able to work for about 90 minutes at a time. He described his pain intensity as moderate, but noted that there were increasingly frequent episodes of mild pain and discomfort. His EMG baseline for the follow-up visit was 4.9 microvolts and he managed an 18 percent reduction in tension level during the session without benefit of feedback either visual or auditory. In short, he seemed to be maintaining the progress noted through the initial thirteen biofeedback sessions.

CASE 2

Mrs. J was a 39-year-old divorced female complaining of pain in her neck and left shoulder secondary to an automobile accident five years earlier. She also reported spasms in her left trapezius muscle and a crushed left index finger with accompanying phlebitis which contributed to her neck and shoulder pain. Mrs. J was a highly articulate, intelligent woman who appeared perfectionistic in many ways and who set very high standards for herself and others. At the initial treatment session, she reported an average pain intensity level of 4.73 indicating moderately severe pain. Her initial EMG baseline level was 10.8 microvolts, again as compared to a normal, tension free level of 2.5 to 3.5 microvolts. She was successful in lowering her tension level during the first five minutes of the initial session by some 29 percent. The average reading for the last five minutes of this session evidenced still further tension reduction to a level of 5.6 microvolts for a total reduction of 47 percent. By the fifth session, her baseline EMG reading was down to 5.0 microvolts, although she was unable to reduce the level during that treatment session. Her self-report pain ratings indicated a decline in both the frequency and severity of perceived pain; her average rating for the fifth week was 3.20, down by 31 percent and suggestive of a moderate level of pain.

Mrs. J was presented with the relaxation tape on the fourth session and instructed to practice relaxation every day outside of the treatment situation. She was seen for five more biofeedback sessions during which her baseline EMG levels remained between 4.5 and 5.1 microvolts. Her average reduction in EMG activity (tension) within each session was approximately 17 percent and she reported much less pain and discomfort in her neck and shoulder.

At the six week follow-up visit, Mrs. J reported that she practiced the relaxation techniques regularly and that they led to a marked reduction in her degree of pain; she in fact noted that she looked forward to her practice periods each day. Her trapezius EMG baseline level at this time was 4.9 microvolts and she was able to reduce it slightly (12 percent) within the session without the benefit of biofeedback. Her average pain rating at follow-up was 2.82, down by 39 percent from the beginning of treatment and indicative of a mild level of pain.

These and many other cases suggest to us the promising effects of EMG biofeedback therapy in interrupting the pain-tension cycle which generally accompanies the chronic pain syndrome seen in increasing numbers of patients, who do not respond satisfactorily to traditional medical and surgical treatment methods. More than any other treatment approach, biofeedback requires that the pain patient become actively involved in his own rehabilitation program and assume a major share of the responsibility for health. It also offers the pain patient an alternative to continuous pain medication, a problem for most patients who experience pain for more than six months without relief.

CONCLUSION

The evidence reviewed above clearly illustrates that behavioral treatment methods are successful when applied to patients with chronic pain disorders. This is true whether one chooses the operant or respondent approach, both of which may benefit the patient. It should also be made clear that behavioral treatment strategies are aimed not at *curing* the patient's pain directly, but rather at teaching the patient to be more functional in his environment despite his pain experience which itself decreases significantly as a result of changes in pain behavior or reduced levels of muscle tension. Behavioral treatment methods are not competitive with more traditional medical/surgical treatment programs, but simply represent an alternative means of relieving the patient's suffering. They should certainly be considered when the more traditional methods fail to remedy the pain experience, in cases where the evidence for an organic etiology for the pain is not sufficient to warrant surgical procedures, and with patients evidencing a chronic pain syndrome, i.e., whose pain persists despite all attempts to treat it over a long period of time.

REFERENCES

Fordyce, W.E. *Behavioral methods for chronic pain and illness.* St. Louis: Mosby, 1976.

Fordyce, W.E., Fowler, R.S., & DeLateur, B. An application of behavior modification technique to a problem of chronic pain. *Behavior Research and Therapy*, 1968, *6*, 105–7.

Fordyce, W.E., Fowler, R.S., Lehmann, J.F., & DeLateur, B. Some implications of learning in problems of chronic pain. *Journal of Chronic Diseases*, 1968, *21*, 179–90.

Fordyce, W.E., Fowler, R.S., Lehmann, J.F., DeLateur, B.J., Sand, P.L., & Trieschmann, R.B. Operant conditioning in the treatment of chronic pain. *Archives of Physical Medicine and Rehabilitation*, 1973, *54*, 399–408.

Fowler, R.S. Biofeedback in the treatment of pain. In J.J. Bonica (Ed.) *The management of pain.* Philadelphia: Lea & Febiger, 1975, in press.

Jacobson, E. *Progressive relaxation.* Chicago: University of Chicago Press, 1938.

Schultz, J. & Luthe, W. *Autogenic therapy, volume I, autogenic methods.* New York: Grune & Stratton, 1969.

 *Chapter 13*

Alcohol Problems

*Linda C. Sobell**
Mark B. Sobell†

Before discussing behavioral approaches to the treatment of alcohol problems, a brief historical perspective regarding alcoholism is warranted. A quarter of a century ago, professional involvement and attention to the treatment of alcohol problems was virtually nonexistent. In the ensuing years, a variety of formal alcohol treatment programs have emerged, and now most cities have some type of formal care available for individuals with alcohol-related problems. Until recently, however, most of our knowledge about alcohol problems was derived from the personal experiences of recovered alcoholics and from rather perfunctory clinical observations. In a forthcoming book, Pattison, Sobell, and Sobell (in press) have summarized this body of phenomenological knowledge as *traditional concepts of alcoholism* and concluded that several fundamental assumptions underlying the traditional model of alcoholism have been seriously contradicted by new clinical and experimental evidence. This new body of data, taken as a whole, compel a reformulation of our thinking about "alcoholism."

One of the assumptions of the traditional model which has been seriously questioned is the idea that some persons—"alcoholics"—suffer from a progressive and irreversible disease process—"alcoholism." In light of the accumulating evidence, it appears that there is no separately definable entity which can be identified as "alcoholism" (Pattison, et al., in press). Rather, there appear to be multiple situations which have in common that some persons suffer adverse

*Dede Wallace Center, Nashville, Tennessee and Vanderbilt University.
†Vanderbilt University, Nashville, Tennessee.

consequences as a result of using alcohol. Consonant with emerging clinical and experimental findings, alcohol problems are better summarized as a variety of syndromes characterized by adverse physical, psychological, and/or social consequences of drinking. The emerging concepts of alcohol dependence further suggest that all individuals who drink are at some risk of developing alcohol problems and can be considered as lying along a continuum, ranging from nonpathological drinking to severely pathological drinking (Pattison, et al., in press). This, of course, differs considerably from the traditional dichotomous view of individuals as either "alcoholic" (or prealcoholic) or not alcoholic.

Regardless of etiology, drinking problems are manifested as complex and broadly generalized behavior patterns. In this regard, when discussing behavioral treatment approaches to alcohol problems, it is important to distinguish between more sophisticated behavioral approaches, as will be discussed in this chapter, and simple-minded conceptions which are limited to surface considerations of merely the drinking response and its modification. Finally, anyone who applies behavioral approaches to the treatment of alcohol problems should have a knowledge of experimentally derived principles of behavior and an understanding of how to apply these principles to human behavior in naturalistic settings.

THE FUNCTIONAL ANALYSIS OF DRINKING BEHAVIOR

In our society, the use of alcohol is a frequent and highly complex behavior which involves multiple behavior patterns. A functional analysis of the behavior of drinking alcohol would suggest that drinking serves different functions for different individuals in different contexts. By this reasoning, the fact that some people develop drinking problems and others do not is dependent, in part, upon a given individual's internal and external environment, including that individual's biological makeup, sociocultural factors, past learning history, and features of the prevailing situation.

In the last five years, a variety of behavioral treatment approaches for drinking problems have been developed. These new approaches should not be confused with earlier approaches which were based largely on methods of classical aversive conditioning. The more recent approaches share a more comprehensive consideration of drinking as a discriminated operant behavior. That is, drinking is conceptualized as occurring in certain situations and not in others (a discriminated behavior). Further, drinking behavior, problem or nonproblem, is hypothesized as being learned—acquired and maintained—as a function of its consequences (an operant behavior). More specifically, the consumption of alcohol is preceded by certain events (antecedents) and followed by various consequences.

Drinking, a behavior that can be easily identified and quantified, has many obvious antecedents and consequences. A behavioral view of drinking decisions appears in Figure 13–1 and Table 13–1 and will be referred to as a "functional analysis model of drinking" (Sobell, Sobell, and Sheahan, 1976). This model portrays behavioral options for a given individual in a given situation. It contrasts with single causal models which might suggest, for instance, that simply "stress" or "boredom" lead to problem drinking.

The functional analysis model simplifies, classifies, and arranges complex clinical data in a meaningful way. Further, since there are multiple opportunities for behavioral interventions in nearly all cases of alcohol-related problems, the model can suggest alternative ways to effectively promote behavior change. That is, what types of treatment strategies and interventions are most likely to be both beneficial and efficient for the client? Additionally, the model can suggest where useful data are missing.

One advantage of the functional analysis model is that it demonstrates that any individual who uses alcohol may engage in problem or nonproblem drinking. Further, it calls attention to the fact that drinking is always preceded by some complex of setting events (antecedents) and followed by certain consequences related, most importantly, to the individual's own environment and the nature of the drinking itself. Thus, the functional analysis of drinking, and more specifically problem drinking, is a highly complex and intricate task, involving far more than the mere act of drinking. An understanding of this conceptualization is crucial to the development of individualized behavioral treatment plans and goals. In this regard, a functional analysis of drinking problems carefully considers the learning history of each individual and that person's past and present resources and deficiencies. In this way, a treatment sequence is tailored as specifically as possible to meet the needs of each individual and designed to maximize generalization of the treatment effects to the extra-treatment environment.

The functional analysis model also provides an idiosyncratic definition of behavior labeled as problem drinking. The degree of problem drinking for any individual is defined by the total resultant consequences of that behavior. Applying the model to specific cases, it becomes evident that what constitutes a problem for one person may not be a problem for another. Take, for example, an individual

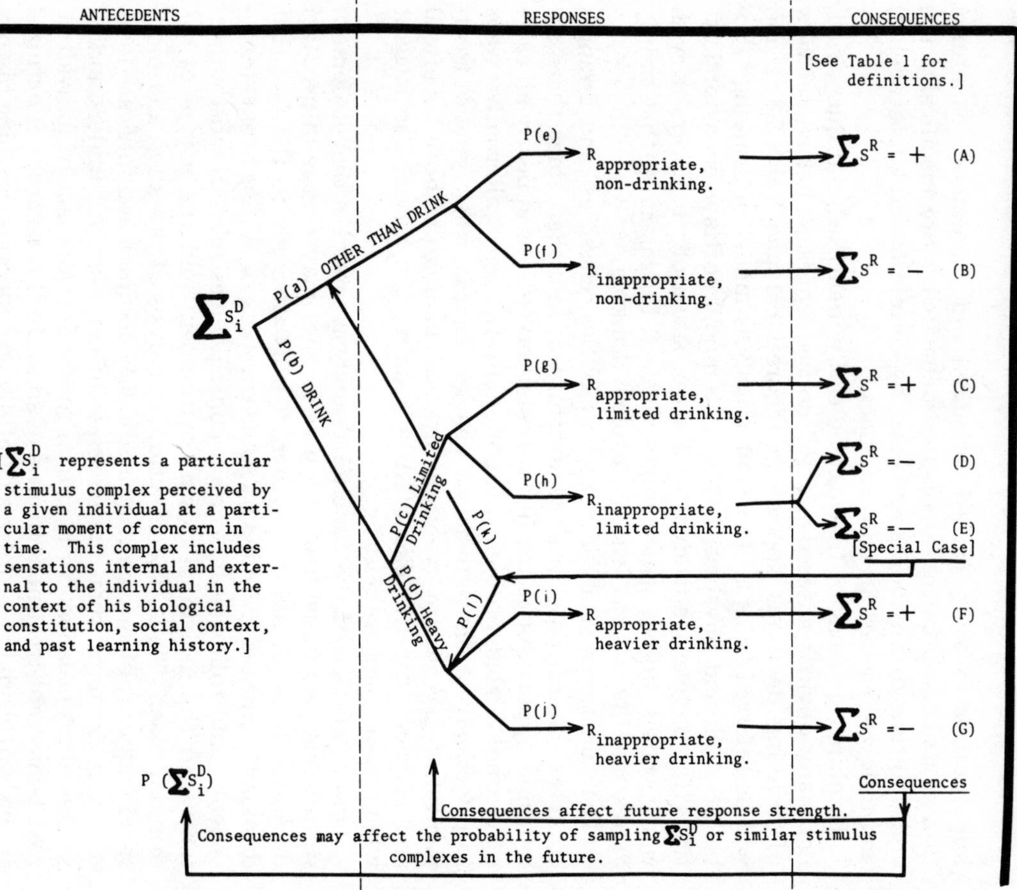

Figure 13–1.
General format for functional analysis of drinking behavior. From: Sobell, M.B., Sobell, L.C., and Sheahan, D.B. Functional analysis of drinking problems as an aid in developing individual treatment strategies. *Addictive Behaviors*, 1976, *1*. 127–132. Permission to reprint granted by Pergamon Press, Ltd.

Table 13–1. Definition of Consequences Complexes, and Examples of Responses and Consequences to Complement Figure 13–1[a]

Code	*Consequence Complex Definition and Examples*	*Response Examples*
A	Consequences are predominantly rewarding or neutral. Typically, rewarding long-term consequences, with either rewarding or neutral short-term consequences.[b] Examples: Paycheck, promotion, praise from others, etc.	Appropriate, nondrinking: Going to work, expressing affection, being assertive, etc.
B	Consequences are predominantly aversive. Typically, aversive long-term consequences, with rewarding or neutral short-term consequences. (When such behaviors occur repetitively, short-term consequences are effective rewards in all cases.) Examples: Damaged business or personal relationships, being arrested, verbal derogation, etc.	Inappropriate nondrinking: Assault, excessive sleeping, sulking, etc.
C	Consequences are predominantly rewarding or neutral, as for code A. Examples: Social acceptance and attention, invitations to parties, etc.	Appropriate, limited drinking: Typical social drinking, religious ceremonial drinking, dinner cocktail at restaurant, etc.
D	Consequences are predominantly aversive, although control exerted by short-term rewards as for code B. In some situations consequences are sufficient to change ΣS_i^D complex, despite punishing elements.[c] Examples: Warned by supervisor not to drink before work again, relax but meet no new friends, etc.	Inappropriate, limited drinking: Before work day, at an AA meeting, in locations where prohibited, to relax recurrent stress, to cope with loneliness, etc.
E	Similar to sequence code D, but consequences not sufficient to eliminate or make ineffective ΣS_i^D. This can lead to heavier drinking, or alternative nondrinking responses.[c] Examples: Relaxation not sufficient, lose job, act foolish attempting to socialize, etc.	Inappropriate, limited drinking: as for code D.

(Table 13–1. cont'd overleaf . . .)

Table 13–1. continued

Code	*Consequence Complex Definition and Examples*	*Response Examples*
F	Consequences are predominantly rewarding or neutral, as for code A. Examples: Social acceptance and praise sufficient to compensate for hangover, use of social excuse of drunkenness to rationalize flirtation, etc.	Appropriate, heavier drinking: Ritual drinking in some cultures, beer parties, drinking to drunkenness with preparations to minimize risk—such as not driving.
G	Consequences are predominantly aversive, as for code B. There is an increasing probability of highly aversive long-term consequences as physical dependence becomes more likely. Increasing threat to all areas of life functioning. *Increasing probability of being defined as Alcohol Abuse.* Examples: Being arrested, being physically ill, divorce, poor job record, death, etc.	Inappropriate, heavier drinking: Passing out to cope with stress or boredom or loneliness, morning drinking to relieve hangover, drinking to excess in any situation where performance is important, drinking to the acquisition of physical dependence, etc.

[a]The general contingency diagram model, as presented here, has been simplified and abbreviated. A more elaborate model could expand greatly on further sequence possibilities, such as the development of physical dependence on alcohol, the possibility of various arrests or medical complications, feedback loops and choice points for the termination of drinking, and so on.

[b]One common characteristic of these situations is that the response is sufficient to change the ΣS_i^D, aversive intensity, deprivation levels, or other elements of the contingency so that major features of the original ΣS_i^D are either no longer present or no longer effective.

[c]In both contingency sequence codes D and E, there exists the potential for developing psychological dependence on drinking, with destructive long-term consequences influencing behavior less than short-term rewards. Sequence type E is particularly risky when it is followed by sequence type G—e.g., when heavier drinking *does* provide adequate sedation.

From: Sobell, M.B., Sobell, L.C., and Sheahan, D.B. Functional analysis of drinking problems as an aid in developing individual treatment strategies. *Addictive Behaviors*, 1976, *1*, 127–132. Permission to reprint granted by Pergamon Press, Ltd.

whose livelihood depends on driving and who loses his drivers license as a result of a drunk driving charge. This person's drinking may well cause life health dysfunction in terms of vocational and financial problems. Conversely, a person who is extremely wealthy and similarly loses his drivers license as the result of a drunk driving conviction may experience little, if any, serious life health dysfunction, as he can probably afford to take a cab or pay someone to provide him with transportation until the driver's license is returned. Thus, alcohol-related dysfunction varies from individual to individual in terms of the factors leading to drinking, the nature of the drinking, and the nature of the ensuing consequences.

For the functional analysis model to have practical value for both client and clinician a caveat is in order. An overly simplified model, limited to gross generalities, may produce either too few therapeutic strategies or else overly simplified and perhaps indiscriminately applied treatment strategies. Thus, individual treatment plans need to be developed based on a *comprehensive* and careful consideration of the individual's life history, present environment and known physical condition. Used in this manner, the model can serve as a framework to generate ideas for individual treatment strategies. It also provides a structure which forces the clinician to become aware of the behavioral complexities of drinking and the possibility of unanticipated consequences.

BEHAVIORAL TREATMENT STRATEGIES

The phrase, "behavioral treatment of alcohol problems," describes several therapeutic modalities. However, before discussing particular techniques, two general behavioral orientations will be described. The first, a "broad-spectrum" behavioral approach, involves developing a treatment plan by combining a variety of techniques deemed appropriate for a given case. A broad spectrum approach is based on the notion that no single method is optimal for treating all problems and all persons. Therefore, an emphasis is placed on tailoring treatment to each case. Such an approach for the treatment of alcohol problems was first reported by Lazarus in 1965. The second general orientation, a "narrow-band" behavioral approach (Lazarus, 1971), refers to using a limited array of therapeutic techniques (i.e. using only systematic desensitization and relaxation training) for treating a wide variety of problems. Although a narrow-band approach has obvious value when used in controlled research and with particular pathologies (i.e. phobics), the population of persons with alcohol problems has been demonstrated to be extremely diverse (reviewed in Pattison, et al., in press). In this regard, a broad-spectrum approach appears most appropriate for behavioral treatment of individuals with alcohol problems.

Depending on the specific characteristics of a case, the drinking treatment goal for a client may range from nondrinking (total abstinence) to some type of limited, nonproblem drinking. In general, the behavioral treatment goal for individuals with alcohol problems can be stated as a *reduction in drinking problems to an ideal of no drinking problems.* In some cases, this ideal may be achieved without a full cessation of drinking (see review of 74 studies in Pattison, et al., in press), while in other cases even a prolonged period of abstinence may not be sufficient to fully ameliorate consequences which have resulted from previous drinking.

While differing in application, most behavioral treatment approaches to alcohol problems share the following characteristics:

1. It is assumed that drinking behavior, and some of the effects of alcohol on other behaviors (e.g. risk taking, aggression), are acquired, i.e. learned. Further, it is assumed that the learned characteristics of drinking behavior can be modified.
2. Drinking behavior is usually dealt with in a direct manner, often by introducing drinking into the treatment strategy (e.g. in inpatient programs) or by monitoring any drinking that occurs during treatment. Drinking decisions are viewed as critical events in syndromes of alcohol problems and, thus, the circumstances surrounding drinking decisions serve as focal points for determining the functions of each individual's drinking.
3. Emphasis is placed on operationally specifying treatment procedures and assessing treatment effectiveness using empirical methods.

In the following description of treatment methods, general behavior therapy procedures are accorded brief mention, while techniques primarily developed or adapted for use in treating individuals with alcohol problems are given more attention. For a more in-depth explanation of specific procedures, the reader is referred to a number of comprehensive reviews (Briddell and Nathan, 1975; Miller, in press; Nathan and Briddell, in press; Nathan and Marlatt, in press; Sobell and Sobell, in press).

Problem Solving Skills Training

Sobell and Sobell (1972, 1973a, 1975) recently developed a behavioral technology which they refer to as "Problem Solving Skills

Training," which is based on a functional analysis of drinking. This is a highly specialized broad-spectrum behavioral treatment procedure which focuses strongly on identifying and evaluating multiple opportunities (behavioral options) for treatment intervention. Basically, the training incorporates a four-stage procedure:

Stage 1—Problem Identification: Clients are first trained in ways to operationally define (identify) specific circumstances and events which have resulted in drinking problems in the past or which are likely to do so in the future. That is, what particular environmental factors and/or internal (physical) stages set the occasion for problem drinking behavior? This almost always involves identifying a complex of factors. The primary objective of this stage is to gain sufficient information about the drinking problems so that appropriate treatment strategies can be delineated. For instance, if a client labels lack of job advancement as a problem but fails to mention that he lacks the necessary educational background to qualify for a desired position, resulting treatment strategies would probably be inappropriate and nonbeneficial for the client. Essentially, this stage could be conceptualized as an ecological consideration of drinking behavior.

Stage 2—Delineation of Behavioral Options (Alternative Responses) to Problem Drinking: Clients are assisted in generating a series of possible alternative behavioral responses to problem situations. It is important to note that in this stage value judgments regarding the delineated options are specifically avoided. So, for example, if the problem involved financial indebtedness, several possible options include declaring bankruptcy, obtaining a consolidation loan, ignoring the situation, robbing a bank, committing suicide, drinking, taking drugs, taking a second job, and so on. While these alternative behaviors have varied short- and long-term anticipated consequences, they nevertheless are actual behaviors engaged in by some individuals in similar situations.

Stage 3—Evaluation of Each Behavioral Option for Its Possible Outcome: Clients are asked to evaluate each of the potential behavioral options delineated in Stage 2 for their probable short-term (immediate) and long-term consequences. At this stage, emphasis is placed on recognizing and developing appropriate behavioral alternatives. In this context, relative "appropriateness" is defined as the *total anticipated consequences* of a behavior. It is important for the client to be aware that all behavioral options will generate *both* short- and long-term consequences, and that the *total* (short- *and* long-term) consequences of behavioral options need to be evaluated before deciding whether or not particular behaviors are appropriate.

From the functional analysis model in Figure 13–1, it is apparent that some behavioral options, albeit not involving drinking, can still cause serious life health dysfunction. To take an extreme example, again consider an individual who has financial difficulties. If the person decides to resolve his problems by robbing a bank, it is likely that engaging in such nondrinking behavior will result in severe life dysfunction (i.e. prison sentence).

Using the functional analysis model in Figure 13–1 and Table 13–1, a partial understanding of why people might drink in response to problem situations can be derived. While the behavioral option of heavy prolonged alcohol consumption usually has associated long-term deleterious consequences, engaging in such behavior is often initially (short-term) rewarding and may even allow the individual to avoid the prevailing situation.

The most significant point to be communicated to clients in this stage is that the best behavioral option is often *not immediately rewarding.* In this regard, while taking a second job might be evaluated as the behavioral option having the best long-term consequences for solving one's financial dilemma, the immediate (short-term) consequences of working a second job are somewhat punishing (e.g. decreased recreational time; increased tiredness; less time to spend with friends and family). A *focus on total consequences* of behaviors is the crux of the functional analysis model of drinking.

Stage 4—Employing the Behavioral Option(s) Evaluated to Have the Best Probable Total Outcome: Finally, the client actually is trained in and then practices the behavioral option(s) evaluated as having the best total consequences, even if in some cases the chosen alternative may be expected to incur some negative consequences. In this stage, various psychotherapeutic and behavioral techniques (i.e. shaping, role playing, relaxation training, biofeedback, etc.) are used as necessary. The treatment methods and techniques used are tailored to both the individual and the specific behavioral option.

The behavioral technique of Problem Solving Skills Training, unlike many alcoholism treatment modalities, analyzes treatment operations on a continuing basis and directly involves the client in the ongoing treatment process. Moreover, it is different from most other approaches to the treatment of alcohol problems in the following ways:

1. The treatment approach is tailored to the client rather than vice-versa.

2. By gearing the model to the client, the judgmental aspect of what is and is not appropriate is removed, simply because behavioral consequences are specific to individuals and circumstances.
3. Behaviors and situations are precisely defined and evaluated.
4. The use of vague terminology, such as "dependency needs," "power needs," "inadequacy" and/or "alcoholism" is avoided.
5. There is an increased awareness of the powerful influence of short-term consequences on perpetuating drinking.
6. There is an increased awareness that many "appropriate" behavioral options have primarily delayed (long-term) rewarding consequences.
7. As clients become better able to define, evaluate, and understand the influences upon their behavior, their life problems, correspondingly become less mysterious and capable of solution. This is attributed to the client being an active participant in his own treatment and life planning.

The Problem Solving Skills approach is a general behavioral treatment strategy which assures that a variety of highly specific and specialized behavioral treatment procedures are considered whenever a problem situation arises. Therefore, many of the following specific treatment procedures may at times be subsumed under Stage 4 of Problem Solving Skills Training rather than constituting the entire treatment.

Relaxation Training and Systematic Desensitization. The technique of progressive deep muscle relaxation (Jacobson, 1938) is often used by behavior therapists to train clients to relax. Relaxation training is particularly useful when used as part of a systematic desensitization treatment (Wolpe, 1969). Systematic desensitization is a well defined procedure used to diminish specific fears. In a graded manner, the client is repeatedly exposed to imagined or real aspects of the phobic situation. This is done under conditions which prevent or minimize the arousal of anxiety. Studies using systematic desensitization and relaxation training in the treatment of alcoholics have been reported by Kraft and Al-Issa (1967) and Kraft (1969).

Assertion Training. Some persons may have drinking problems because they lack appropriate emotional expressiveness or assertiveness. Assertion training is a behavioral method which utilizes the procedures of role playing, modeling, social coaching, role reversal, and social rewards to shape assertive skills. Such skills should not be confused with aggressive behaviors. A case study describing the use of this method with a male alcoholic has been reported by Eisler et al., 1974).

Contingency Management. Contingency management consists of arranging a person's environment so positive consequences will follow desired behaviors with either no consequences or negative consequences contingent upon nondesired behaviors. This method uses the basic behavior management techniques fundamental to token economies. A recent extension of these procedures to deal with Skid Row alcoholics has been reported by Miller (1975). In collaboration with agencies (e.g. Salvation Army, Union Rescue Mission, etc.) serving the Skid Row community, Miller arranged for some randomly selected Skid Row alcoholics to receive various goods and services (i.e. clothing, cigarettes, etc.) if and only if they were found to be sober via a breath test. In contrast to a comparison group of alcoholics not accountable for their sobriety, the contingency management group showed a significant decrease in level of intoxication and in number of arrests over a two month period and a significant increase in number of hours employed for pay.

An excellent example of the contingency management approach was also reported by Hunt and Azrin (1973), who developed an individualized broad-spectrum "community-reinforcement" network for chronic alcoholics whereby social, vocational, recreational and familial rewards were made contingent upon continuing sobriety. Compared to matched alcoholics not receiving the behavioral intervention, the "community-reinforcement" group spent less time drinking, unemployed, away from home or institutionalized during the six months following treatment.

Finally, Bigelow, Liebson, and Lawrence (1973) used a similar technique as part of an occupational alcoholism program. Employees whose jobs were in jeopardy as a direct result of excessive drinking were given the opportunity to work contingent upon daily Antabuse ingestion.

Behavioral Contracting. Behavioral contracting is similar to contingency management. Essentially, the process is one of explicitly defining a set of behaviors and their associated consequences. The contract is usually negotiated between two parties (i.e. husband and wife) and stated in writing, although other arrangements are possible. Sometimes such explicit written agreements are necessary for achieving change. Behavioral contracting assures that all parties agree to expected behaviors, appropriate reactions, and how behavior change will be recognized and rewarded. Behavioral contracting is very helpful in the initial stages of treatment as it can build in early recognition of behavior changes and thereby, motivate clients to make continued life changes. Miller (1972) has reported the successful use of behavioral contracting between an alcoholic and his wife to bring about a maintained pattern of controlled drinking.

Aversion Conditioning. This method summarizes a number of different procedures which attempt to extinguish drinking behavior by pairing components of drinking behavior (e.g. the sight, smell, and taste of alcoholic beverages) with aversive events. Through a process of Pavlovian (classical) conditioning, the drinking behavior is expected to come to elicit aversive reactions similar to those elicited by the aversive event. The aversive event can be electric shock (set at painful but harmless levels), chemical stimulation (typically an emetic like Emetine or Apomorphine), or imagined aversive events (generated as the result of a behavioral procedure called covert sensitization, see Cautella, 1970). The general method of aversion conditioning was first used by Kantorovich in 1930, well before the advent of modern behavior therapy. Recently, researchers have begun to seriously question the supposed efficacy of electrical aversion conditioning. Further, it has been suggested that any positive effects which do occur apparently have little to do with the development of a conditioned aversion (Rachman and Teasdale, 1969; Wilson, Leaf, and Nathan, 1975; Nathan and Briddell, in press). Aversion conditioning by chemical and covert sensitization methods have similarly been suspect, but clear empirical tests of the ability of these procedures to produce conditioned aversion have not yet been performed. The reader is cautioned that, in the words of Nathan and Briddell (in press) "none of the aversive conditioning procedures reviewed above can by itself constitute the treatment of choice for chronic alcoholism."

Avoidance Conditioning. An avoidance conditioning procedure was used by Mills, Sobell, and Schaefer (1971) to shape the drinking behavior of chronic alcoholics to be similar to that of normal drinkers by allowing them to drink but administering mild shocks if they drank inappropriately. While this method was later incorporated into a broad-spectrum behavioral treatment approach (Sobell and Sobell, 1972, 1973a), the authors have since questioned whether the avoidance contingencies were a necessary or effective treatment component.

Blood Alcohol Level Discrimination Training. Blood alcohol level (BAL) discrimination training, developed by Lovibond and Caddy

(1970), is a method whereby subjects are administered beverage alcohol and then requested to subjectively judge their level of intoxication. Breath tests are then administered to determine actual BALs. With feedback, subjects can learn to make relatively accurate estimates of their BALs.

Much controversy surrounds the basis upon which subjects can make accurate BAL estimates (see Caddy, 1976; Nathan and Briddell, in press). In particular, it is unclear whether persons use physical sensations generated by alcohol (e.g., numbness, facial warmth, etc.) as reliable cues or must simply base their estimates on external cues (e.g. knowledge of how much and what strength of alcohol they have consumed over what period of time). Although recent studies had found that normal drinkers could base BAL estimates on internal sensations, this was not the case for alcoholics. However, a recent study (Maisto, 1975) suggests that under properly controlled circumstances even normal drinkers cannot make valid BAL estimates based solely on internal sensations. The utility of the technique, however, lies in the fact that persons can learn to estimate their BALs reliably, even if their BAL estimates are based on more than physiological cues. This technique has strong promise for use in prevention programs.

Self-Monitoring. In reality, it is highly unusual for individuals with alcohol problems to totally stop drinking immediately after entering into a treatment program and never drink again. In this regard, Sobell and Sobell (1973b) had outpatient alcoholics maintain a written log of their daily drinking behavior during the course of treatment. When used in an outpatient setting, this procedure is very valuable in generating information about the functions of a client's drinking. Self-monitoring of drinking involves the client directly in the analysis of his own drinking or potential drinking, promotes discussion of instances when drinking has occurred and, consequently, allows for early treatment intervention if a pattern of increasing or problem drinking becomes evident.

COMPLIANCE: FOLLOWING THE DELINEATED TREATMENT PLAN

Most behavioral treatment approaches recognize that treatment is a collaborative venture between client and clinician. To this end, behavioral treatment plans are usually developed with the client's awareness and agreement. In spite of careful and negotiated treatment planning, however, the problem of compliance—following the delineated treatment plan—is frequently encountered. While research in the area of compliance with behavioral treatment of alcohol problems is virtually nonexistent, the following observations are offered with the caution that they are merely speculative.

It is important to recognize that in terms of time, effort, and modifications of life style, various treatment strategies involve *differential costs for the client.* Therefore, it is often valuable to distinguish between treatment effectiveness and efficiency. An *effective* treatment is defined as a satisfactory resolution of current problems with a high probability of avoiding similar problems in the future. An *efficient* and effective treatment is defined as an attainment of goals while simultaneously requiring the least total change in life style for the client. For example, for a given client either an outpatient or a residential day care program might be evaluated as equally likely to be effective in maintaining short-term sobriety and stabilizing familial relationships. However, if the client were employed full-time, participation in the residential day care program could jeopardize his employment; therefore, in this case outpatient treatment would be evaluated as most efficient.

Considerations of what constitutes both an effective and efficient treatment stem from an assessment of the client's needs, abilities, and immediate environment. When attempting to maximize combined effectiveness and efficiency, it is critical for the therapist to determine what personal cost a client can tolerate in pursuit of treatment objectives. In this regard, an *initial* treatment strategy may be negotiated which delineates changes which the client agrees are attainable and likely to be personally beneficial. While some initial strategies may not be maximally effective, they may contribute to demonstrated short-term positive changes, which in turn are likely to maintain the client in treatment. This initial process can then serve as a basis for the negotiated development of additional treatment strategies which may involve greater cost and commitment for the client.

A matter tangentially related to compliance is inducing the client to report current symptomatology accurately to the therapist. In the area of behavioral treatment of alcohol problems, this involves reporting any and all drinking behavior to the therapist. Since drinking is the *sine qua non* of alcohol problems, it is imperative that the therapist be aware of any drinking which has occurred. Of course, the therapist must recognize that his/her initial reactions to the client's reports of drinking may well determine whether the client continues to report honestly about any drinking that occurs.

Instances of problem drinking during treatment typically occur with great frequency, especially in outpatient alcohol programs. To this end, episodes of problem drinking, while difficult to prevent *in toto*, can be used constructively to provide valuable information about the functions of the current drinking and situations conducive to such drinking. Unfortunately, it is frequently the case that therapists strongly admonish clients whenever they report drinking. A procedure likely to result in greater compliance is to encourage the client to report any drinking that occurs during treatment, and to then explore with the client the potential and actualized consequences (primarily negative) of the drinking. Using such a procedure, we have found that most clients will report drinking instances quite freely (Sobell and Sobell, 1973b). This has consequently, allowed early intervention in cases where clients may have otherwise dropped out of treatment or suffered more serious alcohol-related dysfunctions.

PREVENTION AND BEHAVIORAL APPROACHES

While behavioral treatment approaches to alcohol problems are relatively new, early findings have been impressive and positive. Thus, behavioral approaches might also be expected to have some measurable success in the areas of primary and secondary prevention.

There are two major reasons why behavioral approaches are seen as particularly appropriate for prevention and early intervention programs. First, several of the behavioral treatment techniques can easily be extended to a prevention treatment context. The functional analysis model of drinking, for instance, could easily be adapted for use in prevention. Similarly, self-monitoring, contracting and environmental restructuring could be extended to prevention approaches.

The second reason behavioral approaches are viewed as appropriate for the prevention of alcohol problems relates to the failure of traditional prevention approaches. Traditionally, prevention strategies have focused on educating individuals about alcoholism, emphasizing symptoms associated with various stages in the progressive development of alcoholism (Wilkinson, 1970). This orientation suffers from two serious deficiencies. From an empirical standpoint, recent research (reviewed in Pattison, Sobell, and Sobell, in press) has demonstrated that the concept of a progressive development of alcohol problems characterizes only a small segment of people with drinking problems. From a practical standpoint, traditional orientations to alcoholism prevention offer few strategies for avoiding or minimizing alcohol problems, other than total abstention. In a society where the majority of members drink, it is not surprising that many people are adverse to the prospect of life-long abstinence from alcohol. Considering the large body of recent evidence contradicting the presupposition of an inevitable progression of alcoholism, the need to develop effective and efficient primary and secondary prevention programs has become increasingly apparent. To this end, a recent national study found that only 27.3 percent of adolescents (13 to 18 years of age) were abstainers from alcohol (Rachal et al., 1975). Still another study found that while 92 percent of adult males (age 20 to 30 years) were currently using alcohol, at least 97 percent indicated some prior use of alcohol (O'Donnell et al., 1976).

REFERRAL FOR BEHAVIORAL TREATMENT OF ALCOHOL PROBLEMS

When considering referring an individual for behavioral treatment of alcohol problems, it is important to recognize that health and mental health care providers in all disciplines have long demonstrated a reluctance to treat individuals with alcohol-related problems (Lynn, 1976). Furthermore, there is no evidence to suggest that such an attitude is any less prevalent among behavioral treatment providers. Thus, if a case is evaluated as possibly appropriate for behavioral treatment of alcohol problems, the prospective therapist or treatment program should have a thorough understanding that drinking is a major life problem.

CONCLUSION

In conclusion, two brief cautionary notes regarding behavioral treatment approaches to alcohol problems are in order. First, most of the behavioral approaches to the treatment of alcohol problems have been developed in a research setting and conducted under highly experimental laboratory conditions. Second, while the long-term treatment outcome results of these approaches are positive, they are also limited. Thus, the applicability of behavioral approaches to the treatment of alcohol problems in the general clinical setting and their subsequent efficacy is yet to be fully determined.

REFERENCES

Bigelow, G., Liebson, I. & Lawrence, C. Prevention of alcohol abuse by reinforcement of incompatible behavior. Paper presented at Association for Advancement of Behavior Therapy, Miami, December, 1973.

Briddell, D.W. & Nathan, P.E. Behavior assessment and modification with alcoholics: Current status and future trends. In M. Hersen, R.M. Eisler, and P.M.

Miller (Eds.), *Progress in behavior modification. Vol. 2.* New York: Academic Press, 1975.

Caddy, G.R. Blood alcohol concentration discrimination training: Development and current status. In P.E. Nathan and G.A. Marlatt (Eds.), *Behavioral assessment and treatment of alcoholism.* New Brunswick: Rutgers Center for Alcohol Studies, 1976, in press.

Cautela, J.R. The treatment of alcoholism by covert sensitization. *Psychotherapy: Theory, Research and Practice*, 1970, *7*, 86–90.

Eisler, R.M., Miller, P.M., Hersen, M. & Alford, H. Effects of assertive training on marital interaction. *Archives of General Psychiatry*, 1974, *30*, 643–649.

Hunt, G.M. & Azrin, N.H. The community reinforcement approach to alcoholism. *Behavior Research and Therapy*, 1973, *11*, 91–104.

Jacobson, E. *Progressive relaxation.* Chicago: University of Chicago Press, 1938.

Kantorovich, N.V. An attempt at associative reflex therapy in alcoholism. *Psychological Abstracts*, No. 4282, 1930 (abstract).

Kraft, T. Alcoholism treated by systematic desensitization: A follow-up of eight cases. *Journal of the Royal College of General Practice*, 1969 *18*, 336–340.

Kraft, T. & Al-Issa, I. Alcoholism treated by desensitization: A case study. *Behaviour Research and Therapy*, 1976, *5*, 69–70.

Lazarus, A.A. Towards the understanding and effective treatment of alcoholism. *South African Medical Journal*, 1965, *39*, 736–741.

Lazarus, A.A. *Behavior therapy and beyond.* New York: McGraw-Hill Book Co., 1971.

Lovibond, S.H. & Caddy, G.R. Discriminated aversive control in the moderation of alcoholics' drinking behavior. *Behavior Therapy*, 1970, *1*, 437–444.

Lynn, E.J. Treatment for alcoholism: Psychotherapy is still alive and well. *Hospital and Community Psychiatry*, 1976, *27*, 282–283.

Maisto, S.A. *The effect of expectancy and feedback on blood alcohol level discrimination in heavy drinkers.* Unpublished doctoral dissertation, University of Wisconsin-Milwaukee, 1975.

Miller, P.M. The use of behavioral contracting in the treatment of alcoholism: A case report. *Behavior Therapy*, 1972, *3*, 593–596.

Miller, P.M. A behavioral intervention program for chronic public drunkenness offenders. *Archives of General Psychiatry*, 1975, *32*, 915–918.

Miller, P.M. *Behavioral treatment of alcoholism.* New York: Pergamon Press, in press.

Mills, K.C., Sobell, M.B. & Schaefer, H.H. Training social drinking as an alternative to abstinence for alcoholics. *Behavior Therapy*, 1971, *2*, 18–27.

Nathan, P.E. & Briddell, D.W. Behavioral assessment and treatment of alcoholism. In: B. Kissin & H. Begleiter (Eds.), *The biology of alcoholism, Vol. 5.* New York: Plenum Press, in press.

Nathan, P.E. & Marlatt, G.A. (Eds.) *Behavioral assessment and treatment of alcoholism.* New Brunswick: Rutgers Center for Alcohol Studies, 1976, in press.

O'Donnell, J.A., Voss, H.L., Clayton, R.R., Slatin, G.T. & Room, R.G.W. *Young men and drugs—A national survey.* National Institute on Drug Abuse Research Monograph 5, February, 1976.

Pattison, E.M., Sobell, M.B. & Sobell, L.C. (Eds.) *Emerging concepts of alcohol dependence.* New York: Springer Publishing Co., in press.

Rachal, J.V., Williams, J.R., Brehm, M.L., Cavanaugh, B., Moore, R.P. & Eckerman, W.C. *Final report: A national study of adolescent drinking behavior, attitudes and correlates.* Research Triangle Institute Center for the Study of Social Behavior, April, 1975.

Rachman, S. & Teasdale, J. *Aversion therapy and behaviour disorders: An analysis.* Miami: University of Miami Press, 1969.

Sobell, L.C. & Sobell, M.B. A self-feedback technique to monitor drinking behavior in alcoholics. *Behaviour Research and Therapy*, 1973b, *11*, 237–238.

Sobell, M.B. & Sobell, L.C. Individualized behavior therapy for alcoholics: Rationale, procedures, preliminary results and appendix. Sacramento: *California Mental Health Research Monograph No. 13*, 1972.

Sobell, M.B. & Sobell, L.C. Individualized behavior therapy for alcoholics. *Behavior Therapy*, 1973a, *4*, 49–72.

Sobell, M.B. & Sobell, L.C. Assessment of addictive behaviors. In: M. Hersen & A. Bellack (Eds.) *Behavioral assessment: A practical handbook.* New York: Pergamon Press, in press.

Sobell, M.B., Sobell, L.C. & Sheahan, D.B. Functional analysis of drinking problems as an aid in developing individual treatment strategies. *Addictive Behaviors*, 1976, *1*, 127–132.

Wilkinson, R. *The prevention of drinking problems.* New York: Oxford University Press, 1970.

Wilson, G.T., Leaf, R. & Nathan, P.E. The aversive control of excessive drinking by chronic alcoholics in the laboratory setting. *Journal of Applied Behavior Analysis*, 1975, *8*, 13–26.

Wolpe, J. *The practice of behavior therapy.* New York: Pergamon Press, 1969.

Chapter 14

Noncompliance to Medical Regimen

W. Doyle Gentry*

Compliance or adherence to prescribed medical regimen is perhaps the most crucial issue facing modern medicine today. That is, the extent to which modern medicine is effective in treating various illnesses may depend in large measure on the patient's ability or willingness to follow medical advice, e.g., to take certain medications, restrict one's diet, exercise, and so forth. Medical drugs do not produce miraculous effects in reducing or curing disease if the patient does not take the drugs as prescribed or in fact does not take them at all. The crucial question seems to be: How can the physician insure that his patients will comply with the medical regimen he prescribes so as to maximize their chances for recovery from illness and maintenance of good health?

While a large number of studies have been presented in the medical literature dealing with the issue of noncompliance, which basically is defined as "not following the instructions of a physician," these studies have provided few answers which are helpful to the practicing physician. In fact, many of the studies have produced negative or conflicting findings which further confuse the issue. In a recent review by Kasl (1975), a number of interesting points were made which bear repeating:

1. The traditional approach of looking for stable characteristics of individuals which might predict compliance is of little value. Different forms of compliance are not highly correlated with one

*Duke University Medical Center.

another and compliance in any one form (e.g. taking drugs) is not stable over time.

2. Patients' intentions to comply with medical regimen are poorly correlated with actual compliance behavior.
3. Sociodemographic characteristics are not reliable predictors of noncompliance. Neither age, sex, race, social class, or marital status consistently predict compliance across all situations, although they may determine compliance in specific situations, e.g., older men and younger women evidence poorer adherence to drug regimen in patients with tuberculosis.
4. Compliance seems more related to characteristics of the medical regimen per se than to characteristics of the patients involved. For example, better compliance is associated with single rather than multiple drugs or drug doses, medication taken for relief of symptoms as opposed to prophylactic reasons, and medication taken for short rather than long periods of time.

Rather, Kasl suggests that noncompliance may be more a function of variables in the patient's social environment, which to some extent are beyond the physician's control. He further states that "A doctor who prescribes treatment which consists of alteration of personal habits (smoking and eating) is prescribing treatment which is less obviously medical, *where his authority to insist may be more marginal*,[1] and where the *sanctions available to the doctor are weaker.*" Finally, he notes that some noncompliance may result from the lack of continuous reinforcement from health professionals as well as the social environment and the lack of feedback provided by changes in the patient's symptomatology and through various therapeutic procedures.

Kasl has, in effect, described noncompliance with medical regimen as a behavioral problem subject to behavioral principles and techniques. His emphasis on concepts such as social environment, reinforcement, feedback, as well as self-management and the need to modify patient expectations (cognitions), fits the behavioral framework quite nicely. Unfortunately, to date, behaviorists have offered little beyond speculation to an understanding of noncompliance and the methods by which it might be reduced.

One published study by Zifferblatt (1975) deals with a behavioral analysis of compliance behavior. It suggests that compliance is primarily a function of the environmental events which immediately precede (antecedents) and follow (consequences) it. The antecedent

1. Italics mine.

events are *cues* which tell the patient "this is the occasion to take my medicine," or to resist certain foods, not smoke, exercise, etc. If the cues are highly visible and specific (see Table 14–1), there is a high probability of compliance; if the cues are invisible or ambiguous, the probability is low. The consequent events are seen as reinforcement or punishment depending on whether they constitute a pleasant or unpleasant experience. Relief from pain is indeed a pleasant experience and if it immediately follows injestion of certain medications, the probability is high that the patient will take the medications as prescribed. However, some drugs produce negative side-effects such as dry mouth, dizziness, sleepiness, and gastric upset, and the probability of compliance for these drugs is by comparison much lower. Also, as is evident from Table 14–1, some drugs, as well as things such as exercises and dieting, produce no immediate effects positive or negative since they are taken for preventive reasons and as such also have a low probability of compliance. Zifferblatt notes that the cues for compliance must be *salient*, i.e., have significance for the patient, *compatible* with the patient's daily routine, have a *short latency* between the cue and the compliance behavior, and be *explicit*, i.e., clearly related to the behavior in question. Otherwise, the degree of compliance is low. Table 14–2 provides some examples of the types of cues which contribute to high and low compliance for the taking of medication.

These same factors also play an important role in determining the effect of consequences on compliance. For example, as Kasl noted, the authority of the physician to insist on compliance may not be particularly salient to the patient if the behaviors in question are viewed as nonmedical, e.g., smoking, dieting, etc. Also, the latency of physician reinforcement may be sufficiently delayed following compliance that it has little or no effect on such behavior. Explicitness is equally important, in that it seems unlikely that a statement by a physician to "take care of yourself" or "I'm real pleased that you're taking care of yourself these days," will have any significant effect on the patient's compliance behavior.

Both Kasl and Zifferblatt question the ability of physicians to have a major impact on compliance behavior both because the physician is "reluctant to take an activist, outreach role" in getting patients to comply and because physicians are already harried enough and simply do not have the time to properly attend to compliance problems. Both authors suggest the use of other health care professionals, such as trained nurses or psychologists, to improve compliance, or better yet emphasize the potential for self-management strategies in this area. Techniques for behavioral self-control currently

Table 14–1. Comparison of a Number of Similar Medication Taking Behaviors Through a Functional Analysis

	Antecedents		*Behavior*	*Consequences*		
	Cue specificity	*Event*	*1. Open packet for bottle 2. Mix powder with liquid or take tablet 3. Drink mixture*	*Event*	*Latency*	*Probability of reoccurrences*
(1)	Easily detected and specific to response	Upset stomach	Antiacid	Relief of discomfort	5–10 min.	High
(2)	Easily detected and specific to response	Headache	Headache powder	Relief of headache	10–15 min.	High
(3)	Ambiguous cues-discernable symptoms	None	Aspirin	Avoidance of arthritic pain	Preventive	Low
(4)	Ambiguous	None	Gelatin (brittle nails)	None	Preventive	Low
(5)	Ambiguous	None	Vitamins	None	Preventive nausea	Low
(6)	Ambiguous	None	Diuretic (hypertension)	None	Preventive	Low
(7)						
(a)	Ambiguous	None	Cholestyramine	None	Preventive	Low
(b)	Explicit time or occasion	Buzzer break-fast sponse cue, table	Cholestyramine	Access to breakfast	1 min.	High
(c)	Ambiguous	None	Cholestyramine	$20 bill per ingestion	5 sec.	High

(Reprinted with permission of Zifferblatt, 1975.)

Table 14–2. Examples of Cues Contributing High and Low Compliance for Taking Medication

Cue Dimension	*Probability of Compliance*	
	High	*Low*
1. Salience	Aversive alarm buzzer or watch at work	Spouse reminder the night before
2. Compatibility	Medicine to be taken with meals	Medicine taken before or after meals
3. Latency	Spouse reminder the night before	Secretary reminder at medicine time
4. Explicitness	Vitamin container on kitchen table	Spouse reminder to take medication

exist which might be employed with great success for the compliance problem (Thoresen and Mahoney, 1974). Zifferblatt notes that we can learn to "control our temper" in social situations; why not learn to control our medication intake?

To the extent that changes in patient expectations might determine the degree of compliance behavior, cognitive behavior modification might be employed (Mahoney, 1974). Many of the antecedent cues and covert consequences of compliance or noncompliance could be internalized. The patient could learn to tell himself "It's time for your medicine." in association with meal times and to follow-up the medication intake with a self-statement such as "Good, there you feel better now that you've taken your medicine on time."

Other considerations for improving compliance from a behavioral standpoint include:

1. A step-by-step approach should be used in describing for the patient the desired compliance behavior(s). Many physicians overwhelm their patients with multiple drugs and complex drug doses and in fact require too much change all at once.
2. Attempts should be made to make compliance with the medical regimen as nondisruptive of the patient's normal daily living activities as possible. Compliance should definitely not compete with other sources of reinforcement. Weiss and Engel (1971) found that some cardiac patients failed to participate fully in a biofeedback program which drastically reduced PVC activity and improved their chances of survival, in one case because of a drink-

ing problem and in another case because the patient was "afraid that if his PVCs improved, he might lose his disability benefits" (p. 318). Other examples would include prescribed medicines which require alteration of the family's eating times or which cause drowsiness and prevent social interaction with friends and family.

As was pointed out earlier in this chapter, behaviorists have until now paid little attention to the problem of medical noncompliance. However, it seems clear that noncompliance is not merely a problem for prescribed medical regimen, but also is equally detrimental to behavioral treatment regimens. As the behaviorist extends his principles and techniques for behavioral change more and more into the field of modern medicine, he will surely become more concerned with this problem and will begin to offer more concrete solutions than have been presented herein.

REFERENCES

Kasl, S.V. Issues in patient adherence to health care regimens. *Journal of Human Stress*, 1975, *1*, 5–17.

Mahoney, M.J. *Cognition and behavior modification.* Cambridge: Ballinger, 1974.

Thoresen, C. & Mahoney, M.J. *Behavioral self-control.* New York: Holt, Rinehart, & Winston, 1974.

Weiss, T. & Engel, B.T. Operant conditioning of heart rate in patients with premature ventricular contractions. *Psychosomatic Medicine*, 1971, *33*, 301–22.

Zifferblatt, S.M. Increasing patient compliance through the applied analysis of behavior. *Preventive Medicine*, 1975, *4*, 173–82.

Chapter 15

Assorted Physical Disorders†

*Frank T. Masur, III**

The use of behavioral techniques in the treatment of various physical disorders has become increasingly popular in recent years. Treatment programs based upon a behavioral model of specific physical dysfunctions have been successful in alleviating a number of disorders which had been intractable to more traditional medical interventions. The novelty of these behavioral strategies has added a new dimension to our conceptualization of disease states and in many ways has forced us to focus our attention on a variety of environmental variables that have important implications for our treatment of the "total patient."

Behavioral approaches in medical treatment have reached an applicability which in many ways appears to be limited in scope only by the creativity and ingenuity of the individual practitioner. This is not to say that behavioral interventions are a new panacea, but simply that these techniques warrant inclusion in the armamentarium of the health care professional. In many of the cases which are reported in this chapter, behavioral techniques were successfully employed only after an assortment of medical interventions (e.g., chemotherapy, surgery, etc.) had been found to be of limited value. Successful treatments were particularly dramatic in those instances where the dysfunction had reached life-threatening proportions (e.g., chronic vomiting) or where the physical disorder had all but totally disabled

*Highland Hospital Division, Duke University Medical Center.

†The author wishes to express his thanks to Dr. Thomas Faschingbauer for his valuable editorial assistance and to Jeff Farr who helped in the gathering of relevant bibliographic materials.

the patient (e.g., spasmodic torticollis). Hopefully, by reviewing the various ways in which behavioral approaches have effected significant reductions in physical disorders, we might further stimulate both researcher and clinician in the development and extension of this exciting area.

VOMITING

Infancy

Perhaps one of the most dramatic cases in which chronic ruminative vomiting was successfully eliminated through the use of a behavioral treatment was reported by Lang and Melamed (1969). A nine-month old infant whose life was seriously endangered by persistent vomiting and chronic rumination had undergone extensive medical evaluations to determine the etiology of his condition. No organic basis could be found for his symptoms and several treatment approaches including dietary alterations, the administration of antinausiants, and various changes in the feeding situation provided only short-lived relief. By the time a behavioral approach was considered, the infant was in critical condition with body weight down to twelve pounds. Two days of baseline observation revealed that the infant would regurgitate most of his food intake within 10 minutes of each feeding and that he would continue to vomit small amounts of food throughout the day. Electromyographic (EMG) measurements from muscle potentials recorded just under the patient's chin showed that the onset of vomiting was clearly accompanied by vigorous throat movements characterized by rhythmic, high frequency, high intensity muscle activity. A program of aversive conditioning was initiated following feeding whereby a brief and repeated electric shock was administered to the infant's leg whenever he began to vomit and continued until the vomiting response ended. By the sixth session the child no longer vomited during the treatment periods. The aversive conditioning procedures achieved success in little more than a week, and follow-ups at five months and one year indicated that the patient had exhibited no further vomiting. His weight returned to normal, and he was a healthy, alert, and active child with no physical problems. In this case a rapid recovery from life-threatening chronic ruminative vomiting was produced through brief aversive conditioning therapy in which the vomiting and rumination were treated as maladaptive behavior patterns. Electric shock was used to inhibit the sequence of responses which led to and included vomiting. The authors point out that their use of psychophysiological recordings (EMG) were particularly valuable in helping to provide an objective physical documentation of identifiable responses which were to be altered. No symptom substitution was observed during or after treatment and in fact the child became much more responsive to people and things in his environment.

The effectiveness of aversive conditioning (electric shock) in suppressing chronic vomiting and rumination in infants has received some confirmation in two recent case studies (Cunningham and Linsheid, 1976; Toister et al., 1975). With both infants (9.5 month old male; 7 month old male) an assortment of procedures had been attempted to eliminate their ruminative vomiting but had met with little success. The consequent emaciation from chronic vomiting necessitated the use of fast-acting behavioral interventions and in both cases the delivery of an electric shock contingent upon vomiting brought a speedy reduction in this maladaptive behavior. Follow-ups (four months and six months) demonstrated the stability of the treatment with neither child exhibiting any more vomiting and both children manifesting healthy weight gains. Since the use of electric shock is often painful and frequently frightening to parents and other professional staff, Sajwaj, Libet, and Agras (1974) sought a different stimulus that might suppress chronic ruminative vomiting. Whenever prevomiting tongue movements were observed in a six month old infant whose life was jeopardized by her chronic vomiting, the authors squirted approximately 10 cc's of unsweetened lemon juice in her mouth. After 12 treatments the child no longer regurgitated her food, and concurrent with this reduction in rumination was a significant increase in weight and a noticeably positive change in the infant's response to others. A one year follow-up revealed stable treatment gains. The authors note that this conditioning procedure may have been the result of forcibly injecting fluid into the infant's mouth and that the unpleasant nature of the lemon juice may be irrelevant. Although this procedure, unlike electric shock, can be easily used by paraprofessional personnel and is not likely to be abused, two medical complications may arise from the use of lemon juice in this type of treatment. First, since lemon juice is acidic it may irritate the sensitive mucosa of the mouth. Secondly, and more importantly, the possibility of the patient aspirating the lemon juice into the lungs must be carefully considered and monitored since this would be likely to produce serious medical complications.

Mental Retardation

White and Taylor (1967) employed aversive conditioning procedures to treat the chronic ruminative vomiting of two mentally retarded hospitalized patients (23 year old female; 14 year old male).

Mild electric shock was administered whenever the patient would display throat, eye, or coughing gestures that had served as signals for vomiting. The authors suggest that the shock served to "distract" the patients and whenever other naturally occurring environmental variables served as distracters shock was not administered. Because of this approach shock was presented on a variable basis and this may account for why the response to treatment was also variable from day to day. Although significant improvement was noted for both patients after one week of treatment and again at one month follow-up, the variable use of the aversive conditioning procedures makes it difficult to establish whether a functional relationship between decreased rumination and shock administration actually exists. However, a number of other reports have confirmed the efficacy of aversive conditioning in significantly reduced or totally eliminating chronic vomiting in retarded patients (Kohlenberg, 1970; Luckey, Watson, and Musick, 1968; Watkins, 1972). In each case electric shock was administered upon the onset of vomiting or upon observing reliable prevomiting behavior (e.g., tensing of the abdomen). The response to treatment is generally quick although the relatively large number of shocks delivered in vomiting-control studies suggests that this maladaptive behavior is often highly resistant to treatment. With reduced vomiting, patients typically show healthy weight gains although follow-up data indicate the need for occasional "booster" sessions if vomiting returns. In this regard aversive conditioning techniques appear to be effective in eliminating chronic vomiting although frequently there is a definite need for other behavioral interventions to maintain the treatment gains.

Vomiting, as a behavior, produces consequences for the patient especially in the way that family members, teachers, or hospital personnel respond to the patient after each vomiting episode. In some instances, therefore, treatment programs can be aimed at altering the conditions that follow vomiting without the need for the direct use of aversive conditioning. Azrin and Wesolowski (1975) have reported the successful utilization of a "positive practice and self correction" approach in the elimination of habitual vomiting with a 36 year old profoundly retarded woman. Seclusion for 30 minutes after each vomiting episode had had no appreciable effect on vomiting frequencies. Therefore, whenever the patient vomited she was required to clean it up, change her clothes, and to change her bedsheets if they had been soiled (self-correction). After doing so she was required to engage in 15 practice trials in the correct manner of vomiting (positive practice) i.e., going to the bathroom, bending over the toilet, etc.

Within five weeks vomiting, which had been highly resistant to a number of treatment attempts, was virtually eliminated and remained so at the follow-up one year later.

Wolf et al., (1965) suggested that the vomiting behavior of a 19 year old retarded girl was being maintained by the rewarding consequences of being removed from the classroom. Consequently, the teacher was instructed to continue class as usual despite the child's vomiting and within six weeks vomiting was reduced to zero. To determine whether this reduction was the result of the treatment program and not extraneous uncontrolled variables the authors had hoped to temporarily reverse their procedure and to reinstate the vomiting. However, the child's vomiting never returned, leaving the authors with no response to reward. From an experimental standpoint their inability to reinstate the "deconditioned" behavior limits our ability to attribute the active treatment process to the procedures which were used. Nevertheless, from a practical standpoint this procedure does seem to have relevance in treating this type of vomiting behavior.

Neuroses

All of the cases reported thus far have involved the behavioral treatment of chronic vomiting in infants or retardates. With adult patients who are of normal intelligence, aversive conditioning procedures may be of limited value in eliminating vomiting. Fortunately, other methods have shown some success.

Lang (1965) reports the case of a 23 year old registered nurse treated for anorexia nervosa and nervous vomiting. Vomiting coupled with decreased food intake had worsened six months prior to treatment and the patient had lost 20 pounds. When no organic pathology could be found, a behavioral oriented treatment approach was initiated which consisted of relaxing the patient with deep muscle relaxation exercises (Jacobson, 1938), and then having her visualize the various scenes which had previously caused her to become tense. Hierarchies dealing with each of the three situations eliciting anxiety (travel, being disapproved of by significant people, and being the center of attention) were constructed in this systematic desensitization approach. When the patient could successfully visualize a scene without feeling anxious, the therapist proceeded to the next scene on the hierarchy. In this way she was gradually taught to tolerate situations which previously elicited anxiety responses. Teaching the patient to become more assertive in her responses to others was also an important part of the therapy procedure.

Lang failed to provide any data concerning vomiting frequency but states at a one year follow-up the patient was significantly improved. When work and social pressures were sufficiently high the patient's response of anxiety, nausea, and avoidance would result but the treatment had markedly raised the threshold at which these responses occurred.

Burgess (1969) reported an interesting case of an 18 year old college coed who first vomited following a date on which she had consumed a large quantity of alcohol. Thereafter vomiting would occur the morning after each date despite variations in the individuals she dated, the nature of the date, the locale, presence or absence of drinking behavior, or sexual behaviors during the dating situation. Vomiting never occurred in the absence of dating, and a consistent overall sequence of dating, sleeping, and vomiting the next morning was demonstrated. Treatment consisted of advising the patient in dating patterns which disrupted the date-sleep sequence. The patient was instructed to date everyday and to gradually increase the time spent on each date by 15 to 30 minutes, beginning with one hour daytime dates. The patient was also instructed to avoid alcohol intake, to date in public places for the first three to five dates, and to restrict heavy petting. Treatment was conducted for four one hour sessions over a two week period and vomiting behavior was quickly reduced. Follow-up reports at one month and one year indicated that the patient had returned to a normal dating routine and vomiting had not reoccurred. The author discussed this case within the framework of a classical conditioning paradigm. While the original vomiting experience was probably a result of alcohol intake and excessive fatigue, the date-sleep-vomit sequence seems to have become incidentally conditioned.

Alford, Blanchard, and Buckley (1972) were able to effectively treat a 17 year old woman who had a 10 year history of hysterical vomiting episodes. Treatment consisted of withdrawing all social attention and contacts from the patient whenever she exhibited vomiting behavior. Vomiting was quickly eliminated and seven months after discharge the patient remained asymptomatic. This behavioral approach does have value in eliminating chronic hysterical vomiting particularly when it can be determined that social variables (e.g., attention) are acting as reward systems which maintain the maladaptive pattern.

Mogan and O'Brien (1972) utilized a counterconditioning technique in the treatment of a 60 year old woman who had been vomiting for six weeks following an acute myocardial infarction (MI). Just before her MI the patient had become depressed, had developed a headache, and began to vomit. During the six weeks recovery from her MI the patient continued to vomit despite antiemetic medication. A fluid diet did not stop the vomiting and continuous intravenous therapy was required to repair excessive fluid loss. Extensive physical workups demonstrated no organic basis for the patient's vomiting and she was discharged only to return two weeks later, having lost 18 pounds. Behavior therapy was based on the assumption that vomiting behavior had become associated with feelings of depression. A counterconditioning technique was employed to inhibit reverse peristaltic activity. Ginger ale, administered orally in amounts too small to elicit vomiting, produces normal forward peristaltic movements (Nelson 1954, pg. 669). The patient was instructed to take one sip of ginger ale every 15 minutes she was awake. Vomiting frequencies were reduced from 15 to zero times per day by the end of the second day of treatment. On the third day, ginger ale intake was discontinued and the patient was able to take fluids and solids. Two week and five month follow-ups demonstrated the patient to be free of vomiting. Other behavioral techniques had also alleviated much of the patient's depression.

Finally, a similar strategy was utilized in the training of a response that was incompatible with retching (Stoffelmayer, 1970). The patient, a 30 year old woman, would immediately begin to retch, gag, and near-vomit upon the insertion of dentures. Since the dental surgeon was able to pass a finger over the patient's soft and hard palate without any adverse reaction, the patient's symptoms were interpreted to be a conditioned response to the dentures and were treated accordingly. Since reading is a response that is incompatible with gagging, the patient was directed to read very quickly out loud when her dentures were inserted into her mouth. Short reading periods of only a few seconds duration were begun and by gradually increasing the length of the reading material the woman was able to withhold her dentures for prolonged periods of time. Ten treatment sessions (each 15 minutes in length) enabled the patient to maintain her dentures in place without gagging for up to six hours. Eating and other social behaviors produced no discomfort and on four week and six month follow-ups the patient was symptom free.

DIARRHEA

Bockus (1969) has noted that functional disorders of the gastrointestinal system are relatively common. Frequently, however, as is the case with many psychosomatic disorders, diagnoses are made by exclusion only when specific organic pathology cannot be determined. This is often the case with "emotional diarrhea" even though the patient often complains of being emotionally tense and motility studies suggest that the patient has abnormally high levels of intestinal activity (Chandler, 1963). Cohen and Reed (1968) have reported the successful treatment of two patients with "nervous diarrhea" in which the condition was exacerbated when the patients were required to travel. The first patient was a 20 year old male with a four year history of diarrhea; the second a 30 year old male with a seven year history. Physical examinations were negative and both patients had been seen in psychotherapy prior to the utilization of behavioral techniques. Treatment procedures were explained to the patients in a way that suggested that the physical symptoms were manifestations of anxiety which they had "learned to associate with certain provoking situations." The basic thrust of therapy was to train the patients in deep relaxation exercises and to desensitize them to the images of the provoking situation and of the symptoms themselves. When the patient was relaxed each item in the anxiety hierarchy was presented in turn. No item was presented until the preceding, less stressful, scene could be imagined without anxiety. The patient's clinical state was reviewed when each hierarchy was reviewed at the weekly session. Two measures of change in severity of symptoms were used: frequency of diarrhea and freedom of activity. Both patients rated themselves as having increased their freedom of activity and decreased the number of diarrhea incidents per day, although neither improvement was remarkable. A follow-up over a period averaging six months showed that improvement was maintained and no symptom substitution was evident. The authors postulated a mechanism by which nervous diarrhea may have become a conditioned response to stressful situations, though they were unable to specify which of many factors (including the doctor-patient relationship, relaxation, and desensitization) were influential in the successful treatment of their patients.

Hedberg (1973) reported the successful treatment of a middle age married woman with a case of chronic diarrhea associated with interpersonal anxiety. The patient averaged 10 bowel movements per day. Her inability to control her bowel movements for more than 30 seconds resulted in an average of three "accidents" per week. Her previously active social life had become extremely restricted and she had terminated all of her community activities. The patient's chronic diarrhea had been a problem for 22 years and despite numerous consultations, two years of attending Neurotics Anonymous, and two years of individual psychodynamic therapy, little or no relief had been achieved. At the time of behavioral interventions she had begun to restrict herself to situations in which she could be within 15 seconds of an available bathroom. The treatment approach utilized deep muscle relaxation as well as systematic desensitization. Three personal hierarchies were constructed to deal with her various interpersonal anxieties. An additional hierarchy was used in which the proximity to a bathroom was the primary variable. Twelve individual sessions of systematic desensitization over a six week period constituted the total treatment process. Two months later the patient was given four "booster" sessions for additional learning and two years later, two further booster sessions in an evaluation interview. At the third treatment session the patient freely terminated her medications and reported noticeable symptom relief and increased energy. Bowel control was achieved by the eighth session and was maintained at a two month follow-up. Her social life had also improved. At the time of her two year follow-up the patient was defecating once daily and was able to control her bowels for hours if it was not convenient for her to go to the bathroom. Considering the dramatic results the author suggests that systematic desensitization appears to be a highly effective method in the amelioration of functional chronic diarrhea.

Biofeedback training is a procedure in which an individual is provided with informational feedback about the functioning state of physiological processes, usually outside of normal conscious awareness. The individual, through cognitive mediators, responses in the central nervous system, or by directly influencing the autonomic nervous system, can then gain control over the physiological system. A variety of clinical conditions have been studied and treated within the biofeedback paradigm (Blanchard and Young, 1974).

Furman (1973) utilized biofeedback in the treatment of five female patients suffering from functional disorders of the lower gastrointestinal system. In each of his patients, ranging in age from 15 to 62 years, no organic pathology could be found. Furman began his treatment approach with the assumption that bowel sounds of all varieties were directly proportional to the level of peristaltic activity. Since abnormal hypermotility appears to be related to functional diarrhea, therapy was directed at training the patients to decrease the abnormally high activity from the colon and small intestines. This was accomplished by attaching an electronic stethoscope to the patient's abdomen and amplifying the sound to be played back through a loudspeaker so that the patient was able to directly hear her intestinal sounds. During the treatment sessions the patient was asked to alternately increase or decrease paristaltic activity while the bowel sounds were being monitored. Dramatic, symptomatic improvement consistently occurred as or just before autonomic control became apparent in the treatment sessions. Significant improvement was reported for all five patients, even those who had experienced a life time of functional diarrhea and who had been virtually toilet bound. However, no quantified data were reported and it is difficult to assess the actual degree of symptomatic relief that these patients obtained. The author theorized that the most likely explanation for the dramatic improvement in the patients' conditions was the desensitizing effect of the training situation. He speculated that because the patients were relaxed and unstressed during the sessions they began to learn that motility of the gastrointestinal tract need not be related to anxiety. Thus the major association of anxiety and hypermotility was broken. Similarly, the relief of overall distress and the resumption of more normal life patterns were very rewarding to patients and most likely helped to maintain the clinical improvement.

All three of the cases reported thus far in the treatment of chronic functional diarrhea have utilized techniques which employ relaxation strategies. A combination of relaxation exercises, systematic desensitization, and biofeedback techniques may provide a particularly beneficial approach in the treatment of this disorder.

POLLAKIURIA

Pollakiuria is a disorder in which the patient manifests excessively high frequencies of daily urinations. Asnes and Mones (1973) stressed the distinction between pollakiuria and polyuria. Pollakiuria is used as a descriptive term which refers to an excessive number of urinations per day, whereas polyuria is defined as the passage of an increased volume of urine. While polyuria and pollakiuria usually occur together, it is important to note that a patient may suffer from excessive urinations without actually producing an overabundance of urine. That is, the volume of urine produced is normal but the voiding rate is exceptionally high. Crominas and Rallo (1971) noted that there is a derth of literature on pollakiuria which may be due to the fact that this disturbance, though not uncommon, rarely reaches debilitating proportions. When it does, they speculate that it is typically associated with some organic dysfunction and is therefore treated independently by a urologist. A number of cases, however, have been reported in which pollakiuria did not have an organic etiology and was subsequently treated through behavioral approaches. Jones (1956) successfully treated a 23 year old woman with excessive urinations through a conditioning procedure that was first used by Bykov (1957). The procedure consisted of conditioning the patient to tolerate greater volumes of saline solution which were injected into her bladder via a catheter. The patient was told that her bladder volume would be equal to the pressure displayed to her on a manometer. The treatment consisted of associating the patient's urinary urge with a specific manometer reading and then gradually shaping the patient to tolerate greater volumes of urine by providing her with falsely lowered manometer readings. Generalization of therapeutic gains was accomplished through the use of further deconditioning techniques.

Taylor (1972), assuming that anxiety was the causal factor in the excessive urination of a 15 year old female, used muscle relaxation and systematic desensitization in his treatment approach. The patient reported intermittent difficulties with excessive urination for nine years with an acute exacerbation in her condition during the academic year just prior to seeking therapy. Three anxiety hierarchies were devised which directly involved the patient's riding to school, being in school, and participating in classroom activities. Although Taylor did not provide any quantitative data on urination frequencies, he reports that they were normal at the end of three months of treatment and again at a four month follow-up.

Poole and Yates (1975) reported the successful treatment of a 24 year old college male who was suffering from excessive frequency of urination. Their previous analysis of this patient (Yates and Poole, 1972) indicated that the patient indeed had frequent urinations and was not simply troubled by the urge to urinate frequently. Their development of normative data suggested that within the age range of 18–25 years excessive frequency of urination may be statistically defined as a rate exceeding eight times per day during the waking period. In terms of sleeping time, an habitual frequency of urination of one time per night is statistically abnormal. The patient recorded diurnal urination frequencies ranging from 21 to 38 times per day. Sleeping period urinations ranged from 4 to 19 per night. Both frequencies were clearly abnormal. Since the patient had apparently developed a pattern of responding to minimal bladder stimulation, it was decided to devise a system whereby he could respond instead to time-bound cues. Treatment, therefore, consisted of requiring the patients to refrain from urinating for progressively longer periods of time during a 12 hour period each day (Fixed Period) while allowing him to urinate freely during the remaining 12 hours (Free Period). The patient was seen once weekly for 10 to 15 minutes during which time his daily urination records were collected for analysis. Over a 31 week treatment period, urination frequencies declined to within normal limits during both the fixed 12 hour period and free 12 hour period. A one year follow-up demonstrated that normal urination frequencies had been maintained.

Masur (1976) has reported the case of a 35 year old female who had been troubled by pollakiuria for over three years. Extensive physical examinations failed to provide any organic basis for frequencies of urination which at times reached 15 to 20 times per day. The use of systematic desensitization was considered inappropriate in this case since no specific anxiety-producing situations were evident. Instead, the patient was taught deep muscle relaxation and was placed on a "urination schedule" which specified the precise times each day that she was to urinate. The original urination schedule was based on the average length of time between the patient's urinations during the baseline observation period. Intervals between urinations were then gradually lengthened and a number of self-modification techniques were suggested to help her meet the demands of her urination schedule. These included talking on the phone, taking brisk walks, practicing relaxation exercises, and other behaviors incompatible with urinating. Self reported urination frequencies, which had reached debilitating proportions, were reduced to normal adult levels (5 times per day) after five months of weekly individual treatment. Follow-up over a four year period revealed a stable pattern of normal urinations with no symptom substitution evident.

Finally, van der Ploeg (1975) reported the treatment of a 14 year old boy with an excessive urge to urinate interacting with a school phobia so as to further exacerbate the urinary urge. The treatment consisted of a desensitization-varient approach in which stories were told to the boy to inhibit anxiety and consequently the urge he had to urinate. At the time of treatment the patient was urinating between 15 and 20 times per day. He had started to avoid all social situations and stayed at home most of the time. Since the child would "forget" the urge to urinate for several minutes while talking about his favorite hobby, sailing, items from his pleasant sailing experiences were counterposed in imagination with school images. Within five weeks of treatment, the patient's urination frequency at home and at school had returned to normal and he no longer experienced an excessive urge to urinate nor excessive frequencies of urination. An 18 month follow-up demonstrated no relapse.

SPASMODIC TORTICOLLIS

Spasmodic torticollis is a disorder of the cervical muscles (particularly the sternocleidomastoid muscle) which results in an abnormal positioning of the head, colloquially termed "wry neck." The patient's head is usually turned to either the right or left, depending upon the muscles involved. Despite advances in diagnostic sophistication and in pharmacologic research, spasmodic torticollis remains a clinical enigma whose etiology is still unclear. For years this condition was notoriously refractory to most of the traditional forms of treatment (Alpers, 1958) but more recently a number of behavioral techniques have met with some success in alleviating this often totally disabling condition.

Agras and Marshall (1965) employed the techniques of negative practice in the treatment of two patients with spasmodic torticollis. Negative practice consists essentially of directing the individual to consciously perform the actual behavior that one is attempting to reduce. According to Hull (1943), this constant repetition will produce a drive state which will inhibit the response. A 38 year old woman with spasmodic torticollis was taught to duplicate the head movements in her condition some 200 times in each daily treatment session. This was increased to 400 times per day in home practice exercises and after four weeks significant improvement was noted. Seven and 22 month follow-ups show the patient to be asymptomatic. A 59 year old female treated with the same procedures showed a worsening in her condition. She was unable to voluntarily practice her exercises, particularly returning her head to a resting position. This suggests that returning the head to a resting position may be a critical variable to consider before choosing negative practice in the treatment of torticollis.

Brierly (1967) reported the treatment of two patients with torticollis using an aversive conditioning technique. A special headgear apparatus was constructed which administered a mild electric shock to the patient's wrist when head positioning was abnormal. The apparatus could be adjusted so that the patient was gradually "shaped" to produce increasingly normal head positions. To encourage consciously controlled head movement, patients were instructed to read material that was projected on a wall in front of them. Treatments were held weekly until observable improvement was obtained. One patient demonstrated improvement by the fourth session and remained essentially symptom free at two and a half month and one year follow-ups. The second patient responded more slowly but was significantly improved after ten treatment sessions. A six month follow-up revealed no relapse but at 18 months when placed under severe stress this patient again began to manifest torticollis symptoms. Brierly also noted that the use of aversive conditioning procedures is contraindicated with patients who manifest high anxiety or multiple neurotic traits.

Bernhardt, Hersen, and Barlow (1972) developed a simple and precise method of measuring torticollis. A horizontal grid was placed over a videotape TV monitor and an observer would activate a timer whenever the patient's head was positioned beyond a critical level. In this way the percentage of torticollis positioning per session could be accurately measured. A 50 year old male patient, presenting with symptoms of torticollis, alcohol abuse, and paranoid ideation, was instructed to keep a light off that flashed when he was in a torticollis position. The result of this "negative feedback" approach was a significant decrease in the percentage of torticollis positioning from baseline per ten minute session. Unfortunately, the authors reported no data on clinical improvement or follow-up measurements.

Meares (1973) has postulated a model for the etiology of spasmodic torticollis which is based upon the assumption that fortuitous head movements in the direction of the torticollis produce anxiety which the ensuing muscle spasm momentarily reduces. Muscle spasms may become conditioned since they reduce feelings of anxiety. Meares speculated that since systematic desensitization is an anxiety reducing technique it might prove effective in the treatment of spasmodic torticollis. Systematic desensitization was employed with a 44 year old female with a seven year history of torticollis. Training in muscle relaxation was followed by the presentation of various anxiety hierarchies. At the end of treatment the patient, who previously had not been spasm free for even a minute while awake, was without spasms for hours at a time. Independent assessments by neurologists rated her as "markedly improved" but the author provides no information about follow-up data. While systematic desensitization holds some promise in treating spasmodic torticollis, it may be limited to only those patients displaying or reporting accompanying anxiety. Cleeland (1973) reports a number of case studies designed to assess whether patients with torticollis could modify the intensity and frequency of their spasms. Muscle spasms were paired with cutaneous shock, with an ongoing display of associated muscle activity (EMG feedback), or with a combination of shock and feedback. Ten patients, nine with spasmodic torticollis and one with retrocollis, served as subjects. The four male and six female patients ranged in age from 16 to 24 years. Surface electrodes were placed near the anterior border and just above the clavicular attachment of both the left and right sternocleidomastoid muscles. Shock and/or EMG feedback were presented to the patient contingent upon predetermined specified changes in muscle activity. The number of treatment sessions ranged from 18 to 23 depending upon the patient's clinical improvement. Results indicated that three patients displayed "marked improvement" (defined as no spasmodic muscle activity on follow-up EMG measures and no reported spasmodic action outside the laboratory). Three other patients showed "moderate improvement" (defined as reduced EMG activity on follow-up, assessment from an independent neurologist of significantly reduced head deviation and spasmodic activity, and self reported reductions of head deviation and spasmodic activity outside the laboratory). The remaining two patients were judged to have manifested no significant improvement. The most significant clinical improvement was shown by young patients for whom spasmodic torticollis was a symptom of relatively short duration.

Brudny, Grynbaum, and Korein (1974) have successfully used auditory and visual displays of muscle activity (EMG feedback) in the treatment of nine spasmodic torticollis patients. Seven men and two women, with ages ranging from 20 to 58 years, had torticollis symptoms ranging from 9 months to 15 years duration. All of the patients had received conventional forms of medical or surgical treatment and five patients had been seen in psychotherapy. A form of combined feedback, aimed at decreasing activity in the spasmodic muscle while simultaneously increasing the contractions and strength of the usually atrophied contralateral muscle was found to be especially helpful. Apparently the EMG feedback provided the patients with information concerning levels of muscle activity for which they had lost the usual proprioceptive feedback. The feedback apparatus was designed to allow for a gradual "step up" in the pattern of muscle activity required to produce a feedback signal. In this way the patients could be taught, in a step by step manner, to produce head and neck positions that demanded better performance. Treatment sessions lasting approximately one hour, were held 3 to 5 times per week and averaged 10 weeks. A home program of daily maximal isometric contractions of the previously atrophied muscles was stressed. This therapeutic technique was judged to be effective since three of the nine patients improved to where, after treatment, they were able to maintain neutral head positions for months without feedback and three other patients could maintain neutral positions for hours. Three patients needed further training and "booster sessions" yet no patient had difficulty responding or understanding the treatment procedure. Improved interpersonal relationships, reduced depression, and increased self-assurance were seen uniformly. Since this treatment procedure is noninvasive, free of side effects, and often successful where other conventional methods have failed, it may represent a major therapeutic advance in the treatment of spasmodic torticollis.

Previous research (Jacobs and Felton, 1969) with visual EMG feedback has established that patients with diagnosed neck injuries (involving upper trapezius) are able to significantly reduce abnormal muscle activity to a normal level. The ability of visual feedback to facilitate muscle relaxation suggests that EMG feedback can be a valuable technique in the rehabilitation of certain muscle disorders.

Williams (1974) reported the use of a novel biofeedback strategy in the treatment of a 36 year old woman with an 18 month history of torticollis. Hypothesizing that the induction of heart rate slowing might produce decreased muscle activity, the patient was provided with visual feedback of her heart rate and was instructed to use this feedback to help her learn to relax. Treatments consisted of five sessions over a four week period. EMG measurements were taken from the left sternocleidomastoid muscle to assess whether reductions in the muscle tension were related to heart rate slowing. Both within and across sessions the patient was able to slow her heart rate and become more relaxed with a comcomitant alleviation of torticollis whether measured by EMG or clinically observed. However, as her physical condition improved, her psychological condition began to deteriorate to the point where psychiatric hospitalization was necessary. This has important implication for clinicians using biofeedback techniques in treating patients in whom underlying psychic conflicts may be significant. Since the presenting symptom may serve as a mask for serious psychopathology, removing the symptom may render the patient defenseless. The clinician utilizing this approach should be prepared to manage such psychological complications should they occur.

Finally, Ericksen and Huber (1975) successfully employed a simple technique for the treatment of spasmodic torticollis with a 29 year old schizophrenic male. The procedure required the patient to make small head movements in synchronization with the beat of a metronome. A reference point on the wall in front of the seated patient was centered in his visual field when his neck was in the tonic (left) position. Upon instruction, and with the beat of the metronome (40 beats per minute), the patient made small head movements to the right to center his gaze upon a target visual stimulus taped on the wall one foot to the right of the original reference point. Each of these small turns required the patient to move his head approximately five degrees to the right. The patient practiced this procedure for 10 minute periods each day. Every two days the target stimulus was moved one foot further to the right, thus requiring the patient to gradually increase his head turning until he finally was able to position his head a full 180 degrees from his original tonic position. The patient was instructed to stop his metronome training for five minutes whenever his head turning caused him spasm or pain and then to continue after a rest period. After eight sessions of training the patient had regained complete voluntary control of his neck muscles and remained symptom free at nine month follow-up.

EPILEPSY

Behavioral interventions in epilepsy and other seizure disorders have been utilized with some success in a number of cases where traditional forms of chemotherapy have provided only limited improvement. Frequently this has involved conceptualizing the actual seizure as the last phase or "terminal link" (Zlutnick, Mayville, and Moffat, 1975) in a complex behavioral chain. Treatment, therefore, becomes directed toward modifying behaviors that reliably precede the seizure climax. Efron (1956), for example, treated a 41 year old female with a 26 year history of 7 to 18 seizures per month. Since the patient experienced a vivid preseizure aura that included a powerful olfactory hallucination, it was hypothesized that the introduction of an extraneous powerful odor prior to this experience might arrest the seizure course. A number of compounds were tried and the results indicated that any powerful unpleasant odor could reliably abort the seizures. This form of "counterstimulant" therapy, as it was termed by the author, appears to be effective in those cases in which a well defined aura precedes the seizure state. In a second study (Efron, 1957) with the same patient, a classical conditioning procedure was used to form an association between the noxious odor which arrested her seizures and the sight of a silver bracelet. Continued pairing of the bracelet and odor (jasmine) eventually resulted in the patient being able to use the sight of the bracelet alone to arrest her seizures. Eventually, merely thinking intently about the bracelet proved sufficient to inhibit seizures. The patient remained entirely seizure free for 14 months though later follow-up revealed occasional seizure activity.

Similarly, Daniels (1975) was able to effect a significant decrease in grand mal seizures with a 22 year old female whose seizures occurred one to three times per week. She would usually experience an anticipatory aura involving a complex thought sequence. Her aura would include feelings of excitement, depression, or anticipation, followed by nausea and thoughts concerning the safety of her family. Following her seizure episodes observers inevitably responded with a good deal of concern and attention, which may have served to reinforce the seizures. To abort the thought sequence aura the patient was taught a "thought-stopping" technique. This essentially involved her subvocally yelling "Stop!" and then immediately visualizing a pleasant, relaxing scene. Additionally she was taught to imagine having seizures to which no one paid any attention and staff members were instructed to ignore her seizure behavior. This combination of procedures resulted in a significant decrease in seizures and the patient remained asymptomatic for 16 weeks. Seizures briefly returned following a number of stressful life events, but then abruptly stopped for two more months. A six month follow-up revealed an average seizure frequency of only one per month. Although this approach appears to have been of some value in reducing seizures the inconsistency of the treatment gains warrants attention.

Zlutnick, Mayville, and Moffat (1975) also employed an abrupt interruption to break the behavioral chain preceding seizures. Patients were chosen only if they manifested a seizure that could be easily identified by independent observers, had at least one seizure per day, and had been formally diagnosed as epileptic. Three males and two females, ranging in age from 14 to 17 years, displayed easily observable preseizure behavior (e.g., fixed stare, arm raising, lowered motor activity, body tensing, etc.). Whenever these preseizure behaviors occurred the therapist would shout "No!" loudly and sharply and then grab the patient by the shoulders and shake him once vigorously. Seizure frequency was reduced for four of the five children. It was also found that this therapy approach could be effectively used by appropriately trained parents and other nonprofessional personnel.

Other procedures for the reduction of epileptic seizures have been developed which depend upon the structuring of specific reward systems. Balaschak (1976) has recently reported the successful implementation of a behavioral approach to reduce the seizure frequency in an 11 year old epileptic girl. The child's teacher was directed to shift the focus of attention from seizures to seizure-free time periods. A chart of seizure free "good times" was kept by the teacher whereby the child was rewarded with verbal praise and candy at the completion of totally seizure-free work periods. Seizures, which had occurred at an estimated frequency of three times per week were reduced to one per week at the end of treatment. Unfortunately the child's teacher was unwilling to reinstate the treatment program following the child's lengthy absenteeism due to mononucleosis. Consequently, seizures returned to pretreatment levels. Gardner (1967) was similarly able to train the parents of a 10 year old girl to effectively reduce the frequency of psychogenic seizures. Some weeks prior to her first seizure episode the patient had displayed a number of temper tantrums that "looked like convulsions." Assuming that parental attention and concern had served to reinforce and maintain the "seizures," Gardner taught her parents to not only ignore seizure behavior but also to reward the patient for any and all appropriate nonseizure behavior. Within two weeks the seizures dropped to zero. At a 26 week follow-up the parents were instructed to deliberately reinstate attention for inappropriate behaviors including seizures, and within 24 hours the patient manifested another episode. The parents were then directed to resume the treatment program with a consequent reduction in seizures. These results demonstrated the functional relationship between parental attention and the manifestation of psychogenic seizures in this patient. A 30 week follow-up showed the patient to be free of all seizure behavior.

Iwata and Lorentzson (1976) have also used reward systems to reduce the seizure-like behavior of a 41 year old nonambulatory retarded male. The treatment consisted of increasing the patient's daily activities with recreation therapy, music therapy, playing on the children's ward, etc. as well as rewarding the patient with his favorite beverage (root beer) whenever he had not exhibited a seizure during a specified 20 minute time period. Additionally, a "time out" procedure was used whereby the subject was put to bed at the onset of the seizure and completely ignored until the seizure terminated, at which time he was able to resume his scheduled activities. Seizures, which on the average had occurred approximately 12 times per week, were reduced to near zero after 10 weeks of treatment. As the patient progressed, the need for the use of "time out" procedures was dramatically reduced and later in the therapy program the patient was given money to buy his own root beer contingent upon the absence of seizures. The authors note that this combined treatment procedure makes it difficult to isolate those variables most influential in reducing the patient's seizures. They also note that this type of therapy requires the total cooperation of ward personnel, and often requires a considerable amount of time to implement. However, the data indicate that it should be possible to "fade out" the treatment as the patient's condition progresses.

Aversive conditioning techniques, using the application of mildly painful electric shock, have been successful in reducing the frequency of self-induced seizures with a five year old mentally retarded boy (Wright, 1973). The child would induce seizures by moving his hands back and forth before his eyes and blinking while looking at a light source. Observation by the patient's mother and neurologist confirmed the fact that he was experiencing "several hundred" self-induced seizures per day, each seizure lasting approximately 10 seconds. Conditioning treatment involved five one hour daily sessions over a three day period. At each attempt to self-induce a seizure, an electric shock was administered to the patient. After the third session the boy no longer attempted to induce seizures with his hands. At a five month follow-up the same conditioning procedure was used to arrest seizures induced by eye blinking with similar positive results. A seven month follow-up indicated that a 90 percent reduction in overall self-induced seizures had been maintained.

Parrino (1971) used desensitization in the effective treatment of a 36 year old male whose seizures were provoked by anxiety arousing situations in his environment. Anticonvulsive medication had failed to provide any relief and the patient had been diagnosed as having a progressive neurological disorder characterized by dementia and violent episodes of bizarre muscular movements (Jakob Creutzfeldt Syndrome).

During a thirteen day baseline period the frequency of seizures ranged from 22 to 95 (mean = 58). Deep muscle relaxation exercises and systematic desensitization produced a remarkable decrease in seizure activity over a fifteen week period. Four weeks after discharge the seizure rate was zero. Seizures briefly returned when the patient was placed under high levels of stress and outpatient treatment was continued. At a five month follow-up the patient remained asymptomatic.

A rare but often intractable form of epilepsy is the result of the presentation of specific environmental stimuli which stimulates physiological arousal and percipitates seizures. As a group this form of seizure activity is termed "reflex" or "sensory evoked" epilepsy. A classification of these various epilepsies has been developed (Forster, 1972) which not only relates various seizure inducing stimuli but also specifies the type of behavioral approach which can be effectively utilized in treatment. For over a decade Dr. Forster and his associates at the University of Wisconsin Medical Center have studied and treated a wide assortment of reflex epilepsies. Among the various reflex epilepsies they have successfully treated with conditioning techniques, include stroboscopic induced seizures (Forster, Booker, and Ansell, 1966; Forster and Campos, 1964; Forster, Ptacek and Peterson, 1965; Forster et al., 1964), musicogenic epilepsy (Forster, Booker, and Gascon, 1967; Forster et al., 1965), reading epilepsy (Forster, 1975; Forster, Paulsen, and Baughman, 1969), acousticomotor or startle epilepsy (Booker, Forster, and Klove, 1965) voice-induced epilepsy (Forster et al., 1969) somatosensory or touch evoked epilepsy (Forster and Cleeland, 1969) as well as pattern presentation and eye closure induced seizures (Forster, 1967). Although it is beyond the scope of this chapter to attempt a detailed review of Forster's various conditioning strategies in the treatment of these reflex epilepsies the interested reader is referred to excellent review articles that are available (Forster, 1969a, 1969b, 1969c, 1972, 1975).

Among the various strategies employed by Forster is the complete or partial avoidance of the evoking stimulus. Obviously in many cases (e.g. musicogenic or stroboscopic epilepsy) total avoidance of the eliciting stimuli may not be feasible. In other instances (e.g. reading epilepsy) total avoidance of the provoking stimulus is possible but not practical.

A second approach therefore, consists of altering the evoking stimulus in such a way so as to remove its seizure inducing qualities. For example with the photosensitive patient in whom seizures are induced by stroboscopic stimulation the experimental room is designed so that the strobe light can be presented with the ambient room light level at an intensity high enough to mask the strobe flash. Gradually the ambient light is decreased to where the strobe pulse can be just barely seen and to where no seizure is induced. This procedure is continued until the patient is gradually conditioned to tolerate clearly discernable strobe light flashes. This technique has met with good success in the treatment of stroboscopic induced epilepsy and has been computer automated to facilitate the speed and reliability of the treatment process. (Forster, Booker, and Ansell, 1966). Another method of altering the provoking stimulus is based upon the observation that some forms of reflex epilepsy do not result in seizure when the sensory stimulation is unilateral in form. Thus, some photosensitive patients will not manifest seizures if the strobe light is presented to only one eye. In this way a constant unilateral stimulation renders bilateral stimulation innocuous. It is important, however, for the patient to continually employ home training sessions of unilateral stimulation to maintain the effectiveness of this procedure. For this reason Forster (1972) feels that the treatment procedure represents a conditioning process and not simply an extinction process. To assist the generalization of the therapy process to the patient's environment, Forster has developed an ingenious technique. Initially, innocuous strobe light flashes are associated with audible clicks, thereby developing a conditioned association between nonseizure inducing light flashes and a clicking sound. Specially designed glasses, incorporating a sensitive photoelectric cell and a minature speaker then translate light flashes in the natural environment into clicking sounds that the patient can readily hear. In this way, strobe light flashes that are encountered in the patient's everyday life produce a clicking sound which has previously been conditioned to be innocuous.

Still another method of rendering a provoking stimulus innocuous is to raise the threshold at which the patient responds to the stimulus. With musicogenic and voice induced epilepsy, this is done by continuing the stimulation of the patient throughout the induction of the seizure and into the postictal state. Obviously, reading epilepsy is not amenable to this approach; however, a "vigilance method" has been found to be effective. Treatment consists of instructing the patient to maintain a vigilance for certain cues in the eliciting stimulus and to respond to those cues in some specified way. For example, the patient might be told to slap his thigh or press his fingers together at the occurence of every "a" in the material he is reading. It is often necessary to change the target letter to maintain effective vigilance.

Recently, a case of decision-making-induced epilepsy has been reported (Forster et al., 1975) which has not responded favorably to any of the conditioning techniques that have been found to be effective in the treatment of other forms of reflex epilepsy. Although various forms of reflex epilepsy are relatively rare, when encountered, they are often seriously disabling and quite intractable to traditional treatments. It is a credit to Dr. Forster and his associates that his novel therapeutic approaches have been so successful in treating this condition.

DeWerdt, and Van Rijn (1975) using Forster's vigilance procedures have reported the successful treatment of a 19 year old girl with reading epilepsy. As with Forster's patients, significant reduction in seizures corresponded with objectifiable decreases in pathological EEG activity.

Pinto (1972) treated a 31 year old male with movement epilepsy and a generalized phobic response to being in public (agoraphobia). Treatment consisted of having the patient listen to tape recorded accounts in which he was "flooded" with stories which dealt with his entering the intensely phobic situation and developing a seizure with all of the feared embarrassments. Following each fantasy session the patient experienced the situation *in vivo* without the seizure. Ten fantasy sessions followed by practice were used over three weeks of treatment. Seizures which had occurred with daily frequency were reduced to zero and the patient remained asymptomatic for 16 weeks.

A particular EEG rhythm of 12 to 16 Hz, termed the sensory motor rhythm (SMR), when conditioned in cats renders them resistant to seizures induced by convulsant drugs (Sterman, 1972). Relating these findings to humans suggested a clinical tool which might raise the seizure thresholds of epileptics, and Sterman and his associates have employed SMR biofeedback in the clinical treatment of epilepsy (Sterman, 1973; Sterman and Friar, 1972; Sterman, MacDonald, and Stone, 1974). Treatment consists of multiple long-term biofeedback sessions in which the individual is given information about and incentives for the production of SMR EEG patterns. Feedback is usually provided in both visual and auditory modalities and incentive systems range from monetary rewards to presenting the patient with photo slides of pleasant scenes, contingent upon SMR performance. In some cases a portable biofeedback EEG unit is provided for daily home use. The results of intensive biofeedback training and well controlled experimental procedures indicate that normal human subjects are able to produce significant increases in SMR activity. Clinically, there is a rather remarkable decrease in the incidence of major motor seizures when epileptics are given extensive SMR training. In some cases reductions of 67 percent have been noted though change generally occurs slowly over several months of biofeedback training. In some instances (Sterman, 1972) seizure reduction is accompanied by other positive personality changes and improved sleeping patterns. In other cases marked academic improvement was noted, (Sterman, 1973). These results appear to be specific for the SMR training and are probably not simply due to placebo effects or generalized relaxation training since when SMR training is discontinued a number of patients revert to pretreatment seizure levels and biofeedback techniques must be reinstituted. Thus, home practice and regular "booster" sessions are often necessary components in the total treatment plan.

Recent support for the effectiveness of SMR biofeedback has been presented by Lubar and Bahler (1976) in the treatment of eight severely epileptic patients. The patients, three of whom had varying degrees of mental retardation, represented a cross section of several forms of epilepsy including grand mal, myoclonic, akinetic, focal, and psychomotor. Two patients who had previously displayed multiple weekly seizures were significantly improved and were totally seizure free for periods up to one month. Other patients were able to block many of their seizures with a decrease in both seizure intensity and seizure duration. These data confirm earlier results (Seifert and Lubar, 1975) which indicate that SMR biofeedback training does have clinical relevance in the treatment of several forms of epilepsy. It appears, however, that SMR training is most effective with seizures in which there is motor involvement. The authors suggest that SMR biofeedback training may make a significant contribution to the treatment of epilepsy, particularly where chemical management is unsatisfactory or contraindicated.

Johnson and Meyer (1974) used a combination of relaxation training, EMG feedback, and the feedback of alpha and theta EEG frequencies to develop a low arousal, "antistress" response in an 18 year old female with a ten year history of grand mal seizures. Under chemical management seizures had stabilized at three episodes per month. The patient was taught relaxation techniques which were augmented by EMG biofeedback. EEG training was then administered in 36 sessions over a one year period with training focused upon the production of alpha, alpha-theta, and finally theta EEG patterns. Seizure frequency dropped 46 percent to a mean of 1.5 seizures per month. A three month follow-up indicated that seizures had stabilized at one per month. Although the patient could not terminate a seizure once it began, she was able to recognize the onset of a preseizure aura and could reliably abort the seizure at that point.

NEURODERMATITIS

Neurodermatitis refers to any cutaneious erruption that is the result of emotional stimulation. Topical ointments are sometimes ineffective since they do not relieve the patient's tense emotional state, thereby failing to break the vicious cycle of tension-skin irritation-scratching-skin irritation-tension.

A number of behavioral approaches have been utilized in the treatment of neurodermatitis and other techniques have been developed to eliminate the scratching behaviors which maintain this skin condition. Wolpe (1959) successfully treated atopic dermatitis by systematic desensitization and hypnosis combined with assertive training. Assertive training involves the use of role playing, modeling, and coaching to help patients learn how to effectively express their feelings to others. Although the expression of anger is frequently the focus of assertive training, feelings of love and concern are equally important.

Walton (1960) treated a 20 year old woman with a two year history of neurodermatitis that was exacerbated by continued scratching. An analysis of the patient's history suggested that her skin condition may well have had an organic etiology but that the problem was being maintained due to psychological factors. Excessive concern and attention from family members and the patient's fiance appeared to be powerful rewards for scratching behaviors which consequently perpetuated the skin condition. Treatment was aimed at reducing these "reinforcing" factors by instructing the patient's family and fiance to ignore her scratching and to discontinue all discussions with her of her skin problem. Within two months scratching was eliminated and at three months the condition of her skin was normal. A four year follow-up indicated that the neurodermatitis had not returned.

Similar dramatic results were obtained using a combination of aversive conditioning and relaxation training in the treatment of a longstanding dermatological problem that was worsened by scratching (Ratliff and Stein, 1968). The patient, a 22 year old male college student, had a 17 year history of skin erruptions that had become progressively worse two years before behavioral intervention. A vicious cycle had become established where dryness of the skin led to scratching, which often caused bleeding. Frequent bathing following bleeding further dried the skin. Initially therapy involved the presentation of electric shocks whenever the patient scratched any part of his body. Shock was terminated when the patient stopped scratching and said aloud "Don't scratch." There was a dramatic decrease in the patient's scratching during and initially after his weekly therapy sessions, but between visits his scratching would return. Therefore, an alternative but complimentary strategy was adopted whereby the patient was taught deep muscle relaxation techniques which he was directed to use whenever he felt "the urge to scratch." After five weeks of treatment all maladaptive scratching had been eliminated and the patient's severe skin rash progressively diminished. At six month follow-up the patient was asymptomatic and scratching had not returned.

Urticaria, or hives, is a vascular reaction of the skin characterized by elevated reddish or whitish patches (wheals) which are usually accompanied by itching or prickling sensations (Domonkos, 1971). Daniels (1973) reported the successful treatment of a 23 year old woman with an acute onset of urticaria and a two year history of severe headaches. The patient's skin condition would increase in intensity throughout the day, reaching a peak in the evening where it interfered with sleep as well as sexual intimacies with her husband. Upon further examination it was discovered that wheals erupted following arguments with her husband which usually involved the topics of money and her relationship with members of his family. Treatments consisted of training the patient in deep muscle relaxation and the constructing of anxiety hierarchies pertaining to her interactions with her husband and her in-laws. Additionally the patient was taught to use a technique which required her to vividly imagine scenes from the anxiety hierarchy in which she remained "relaxed and poised" and then to reward herself for this image by then imagining other scenes that she had found pleasurable (e.g., eating ice cream, reading a favorite novel, etc.). This procedure, technically called covert reinforcement (Cautela, 1970), could be practiced at home by the patient and was a valuable addition to standard desensitization methods. After 12 weeks of treatment urticaria symptoms ceased completely and had not reappeared at a two year follow-up.

Allen and Harris (1966) also employed a combination of behavioral techniques in eliminating a five year old girl's excessive scratching. An analysis of the patient's one year scratching history suggested that this behavior was being maintained by attention from the mother and that the behavior could be reduced or eliminated by helping the mother to modify her own response to her child's scratching. Observing the patient with her mother in the laboratory revealed that although the child was a highly capable and competent little girl her mother spoke to her only to criticize, berate, or discipline her. Home observation records also indicated that the patient would remain free of scratching when she was engaged in constructive play, but that when severe scratching did occur the patient's father would often resort to physical punishment that apparently had no therapeutic effect. Treatment consisted of consultation with the patient's mother wherein she was instructed to ignore all scratching behavior no matter how bloody the results. At the same time the child was rewarded with approval and attention whenever she displayed constructive play and did not scratch. A system of tangible incentives and rewards was established whereby the child received a gold star whenever she did not scratch during a 30 minute period. Early in the treatment with the acquisition of every two or three stars the child was given a cookie, candy, or beverage that she liked. Finally more powerful rewards were used whenever the child remained free of scratching for one entire day. These procedures were eventually "faded out" as the patient's improving skin condition met with increased parental approval. At the end of six weeks of treatment the child was free of scratching and her skin sores had completely healed. A four month follow-up demonstrated the stability of the treatment gains.

If one considers maladaptive scratching to be a problem of "self-control" then it is reasonable to assume that it might respond favorably to behavioral techniques which are aimed at self-modification. Watson, Tharp, and Crishberg (1972) acted as consultants to a 21 year old woman with a 17 year history of a scaly itching rash that was being maintained by scratching. The woman was enrolled in a large lecture course on self-modification procedures from which she was able to design and implement a number of self-modification techniques to eliminate her persistent scratching. The first phase of treatment was a process by which the patient taught herself to use behaviors that were incompatible with scratching (e.g., patting, or rubbing) whenever she felt the urge to scratch. Since much of her scratching occurred while sleeping, the patient, just prior to falling asleep, practiced waking herself up to scratch unaffected areas of her skin. Thus scratching became a stimulus for waking up in the night. Further self-modification techniques involved the patient establishing a point system for herself whereby suppressing scratching or substituting stroking or patting for scratching earned points which she then used to "pay for" tangible rewards (e.g., a bath). Twenty days of self-treatment eliminated all scratching and a six month follow-up revealed stable improvement. However, at 18 months itching and scratching had temporarily returned. These were again successfully eliminated through the reinstatement of other self-modification techniques.

BRUXISM

Bruxism is a nonfunctional gnashing and grinding of the teeth that usually occurs while sleeping. Although common (5.1 percent of college students, Reding, Rubright, and Zimmerman, 1966) and frequently leading to serious dental problems, dental procedures such as occlusal correction or night guards have been found to be relatively ineffective (Ayer and Gale, 1969). There have also been few systematic attempts to determine the differential effectiveness of various behavioral strategies with bruxism.

An automated aversive conditioning procedure was developed by Heller and Strang (1973) in the treatment of a 24 year old graduate student who had been grinding his teeth nightly for years. A tape-recorded sampling of his sleep revealed that the patient's audible grinding rate was 1.75 times per minute, a level that was judged to be sufficiently high to warrant the introduction of aversive conditioning procedures. An apparatus was constructed which was capable of monitoring teeth grinding frequency and could deliver an aversive stimulus (loud sound blast) when that frequency reached three times per five second interval. Upon retiring, the patient set up the apparatus and fitted a tiny speaker into his ear. Whenever grinding reached the criterion level he would be awakened by the sound blast. It was found that although bruxism could be significantly reduced using this procedure, teeth grinding was not entirely eliminated. The authors suggest that further research, utilizing a similar treatment design, will be based upon jaw muscle movements which will provide a more sensitive and reliable target behavior. Bruxism is a common problem in those patients that are troubled by temporomandibular joint problems. This combination of symptoms including pain in the face, jaw, masticatory, and cranium stabilizing muscles, and alterations in mandibular function has been referred to as a myofascial pain dysfunction syndrome (Alderman, 1971). Clinicians have long felt that psychological factors played an important role in this syndrome and Gessel and Alderman (1971) undertook a study to assess the effectiveness of muscular relaxation training with this problem. Eleven patients were treated with individual sessions of training in Jacobson's progressive relaxation techniques with special emphasis being placed upon the control of the jaw muscles. Six of the patients, all women, ranging in age from 22 to 41 had good results with this procedure. Treatment failures (two males and three females) were older (mean age = 44) and had longer symptom histories (five years vs. two years). Also there was a significantly higher level of "social disability" and depression among the treatment failures than among those patients who responded favorably. These results suggest that progressive relaxation techniques may be beneficial in the reduction of myofascial pain dysfunction syndrome for some patients but that special attention should be paid to psychological factors such as depression and social disability.

RAYNAUD'S DISEASE

Raynaud's disease is a disorder of the cardiovascular system in which the patient suffers from episodes of vasoconstriction of the small blood vessels in the extremities often producing a three stage color change. The effected area first blanches, then turns to a cyanotic blue, and finally becomes bright red as the spasm is relieved and reactive hyperemia sets in. The patient's effected extremities feel cold to the touch, often produce pain, and in the most severe cases can become gangrenous. All of the behavioral approaches reviewed here involve the use of temperature biofeedback. Schwartz (1973) reported a preliminary investigation involving the treatment of two Raynaud patients (one male, one female). The man demonstrated large increases in blood volume in the foot for which he was given temperature feedback. This patient remained symptom free for one year and then returned for further training due to some relapse in his condition. The woman, however, was not able to demonstrate clinically significant changes in blood volume in her hands and was not helped at all by the procedure.

Jacobson et al., (1973) combined hypnosis and temperature biofeedback in the treatment of a 31 year old male with a three year history of Raynaud's disease. Three sessions of hypnosis and autohypnosis produced no significant elevations in peripheral skin temperature. However, a combination of autohypnosis and temperature feedback resulted in significant elevations in skin temperature (increasing as much as 4.3 degrees Centigrade). By the end of five such treatment sessions the patient could produce treatment and color changes in both of his hands by simply recalling the experimental situation. On seven and a half month follow-up the patient reported that his newly acquired skill had remained effective and that he could continue to control the warmth and color of both hands.

Surwit (1973) in a review of the biofeedback treatment of Raynaud's, concludes that it would be premature to infer that biofeedback was the sole therapeutic agent responsible for improvement. Many cases (Jacobson et al., 1973; Peper, 1972; Schwartz, 1973) included a combination of either hypnosis, autogenic training, assertive training, or relaxation exercises in addition to the biofeedback procedure. At the same time, however, the author notes that supplemental therapeutic procedures such as these may be a necessary part of any comprehensive treatment program involving biofeedback training, not only to insure proper patient motivation but also to assist the patient in developing more adaptive ways of handling environmental and social stresses.

Recently, Blanchard and Haynes (1975) were able to isolate biofeedback training as the important therapeutic factor in the treatment of a 28 year old female with a longstanding problem of moderately severe Raynaud's disease. Following four 40 minute sessions of baseline data the patient was instructed, without feedback, to attempt to raise her hand temperatures by "mental means." Then, six sessions of temperature feedback training were provided, followed again by six sessions of no feedback, and again six sessions of feedback. Results indicated that feedback training was an important factor in teaching the patient hand warming and that at the end of the treatment and on each of three follow-ups (2, 4, and 7 months) the clinical problem of Raynaud's disease was mostly abated. Measurement of the patient's hand temperature across treatment sessions indicated that the biofeedback techniques were effective in increasing her basel hand temperature.

DYSMENORRHEA

Dysmenorrhea, or painful menstruation, independent of organic pelvic pathology, is a common gynecological complaint (Ogden et al., 1970). It has been estimated that the incidence of this disorder ranges from 21 to 80 percent in women of child bearing age (Heald, Sturgis, and Galeagher, 1956; Kessel and Coppen, 1963). When the problem becomes disabling in its intensity and when pharmacologic interventions are ineffective the use of behavioral treatments warrant some consideration.

Mullen (1968) treated a 31 year old woman who had been suffering from a severe case of dysmenorrhea for 21 years. The treatment was concentrated upon the reduction and elimination of menstrual cramps and excluded any attempt at having the patient gain "insight" into her femininity as some psychodynamic therapies might proceed. The patient was seen for 16 sessions over a six month period. Treatment consisted of training the patient in muscle relaxation exercises and in developing an anxiety hierarchy for use in systematic desensitization. One hierarchy concerned the patient's behavior at the approach of, and during, a typical menstrual period. Since the patient became anxious whenever she saw a woman in the final stages of pregnancy, the second hierarchy dealt with items relating to pregnancy. The patient was also directed to practice her relaxation exercises at home and to gradually desensitize herself *in vivo* to the looking at, holding, and wearing of sanitary napkins which had previously become associated with painful menses. Results indicated that the patient became free of pain and anxiety during normal menstruation and continued in her progress at a six month follow-up.

Mullen (1971) has extended this treatment program into a controlled experiment where it was found that the systematic desensitization of individually constructed anxiety hierarchies could be effectively utilized in the alleviation of dysmenorrhea. A no-treatment control group displayed no significant reductions in symptomatology.

Tasto and Chesney (1974) investigated a group procedure for the treatment of primary dysmenorrhea. Patients were taught to associate relaxation exercises with images of reduced menstrual pain with the purpose of transfering this relaxation training to the actual onset of menstrual pain to thereby mitigate its occurence. The seven patients had an average age of 20.2 years, were all nonparous, and were not taking oral contraceptives or hormones. Patients were encouraged to practice these treatment procedures at home. The resulting data suggested that these treatment approaches can be effective in the reduction of dymenorrhea in college age women and that the simplicity of the group approach suggests that less therapy time is involved and that nurses and other paraprofessionals can be easily trained to administer the procedures.

SPASMS

Sachs and Mayhall (1971) have reported the successful treatment of spastic behavior in a 20 year old cerebral palsied male using an aversive conditioning procedure. For eight conditioning sessions, each lasting 30 minutes in length, the patient received a painful electric shock on his hand immediately following gross head movements, or spasms, (irrelevant movements of the arms, legs, or body). Spastic behavior was dramatically reduced by almost 90 percent. The authors do not contend that the spastic behavior of cerebral palsied patients can be totally or even partially eliminated, however, they do recommend that for each patient a thorough examination of spastic behavior be conducted. This is particularly important when there is a good deal of variability in spasticity which may indicate that the spastic behavior is a product of both cerebral dysfunction and learning. Thus, using conditioning techniques, learned spastic behavior can be reduced.

Essential blepharospasm is a disorder of involuntary clonic and tonic spasms of the eyelids and associated musculature that often proceeds along a progressively deteriorating course which can result in the severe or total curtailment of sight-dependent activities. Surgical intervention is sometimes necessary although this form of treatment is often disappointing. Ballard, Doerr, and Varni (1971) have reported the successful treatment of a patient with essential blepharospasm with a combination of biofeedback and shock avoidance procedures. Feedback alone was found to be effective in helping the patient to progressively gain control over his spasm. The absence of spasms on a nine month follow-up suggested that this procedure may be a painless and effective therapy for this and other neuromuscular disorders. Sharpe (1974) treated a 51 year old male with a 10 month history of progressively worsening blepharospasm. It was hypothesized that the spasms had been precipitated by a repeated pattern of closing the eyes in response to eyelid aching, and that the spasms were being maintained by excessive demands to try to open the eye. The patient was taught how to relax, and was instructed never to try to force his eyelids open or to focus attention voluntarily on them if they went into spasm. Simultaneously he was directed to seek out rewards in the environment for keeping his eyes open. Fourteen weeks of therapy, including one week of inpatient treatment, significantly reduced spasms and the patient was able to drive, and to resume his business and social interest. A nine month follow-up demonstrated no deterioration in his condition.

Finally, Butler and Salamy (1975) were able to successfully treat a 28 year old male for chronic muscle spasms in the neck of three year duration. Muscle relaxation training and the construction of anxiety hierarchies were augumented by the use of an electric vibrator which was placed upon the patient's neck when he was instructed to imagine neck positions that usually precipitated spasms. After counterconditioning these imagined head positions the vibrator was also used to eliminate the slight residual tensions elicited by *in vivo* head and body positions. A six month follow-up revealed the stability of the treatment gains which suggests that this treatment approach might be useful in dealing with localized sights of muscle tensions.

VOCAL NODULES

Gray, England, and Mohoney (1965) employed systematic desensitization in the elimination of benign vocal nodules in a 29 year old female. Prior to treatment the patient experienced hoarseness for six months which eventually lead to total voice loss. Laryngeal examination revealed prominent bilateral vocal nodules which were surgically removed with biopsy indicating no malignancy.

Four weeks postoperatively the patient again began to exhibit hoarseness and further examination confirmed the reoccurence of prominent nodules. Hypothesizing that perhaps vocal nodules were developing due to the misuse of her vocal appartus which was the result of pervasive, almost continuous anxiety, the patient was referred for behavior therapy. Training in deep muscle relaxation was used in the systematic desensitization of three anxiety hierarchies involving (a) disciplining her children, (b) her relationship with her husband, and (c) her relationship with another man with whom she was emotionally involved. Despite the patient's resistance to therapy, after 15 treatments over a three week period she was asymptomatic. Laryngeal examinations three days and six weeks after the therapy program ended revealed that the vocal nodules had cleared.

MUSCULAR REEDUCATION

Marinacci and Horande (1960) pioneered the use of the electromyogram in neuromuscular reeducation. Johnson and Garton (1973) have reported the successful application of EMG muscle reeducation in hemiplegia and Andrews (1964) was able to help instruct hemiplegic patients to generate motor unit activity in nonfunctioning muscles. Although it is beyond the scope of this chapter to review the extensive literature on the utilization of behavioral techniques in muscle reeducation, a recent study by Basmajian et al., (1975) will demonstrate the utility of such methods. Twenty adult hemiparetic patients, all of whom had suffered a cerebral vascular accident at least three months prior to the study, manifested "foot drop" (residual foot dorsiflexion paresis). The patients, 20 males and 20 females, were randomly assigned to either conventional physical therapy training or to a combination of physical and EMG biofeedback procedures. Treatments for both groups involved 40 minute sessions three times per week over a five week period. Dependent measures included the strength of dorsiflexion, active range of motion, and functional improvement in walking. The results indicated that while both groups demonstrated positive changes in the range of motion and strength of dorsiflexion, the combined approach of physical therapy and biofeedback training resulted in increases that were twice as great as physical therapy alone. The authors suggest that these results support the effectiveness of biofeedback training as a valuable adjunct to traditional physical therapy with physically handicapped patients.

RECENT DEVELOPMENTS AND LIMITATIONS

Recently, EMG biofeedback has been found to be a useful approach in the treatment of a musician with disabling throat and facial tension (Levee, Cohen, and Rickles, 1976), and in the reduction of chronic dysphagia spastica, a difficulty in swallowing due to constricted throat muscles (Haynes, 1976). Tape recorded relaxation exercises combined with EMG biofeedback has also been found to be effective in reducing the emotional lability of a diabetic woman with the consequent stabilization in her insulin intake (Fowler, Budzynski, and Vandenbergh, 1976). Although these results are promising Gentry (1975) has discussed a number of problems which are raised when one begins to employ behavioral techniques in treating physical disorders. Difficulties arise when a clinician must choose between a number of techniques that may be effective, and when patients are unmotivated to undergo the treatment procedures (e.g., aversive conditioning). Likewise, behavioral interventions rest upon the assumption that the patient possesses the minimal constitutional requirements necessary for the successful learning, relearning, or unlearning of certain physical responses. No matter how motivated that patient may be or how powerful the techniques are, certain physical limitations will place a ceiling upon the extent of physical recovery. Behavior therapists often eschew the need for an understanding of the etiology of a pathological condition. For that reason, this approach is a novel one for many medical practitioners. It is interesting to note that in virtually every case reported in this chapter an organic basis for the physical condition had been ruled out (e.g., vomiting, diarrhea, excessive urination), or was insufficiently understood (epilepsy, spasmodic torticollis, dysmenorrhea, Raynaud's disease). The use of behavioral strategies may be particularly relevant in these instances, especially where high states of tension and environmental factors appear to be maintaining or exacerbating the physical disorder.

It is hoped that this review had provided the clinician with a new perspective on a variety of physical dysfunctions. Many disorders, despite their etiology, are amenable to treatment strategies that are based upon learning principles. The novelty of these approaches should not deter the concerned clinician from attempting to implement these procedures, particularly where life-threatening conditions remain intractable to conventional therapies. In other cases, these procedures may offer viable alternatives to surgical interventions or chemical management, especially when these latter techniques have been found to be relatively ineffective or are otherwise contraindicated.

REFERENCES

Agras, S., & Marshall, C. The application of negative practice to spasmodic torticollis. *American Journal of Psychiatry*, 1965, *122*, 579–582.

Alderman, M.M. Disorders of the temporomandibular joint and related structures. In L.W. Burket (Ed.) *Oral medicine.* 6th edition, Philadelphia: Lippincott, 1971.

Alford, G.S., Blanchard, E.B., & Buckley, T.M. Treatment of hysterical vomiting by modification of social contingencies: a case study. *Journal of Behavior Therapy and Experimental Psychiatry*, 1972, *3*, 209–212.

Allen, K.E., & Harris, F.R. Elimination of a child's excessive scratching by training the mother in reinforcement procedures. *Behavior Research and Therapy*, 1966, *4*, 79–84.

Alpers, B. *Clinical neurology* (4th ed.). Philadelphia: Davis, 1958.

Andrews, J.M. Neuromuscular re-education of hemiplegia with aid of electromyograph. *Archives of Physical Medicine and Rehabilitation*, 1964, *45*, 530–532.

Asnes, R.S., & Mones, R.L. Pollakiuria. *Pediatrics*, 1973, *52* (4), 615–617.

Ayer, W.A. & Gale, E.N. Extinction of bruxism by massed practice therapy. *Journal of the Canadian Dental Association*, 1969, *35*, 492–494.

Azrin, N.H., & Wesolowski, M.D. Eliminating habitual vomiting in a retarded adult by positive practice and self-correction. *Journal of Behavior Therapy and Experimental Psychiatry*, 1975, *6*, 145–148.

Balaschak, B.A. Teacher -implemented behavior modification in a case of organically based epilepsy. *Journal of Consulting and Clinical Psychology*, 1976, *44* (2) 218–223.

Ballard, P., Doerr, H., & Varni, J. Arrest of a disabling eye disorder using biofeedback. *Psychophysiology* 1972, *9*, 271.

Basmajian, J.V., Kukulka, C.G., Narayan, M.G. & Takebe, K. Biofeedback treatment of foot-drop after stroke compared with standard rehabilitation technique: Effects on voluntary control and strength. *Archives of Physical Medicine and Rehabilitation*, 1975, *56*, 231–236.

Bernhardt, A.J., Hersen, M., & Barlow, D.H. Measurement and modification of spasmodic torticollis: An experimental analysis. *Behavior Therapy*, 1972, *3*, 294–297.

Blanchard, E.B., & Haynes, M.R. Biofeedback treatment of a case of Raynaud's disease. *Journal of Behavior Therapy and Experimental Psychiatry*, 1975, *6*, 230–234.

Blanchard, E.B., & Young, L.D. Clinical application of biofeedback training: a review of evidence. *Archives of General Psychiatry*, 1974, *30*, 573–589.

Bockus, H.L. *Gastroenterology* (2nd ed.) Philadelphia: Saunders, 1969.

Booker, H.E., Forster, F.M., & Klove, H. Extinction factors in startle (acousticomotor) seizures. *Neurology*, 1965, *15*(12), 1095–1103.

Brierly, H. The treatment of hysterical spasmodic torticollis by behavior therapy. *Behavior Research and Therapy*, 1967, *5*, 139–142.

Brudney, J., Grynbaum, B.B., & Korein, J. Spasmodic torticollis: Treatment by feedback display of the EMG. *Archives of Physical Medicine and Rehabilitation*, 1974, *55*, 403–408.

Burgess, E.P. Elimination of vomiting behavior. *Behavior Research and Therapy*, 1969, *7*, 173–176.

Butler, P.E., & Salamy, A. Eliminating a conditioned muscle spasm by external inhibition by an electric vibrator. *Journal of Behavior Therapy and Experimental Psychiatry*, 1975, *6* 159–161.

Bykov, K.M. *The cerebral cortex and the internal organs.* New York: Chemical 1957.

Cautela, J. Covert reinforcement, *Behavior Therapy*, 1970, *1*, 33–50.

Chandler, G.N. *A synopsis of gastro-enterology.* Baltimore: Williams & Wilkins, 1963.

Cleeland, C.S. Behavior techniques in the modification of spasmodic torticollis. *Neurology*, 1973, *23*, 1241–1246.

Cohen, S., & Reed, J. The treatment of nervous diarrhea and other conditioned autonomic disorders by desensitization. *British Journal of Psychiatry*, 1968, *114*, 1275–1280.

Crominas, R., & Rallo, J. Urinary retention and nervous pollakiuria. *Revista Clinica Espanola*, 1971, *123/2*, 117–128.

Cunningham, C.E., & Linscheid, T.R. Elimination of chronic infant ruminating by electric shock. *Behavior Therapy*, 1976, *7*, 231–234.

Daniels, L.K. Treatment of urticaria and severe headache by behavior therapy. *Psychosomatics*, 1973, *14*, 347–351.

Daniels, L.K. Treatment of grand mal epilepsy by covert and operant conditioning techniques. *Psychosomatics*, 1975, *16*, 65–67.

DeWeerdt, C.J., & Van Rijn, A.J. Conditioning therapy in reading epilepsy. *Electroencephalography and Clinical Neurophysiology*, 1975, *39*, 417–420.

Domonkos, A.N. *Andrews' diseases of the skin*, Philadelphia: Saunders, 1971.

Efron, R. The effect of olfactory stimuli in arresting uncinate fits. *Brain*, 1956, *79*, 267–281.

Efron, R. The conditioned inhibition of uncinate fits. *Brain*, 1957, *80*, 251–262.

Ericksen, R.A., & Huber, H. Elimination of hysterical torticollis through the use of a metronome in an operant conditioning paradigm. *Behavior Therapy*, 1975 *6*, 405–506.

Forster, F.M. Conditioning of cerebral dysrhythmia induced by pattern presentation and eye closure. *Conditional Reflex*, 1967, *2*(3), 236–244.

Forster, F.M. Clinical therapeutic conditioning in epilepsy. *Wisconsin Medical Journal*, 1969, *68*, 289–291. (a).

Forster, F.M. Conditional reflexes and sensory-evoked epilepsy: The nature of the therapeutic process. *Conditional Reflex*, 1969, *4*(2), 103–114. (b).

Forster, F.M. *Conditioning treatment in reflex epilepsy.* Paper presented at Fourth International Congress of Neurological Surgery, Ninth International Congress of Neurology. New York, September, 1969. (c).

Forster, F.M. The classification and conditioning treatment of the reflex epilepsies. *International Journal of Neurology*, 1972, *9*(1), 73–86.

Forster, F.M. Reading epilepsy, musicogenic epilepsy, and related disorders. In H.R. Myklebust (Ed.) *Progress in learning disabilities*, Vol. III. New York: Grune & Stratton, 1975.

Forster, F.M., Booker, H.E., & Ansell, S. Computer automation of the conditioning therapy of stroboscopic induced seizures. *Transactions of the American Neurological Association*, 1966, *91*, 232–233.

Forster, F.M., Booker, H.E. & Gascon, G. Conditioning in musicogenic epilepsy. *Transactions of the American Neurological Association*, 1967, *92*, 236–237.

Forster, F.M., & Campos, G.B. Conditioning factors in stroboscopic-induced seizures. *Epilepsia*, 1964, *5*, 156–165.

Forster, F.M. & Cleeland, C.S. Somatosensory evoked epilepsy. *Transactions of the American Neurological Association*, 1969, *94*, 268–269.

Forster, F.M., Hansotia, P., Cleeland, C.S. & Ludwig, A. A case of voice-induced epilepsy treated by conditioning. *Neurology*, 1969, *19*(4), 325–331.

Forster, F.M., Klove, H., Peterson, W.G. & Bengzon, A.R.A. *Modification of musicogenic epilepsy by extinction technique.* Paper presented at Eighth International Congress of Neurology, Vienna, 1965.

Forster, F.M., Paulsen, W.A., & Baughman, F.A. Clinical therapeutic conditioning in reading epilepsy. *Neurology*, 1969, *19*, 717–723.

Forster, F.M., Ptacek, L.J., & Peterson, W.G. Auditory clicks in extinction of stroboscope-induced seizures. *Epilepsia*, 1965, *6*, 217–225.

Forster, F.M., Ptacek, L.J., Peterson, W.G., Chun, R.W. M.M., Bengzon, A.R.A., & Campos, G.B. The modification by extinction techniques of stroboscopic-induced seizure discharges. *Archives of neurology*, 1964, *11*, 603–608.

Forster, F.M., Richards, J., Panitch, H., Huisman, R., & Paulsen, R. Reflex epilepsy evoked by decision making. *Archives of Neurology*, 1975, *32*, 54–56.

Fowler, J.E., Budzynski, T.H., & VandenBergh, R.L. Effects of an EMG biofeedback relaxation program on the control of diabetes: A case study. *Biofeedback and Self-regulation*, 1976, *1*(1), 105–112.

Furman, S. Intestinal biofeedback in functional diarrhea: a preliminary report. *Journal of Behavior Therapy and Experimental Psychiatry*, 1973, *4*, 317–321.

Gardner, J. Behavior therapy treatment approach to a psychogenic seizure case. *Journal of Consulting Psychology*, 1967, *31*, 209–212.

Gentry, W.D. Behavioral treatment of somatic disorders. In W.D. Gentry (Ed.) *Applied behavior modification*. St. Louis: C.V. Mosby, 1975.

Gessel, A.H., & Alderman, M.M. Management of myofacial pain dysfunction syndrome of the temporomandibular joint by tension control training. *Psychosomatics*, 1971, *12*, 302–309.

Gray, B.B., England, G. & Mohoney, J.L. Treatment of benign vocal nodules by reciprocal inhibition. *Behavior Research and Therapy*, 1965, *3*, 187–193.

Haynes, S.N. Electromyographic biofeedback treatment of woman with chronic dysphagia. *Biofeedback and Self-regulation*, 1976, *1* (1), 121–126.

Heald, F.P., Masland, R.D., Sturgis, S.H., & Galeagher, J.R. Dysmenorrhea in adolescence. *Pediatrics*, 1956, *20*, 121.

Hedberg, A.G. The treatment of chronic diarrhea by systematic desensitization: A case report. *Journal of Behavior Therapy and Experimental Psychiatry*, 1973, *4*, 67–68.

Heller, R.F., & Strang, H.R. Controlling bruxism through automated aversive conditioning. *Behavior Research and Therapy*, 1973, *11*, 327–329.

Hull, C.L. *Principles of behaviour*, New York: Appleton-Century, 1943.

Iwata, B.A. & Lorentzson, A.M. Operant control of seizure-like behavior in an institutionalized retarded adult. *Behavior Therapy*, 1976, 7 247–251.

Jacobs, A., & Felton, G.S. Visual feedback of myoelectric output to facilitate muscle relaxation in normal persons and patients with neck injuries. *Archives of Physical Medicine and Rehabilitation*, 1969, *50*, 34–39.

Jacobson, E. *Progressive relaxation*, Chicago: University of Chicago Press, 1938.

Jacobson, A.M., Hackett, R.P., Surman, O.S. & Silverberg, E.L. Raynaud's phenomenon: Treatment with hypnotic and operant technique. *Journal of the American Medical Association*, 1973, *225*, 739–740.

Johnson, H.E., & Garton, W.H. Muscle re-education in hemiplegia by use of electromyographic device. *Archives of Physical Medicine and Rehabilitation*, 1973, *54*, 320–323.

Johnson, R.K. & Meyer, R.G. Phased biofeedback approach for epileptic seizure control. *Journal of Behavior Therapy and Experimental Psychiatry*, 1974, *5*, 185–187.

Jones, H.G. The application of conditioning and learning techniques to the treatment of a psychiatric patient. *Journal of Abnormal and Social Psychology*, 1956, *52*, 414–420.

Kessel, N. & Coppen, A. The prevalence of common menstrual symptoms, *Lancet*, 1963, *61*, 1961–1964.

Kohlenberg, R. The punishment of persistent vomiting: a case study. *Journal of Applied Behavior Analysis*, 1970, *3*, 241–246.

Lang, P.J. Behavior therapy with a case of nervous anorexia. In L.P. Ullmann & L. Krasner (Eds.) *Case studies in behavior modification*. New York: Holt, Rinehart, & Winston, 1965.

Lang, P.J. & Melamed, B.G. Avoidance conditioning therapy of an infant with chronic ruminative vomiting. *Journal of Abnormal Psychology*, 1969, *74*, 1–8.

Levee, J.R., Cohen, M.J., and Rickles, W.H. Electromyographic biofeedback for relief of tension in the facial and throat muscles of a woodwind muscian. *Biofeedback and Self-regulation*, 1976, *1* (1), 113–120.

Lubar, J.L., & Bahler, W.W. Behavioral management of epileptic seizures following EEG biofeedback training of the sensorimotor rhythm. *Biofeedback and Self-regulation*, 1976, *1* (1), 77–104.

Luckey, R.E., Watson, C.M. & Musick, J.K. Aversive conditioning as a means of inhibiting vomiting and rumination. *American Journal of Mental Deficiency*, 1968, *73*, 139–142.

Marinacci, A.A. & Horande, M. Electromyogram in neuromuscular re-education. *Bulletin of the Los Angeles Neurological Society*, 1960, *25*, 57–71.

Masur, F.T. A behavior therapy approach to the treatment of pollakiuria (excessive frequency of urination). *Journal of Behavior Therapy and Experimental Psychiatry*, in press.

Meares, R.A. Behavior therapy and spasmodic torticollis. *Archives of General Psychiatry*, 1973, *28*, 104–107.

Mogan, J., O'Brien, J.S. The counterconditioning of a vomiting habit by sips of ginger ale. *Journal of Behavior Therapy and Experimental Psychiatry*, 1972, *3*, 135–137.

Mullen, F.G. The treatment of a case of dysmenorrhea by behavior therapy techniques. *The Journal of Nervous and Mental Disease*, 1968, *147* (4), 371–376.

Mullen, F.G. *Treatment of dysmenorrhea by professional and student behavior therapists*. Paper presented at Fifth Annual Meeting of the Association for Advancement of Behavior Therapy, Washington, D.C. September, 1971.

Nelson, W.E. *Textbook of pediatrics*. Philadelphia: Saunders, 1954.

Ogden, J.A., Wade, M.E., Anderson, G., & Davis, C.D. Treatment of dysmenorrhea: a comparative double-blind study. *American Journal of Obstetrics and Gynecology*, 1970, *106*, 838–842.

Parrino, J. Reduction of seizures by desensitization. *Journal of Behavior Therapy and Experimental Psychiatry*, 1971, *2*, 215–218.

Peper, E. Frontiers of clinical biofeedback. In L. Birk (ed.) *Seminars in psychiatry*, Vol. 5, New York: Grune & Stratton, 1973.

Pinto, R. A case of movement epilepsy with a ogoraphobia treated successfully by flooding. *British Journal of Psychiatry*, 1972, *121*, 287–288.

Poole, A.D., & Yates, A.J. The modification of excessive frequency of urination: a case study. *Behavior Therapy*, 1975, *6*, 78–86.

Ratlif, R.G., & Stein, N.H. Treatment of neurodermatitis by behavior therapy: a case study. *Behavior Research and Therapy*, 1968, *6*, 397–399.

Reding, G.R., Rubright, W.C. & Zimmerman, S.O. Incidence of bruxism. *Journal of Dental Research*, 1966, *45*, 1198–1204.

Sachs, D.A., & Mayhall, B. Behavioral control of spasms using aversive conditioning with a cerebral palsied adult. *The Journal of Nervous and Mental Disease*, 1971, *152* (5), 362–363.

Sajwaj, T., Libet, J., & Agras, S. Lemon-juice therapy: The control of life-threatening rumination in a six-month-old infant. *Journal of Applied Behavior Analysis*, 1974, 7, 557–563.

Schwartz, G.E. Biofeedback as therapy: some theoretical and practical issues. *American Psychologist*, 1973, *28*, 666–673.

Seifert, A.R., & Lubar, J.F. Reduction of epileptic seizures through EEG biofeedback training. *Biological Pyschology*, 1975, *3*, 157–184.

Sharpe, R. Behavior therapy in a case of blepharospasm. *British Journal of Psychiatry*, 1974, *124*, 603–604.

Sterman, M.B. *Studies of EEG biofeedback training in man and cats.* Highlights of 17th Annual Conference: VA Cooperative Studies in Mental Health and Behavioral Sciences. St. Louis, 1972.

Sterman, M.B. Neurophysiological and clinical studies of sensorimotor EEG biofeedback training: Some effects on epilepsy. *Seminars in Psychiatry*, 1973, *5*(4), 507–525.

Sterman, M.B., & Friar, L. Suppression of seizures in an epileptic following sensorimotor EEG feedback training. *Electroencephalography and Clinical Neurophysiology*, 1972, *33*, 89–95.

Sterman, M.B., MacDonald, L.R., & Stone, R.R. Biofeedback training of the sensorimotor EEG rhythm in man: effects on epilepsy. *Epilepsia*, 1974, *15*, 395–416.

Stoffelmeyer, B.E. The treatment of a retching response to dentures by counteractive reading aloud. *Journal of Behavior Therapy and Experimental Psychiatry*, 1970, *1*, 163–168.

Surwit, R.S. Biofeedback: A possible treatment for Raynaud's Disease. *Seminars in Psychiatry*, 1973, *5*(4) 483–490.

Tasto, D.L., & Chesney, M. Muscle relaxation treatment for primary dysmenorrhea. *Behavior Therapy*, 1974 *5*, 668–672.

Taylor, D.W. Treatment of excessive frequency of urination by desensitization. *Journal of Behavior Therapy and Experimental Psychiatry*, 1972, *3*, 311–313.

Toister, R.P., Condron, L.W., & Arthur, D. Faradic therapy of chronic vomiting in infancy: A case study. *Journal of Behavior Therapy and Experimental Psychiatry*, 1975, *6*, 55–59.

Van der Ploeg, H.M. Treatment of frequency of urination by stories competing with anxiety. *Journal of Behavioral Therapy and Experimental Psychiatry*, 1975, *6*, 165–166.

Walton, D. The application of learning theory to the treatment of a case of neurodermatitis. In H. Eysenk (Ed.) *Behavior therapy and the neuroses*, New York: Pergamon Press, 1960.

Watkins, J.T. Treatment of chronic vomiting and extreme emaciation by an aversive stimulus: case study. *Psychological Reports*, 1972, *31*, 803–805.

Watson, D.L., Tharp, R.G., & Krisberg, J. Case study in self-modification: suppression of inflamatory scratching while awake and asleep. *Journal of Behavior Therapy and Experimental Psychiatry*, 1972, *3*, 213–215.

White, J.D., & Taylor, D. Noxious conditioning as a treatment for rumination. *Mental Retardation*, 1967, *5*, 30–33.

Williams, R.B. *Heartrate feedback in the treatment of torticollis: a case report.* Paper presented at Annual Meeting for Psychophysiological Research, Salt Lake City, Utah, October, 1974.

Wolf, M., Brinbrauer, J., Williams, T., & Lawler, J. A note on apparent extinction of the vomiting behavior of a retarded child. In L. Ullmann and L. Krasner (Eds.) *Case studies in behavior modifications*, New York: Holt, Rinehart, & Winston, 1965.

Wolpe, J. Psychotherapy based on the principles of reciprocal inhibition. In A. Burton (Ed.) *Case studies in counseling and psychotherapy*, New Jersey: Prentice Hall, 1959.

Wright, L. Aversive conditioning of self-induced seizures. *Behavior Therapy*, 1973, *4*, 712–713.

Yates, A.J., & Poole, A.D. Behavioral analysis in a case of excessive frequency of micturition. *Behavior Therapy*, 1972, *3*, 449–453.

Zlutnick, S. Mayville, W.J., & Moffat, S. Modification of seizure disorders: The interruption of behavioral chains. *Journal of Applied Behavior Analysis*, 1975, *8*(1) 1–12.

Chapter 16

Concluding Remarks

*John Paul Brady**

This book is concerned with the application of behavior therapy to a number of problems frequently seen in medical practice. To put these applications in perspective, it may be useful to look at the field of behavior therapy as a whole.

Behavior modification therapy as a distinctive, systematic approach to psychiatry and clinical psychology is only two decades old. During this time the concept itself has evolved. The initial notion of behavior therapy as a systematic application of principles of learning (learning theory) to disorders of behavior is now regarded as too narrow. Today behavior therapy is seen in broader terms as an approach to clinical problems which relies on the methods and the results of experimental behavioral science (Brady, in press). Of course, the whole range of behavioral science is relevant to the understanding and modification of behavioral disorders or medical disorders with behavioral components. This includes aspects of behavioral biology at one end of the continuum and social anthropology at the other. However, it is the natural science of behavior qua behavior, experimental psychology, which is central to behavior therapy as an applied clinical discipline. Thus a behavioral approach to psychiatry, clinical psychology and medicine makes extensive use of the methods of the experimental psychologist.

The range of problems that have been treated has also broadened during these two decades. Earlier applications focused on the disorders traditionally of interest to psychiatry and clinical psychology:

*Dr. Brady is Kenneth E. Appel Professor of Psychiatry and Chairman of the Department, University of Pennsylvania, Philadelphia, Pa.

classical neuroses, some aspects of psychotic disorders and chronic, maladaptive behavioral patterns (personality disorders). However, the same methods of analysis and response modification which proved useful with psychiatric disorders are applicable to many medical disorders as well—tension headache, migraine, asthma, and cardiac arrhythmias. These medical applications often entail "biofeedback" procedures which may be considered special instances of operant conditioning. That is, in biofeedback reinforcement contingencies are attached to autonomic responses rather than skeletal muscle responses for the purpose of helping the patient gain control over physiological events which underlie his medical problem. Many of the reports in this book are of this category.

Also represented in the present volume is another and related application of behavior modification principles. This is the modification of behaviors which in themselves do not constitute medical disorders but which have important health consequences (Pomerleau and Brady, 1975). Included here are cigarette smoking, Type A behavior pattern, and overeating. These "disorders of self-control" are of increasing interest to the behaviorally-oriented clinician.

Still another level of application of behavioral procedures is in the prevention of disease (Pomerleau, Bass, and Crown, 1975). This application, although little developed to date, holds enormous potential. By and large the preventive aspect of medicine is neglected by the biomedical community. By training, tradition, and perhaps personality style most physicians and biomedical scientists are oriented more toward disease rather than health. That is, oriented more toward the alleviation of pain and suffering and the cure of disease than towards the prevention of disease and disability. Yet, from a public health point of view, prevention may have more impact than the treatment of disease once it exists. Recent studies by the Long-Range Health Planning Branch of the Ministry of Health and Welfare of Canada are of interest here (Lalonde, 1974). These studies showed that marked improvement in the quality and accessibility of health services in Canada over a twenty-year period resulted in little measurable improvement in the overall health of the nation. Mortality rates were little affected by the development of prepaid national health insurance over a 15-year period although the latter brought extensive health services to all Canadians without cost. What these data reflect is that the principal causes of morbidity and mortality in major developed countries lie in environmental factors and health-related lifestyle behavioral patterns. In a study of a large population at risk, it is difficult to detect the effects of improved facilities for the treatment of existing disease.

Among the important behaviors with serious health consequences, one would list cigarette smoking, the consumption of alcohol, inadequate physical activity, an energy balance that results in excessive weight, a diet that favors hyperlipidemia, etc. Recognition of this recently prompted the National Heart and Lung Institute to sponsor a conference on health behaviors related to the prevention and control of cardiopulmonary disorders (Weiss, 1975). Consider, for example, coronary artery disease, the principal cause of death in the United States. Most of the identified or suspected risk factors in coronary heart disease have large behavioral aspects. Cigarette smoking, obesity, and the Friedman-Rosenman personality pattern A are clearly in this category. Hypertension, another risk factor, is a disorder whose pathogenesis in some individuals relates to body weight, diet, and life-style. The elevated blood pressure of most patients with essential hypertension can be adequately controlled with appropriate medications. However, a high percentage of patients with this disorder fail to adhere to a potentially effective drug regimen, probably because the disease itself is largely asymptomatic for many years (Cardon, 1953). Thus the limiting step in the effective control of hypertension in the individual patient is largely a behavioral issue, inadequate or inconsistent adherence to a prescribed medical plan. Of course, recent developments in behavior therapy procedures offer alternative or adjunctive methods for the treatment of hypertension and hence the reduction of another risk factor in coronary artery disease. Elevated blood cholesterol and possibly elevated triglycerides are additional risk factors. In most cases these can be controlled by dietary means, again a behavioral problem of compliance to a prescribed medical regimen. Adequate regular physical exercise still is another likely factor of a behavioral nature.

Considerations of this kind are leading to efforts by groups of behaviorally-oriented clinicians to develop programs aimed at the simultaneous modification of multiple health-related behaviors in the interest of the prevention of disease (Meyer and Henderson, 1974). Clinical research in this area is at an early phase, however, and many difficult technical problems remain to be solved. The first is to develop and evaluate the behavioral technology to reduce the individual risk factors involved in disease. As this book demonstrates, rapid progress is being made in many health-related behaviors. A second problem is the development of reliable physiological or behavioral measures of successful intervention. This is not an issue with some behaviors such as overeating since the clinician can rely on body weight as a measure of success. It is a problem with behaviors such as cigarette smoking in which most clinicians have simply relied upon self-report as the evidence for treatment outcome.

A related area of research is the issue of multiple-risk factor reduction in a single individual. If a person is able to stop smoking in a behavior intervention program, is he able to more easily gain control over other health-related behaviors such as overeating and dietary indiscretions or is self-control in these various areas largely independent. Successful demonstration that particular physiological indices of risk of cardiovascular disease are successfully controlled by a behavioral program is suggested but not in itself a demonstration of the effectiveness of a program of prevention. Ultimately a large-scale clinical trial is needed to directly ascertain whether such behavioral programs in fact reduce the occurrence of cardiovascular events such as myocardial infarction. This will raise special problems of adequate control groups, and the like.

In summary, behavior modification therapy has demonstrated efficacy and efficiency in the treatment of a wide range of psychiatric disorders. There is growing interest in the application of these procedures to medical illnesses and the modification of behaviors with significant health consequences. These latter applications, subsumed under the term behavioral medicine, hold great promise both for the treatment and prevention of disease.

REFERENCES

Brady, J.P.: Psychiatry as the behaviorist views it. In Brady, J.P., Mendels, J., Orne, M.T. and Rieger, W. (eds.), *Psychiatry: Areas of promise and advancement.* New York: Spectrum Publications, Inc., in press.

Cardon, P.V., Jr.: Relationship of life stress to essential hypertension. *Mississippi Valley Medical Journal*, (July) 1953, *75*, 111.

Lalonde, M.: *A new perspective on the health of Canadians: A working document.* Ottawa, Canada: Ministry of Health and Welfare, 1974.

Meyer, A.J. and Henderson, J.B.: Multiple risk factor reduction in the prevention of cardiovascular disease. *Preventive Medicine*, 1974, *3*, 225–236.

Pomerleau, O., Bass, F. and Crown, V.: Role of behavior modification in preventive medicine. *New England Journal of Medicine*, 1975, *292*, 3–8.

Pomerleau, O.F. and Brady, J.P.: Behavior modification in medical practice. *Pennsylvania Medicine*, 1975, *78*, 49–53.

Weiss, S.M. (ed.): *Proceedings of the National Heart and Lung Institute Working Conference on Health Behavior.* DHEW Publication No. (NIH), 1975, pp. 76–868, Washington, D.C.

Index

About the Editors

Redford B. Williams, Jr. is Associate Professor of Psychiatry and Assistant Professor of Medicine at Duke University Medical Center. He received his medical degree from Yale, where he also completed his training in internal medicine. Before joining the faculty at Duke, he was a Clinical Associate at the National Institute of Mental Health. Dr. Williams' research and clinical interests have been in the general field of psychosomatic medicine, and he has published extensively in the area of psychosocial aspects of cardiovascular disease. He is the recipient of a Research Scientist Development Award from the National Institute of Mental Health.

W. Doyle Gentry, Ph.D. is currently Professor and Head of the Division of Medical Psychology, Department of Psychiatry, Duke University Medical Center. He is also a Lecturer in the Psychology Department at Duke University and Senior Fellow in the Duke University Center for the Study of Aging and Human Development. He received his doctoral degree from Florida State University in 1969 and has been on the faculty of Duke University Medical Center since that time. In addition to geropsychology, his clinical and research interests include psychosomatic medicine, human and infrahuman aggression, and behavior therapy. He has authored numerous publications in scientific and professional journals and is editor of *Applied Behavior Modification* and co-editor of *Psychological Aspects of Myocardial Infarction and Coronary Care.*

About the Contributors

A. Barney Alexander, Ph.D. is currently Head of the Psychophysiology Laboratory at the National Asthma Center, Denver, Colorado. He received his doctorate in clinical psychology from Indiana University in 1970. He is a member of the Association for the Advancement of Behavior Therapy, the Biofeedback Research Society, and the Society for Psychophysiological Research, as well as an editorial advisor to several behavioral journals. He has published numerous papers dealing with the effectiveness of behavioral intervention in treating asthmatic behavior.

Guillermo A. A. Bernal is a candidate in the doctoral program in clinical psychology at the University of South Carolina. He is an Instructor in the Division of Medical Psychology, Department of Psychiatry, Duke University Medical Center, and Assistant Director of the Clinical Biofeedback Laboratory at Duke Hospital. His professional interests include psychosomatic medicine, psychotherapy, and psychological assessment.

Edward B. Blanchard, Ph.D. is Professor of Psychology, Department of Psychiatry, at University of Tennessee Center for the Health Sciences and Adjunct Professor of Psychology at Memphis State University. He received his doctorate from Stanford University in 1969 and was previous Professor of Psychiatry and Director of the Psychology Internship Training Program at the University of Mississippi Medical Center. He is a Diplomate in Clinical Psychology and is a consulting editor to numerous psychological journals. He has published over 60 scientific and professionals works in fields including: biofeedback and behavior modification, sexual problems and therapy, psychopathic deviency, and family medicine.

Thomas D. Borkovec, Ph.D. is an Associate Professor of Psychology at the University of Iowa, where he has been since receiving his doctorate in clinical psychology from the University of Illinois in 1970. He is a member of several professional organizations including the American Association of Biofeedback Clinicians, the Association for the Advancement of Behavior Therapy, and the American Association for the Advancement of Tension Control. He has published over 25 scientific and professional papers dealing primarily with behavior therapy, and is co-author (with D.A. Bernstein) of a book entitled *Progressive Relaxation Training.*

Patrick A. Boudewyns, Ph.D. is Chief of the Psychology Service, Durham V.A. Hospital, and Associate Professor of Medical Psychology, Department of Psychiatry, Duke University Medical Center. He received his doctorate from the University of Wisconsin in Milwaukee in 1968 and was previously on the faculty of the University of Iowa and Chief of the Psychology Service, Iowa City VA Hospital. He is a member of the Association for the Advancement of Behavior Therapy and the Biofeedback Society. He has published numerous articles on behavior therapy and has recently been appointed Director of the Behavior Change and Self-Control Clinic at Duke University Medical Center.

John Paul Brady, M.D. is a Kenneth E. Appel Professor of Psychiatry and Chairman of the Department of Psychiatry at the University of Pennsylvania School of Medicine. He received his medical degree from Boston University in 1955 and completed his psychiatric residency at the Institute of Living, Hartford, Conn., in 1959. He was formerly a Research Psychiatrist and Assistant Professor of Psychiatry at the Indiana University School of Medicine. He is board certified by the American Board of Psychiatry and Neurology, is a member of numerous professional organizations in the fields of medicine, psychiatry, and psychology, and has been a member of the American Psychiatric Association Task Force on Behavior Therapy. He is cofounder and associate editor of the journal *Behavior Therapy*, is on the editorial board of the *Journal of Behavior Therapy and Experimental Psychiatry*, and is an editorial consultant to the journal *Biofeedback and Self-Regulation.* He has to date published well over 100 articles and book reviews dealing with various topics including: hysterical blindness, sex therapy, behavioral treatment of stuttering, psychiatric training, and behavior therapy for hypertension.

James E. Byassee, Ph.D. is currently a Clinical Associate in Medical Psychology, Department of Psychiatry, Duke University Medical Center, and Director of Clinical and Administrative Services for the Halifax County Mental Health Center, Halifax, North Carolina. He received his doctorate in clinical psychology from the University of Louisville in 1975. His primary interest is in the area of behavioral treatment of essential hypertension.

Bernard T. Engel, Ph.D. is currently Chief of the Section of Psychophysiology and Chief of the Laboratory of Behavioral Sciences at the Gerontology Research Center, National Institute of Aging. He is also an Associate Professor of Behavioral Biology at Johns Hopkins School of Medicine. He received his doctorate from the University of California, Los Angeles, in 1956 and has previously been on the faculty at the University of California School of Medicine and Michael Reese Hospital. He is a past president of the Society for Psychophysiological Research. He has published over 50 scientific papers and chapters dealing with psychosomatic disorders, behavioral treatment of heart rate problems and fecal incontinence, and physiological correlates of hunger and pain.

John Paul Foreyt, Ph.D. is Assistant Professor of Experimental Medicine and Psychology at Baylor College of Medicine and Project Director of the Diet Modification Clinic, which is part of the National Heart and Blood Vessel Research and Demonstration Center. He received his doctorate in clinical psychology from the Florida State University in 1969 and has previously been a faculty member at Florida State University and project director of the Behavior Modification Program, Florida State Hospital, Chattahoochee. He has published numerous papers on the behavioral treatment of eating disorders and is editor and co-editor of three texts: *Mental Examiner's Handbook*, *Obesity: Behavioral Approaches to Dietary Management*, and *Behavioral Treatments of Obesity*.

Frank T. Masur, III, Ph.D. is an Assistant Professor in the Departments of Family Medicine and Psychiatry at the University of Tennessee Center for Health Sciences, Memphis. He received his doctoral degree in clinical psychology from St. Louis University in 1977 and completed his internship training at Duke University Medical Center. His primary interests include biofeedback therapy, diagnosis and treatment of psychosomatic disorders, and sexual dysfunction.

E. Wayne Sloop, Ph.D. is currently Unit Manager, Child Development Center, Lynchburg, Virginia. He received his doctorate in clinical psychology from Florida State University in 1969 and has previously been on the faculty of Winthrop College, the West Virginia University Medical Center, and Lynchburg College. He has authored several papers and chapters on the topics of behavioral treatment of enuresis, parents as behavior modifiers, and psychology technicians as paraprofessionals. He also is involved in private practice, specializing in behavioral treatment of child disorders.

Linda C. Sobell, Ph.D. is Director of Alcohol Programs at the Dede Wallace Mental Health Center, Nashville, Tennessee, and an Adjunct Instructor in the Psychology Department at Vanderbilt University. She received her doctorate in clinical psychology from the University of California at Irvine in 1976. She is a consulting editor for the *Journal of Studies on Alcohol* and a member of the editorial board of *Addictive Behaviors*. She has published over 25 papers, chapters, and books, including (with M.B. Sobell) *Behavioral Treatment of Alcohol Problems*.

Mark B. Sobell, Ph.D. is currently Associate Professor and Director of Graduate Research and Training on Alcohol Dependence, Department of Psychology, Vanderbilt University. He received his doctorate from the University of California at Riverside in 1970 and has previously been a research psychologist at Patton State Hospital and a Clinical Instructor in the Department of Psychiatry and Human Behavior, University of California College of Medicine at Irvine. He is a consulting editor to numerous professional journals including *Behavior Therapy* and the *Quarterly Journal of Studies on Alcohol*. He has authored over 30 papers, chapters, and books dealing with the behavioral treatment of alcohol problems, including (with E.M. Pattison and L.C. Sobell) *Emerging Concepts of Alcohol Dependence*.

Richard M. Suinn, Ph.D. is Professor and Head of the Department of Psychology at Colorado State University. He is also associated with the Sports Medicine Team and the U.S. National and Olympic Ski Teams. He received his doctorate in clinical psychology from Stanford University in 1959, and has previously been on the faculty of the Stanford University School of Medicine and the University of Hawaii. He has authored four books and numerous articles dealing with behavioral treatment of anxiety-related disorders including cardiac stress.